2018

Why the COCKS FIGHT

Dominicans, Haitians, and the Struggle for Hispaniola

Michele Wucker

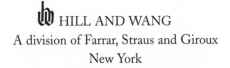

HILL AND WANG

A division of Farrar, Straus and Giroux

New York

Hill and Wang

A division of Farrar, Straus and Giroux

19 Union Square West, New York 10003

Disributed in Canada by Douglas & McIntyre Ltd.

Printed in the United States of America

Designed by Lisa Stokes

First edition, 1999

Library of Congress Cataloging-in-Publication Data
Wucker, Michele, 1969–
    Why the cocks fight : Dominicans, Haitians, and the struggle for
Hispaniola / by Michele Wucker.
        p. cm.
    Includes bibliographical references and index.
    ISBN 0-8090-3719-X (alk. paper)
    1. Dominican Republic—Relations—Haiti. 2. Haiti—Relations—
Dominican Republic. 3. Dominican Republic—Relations—United
States. 4. United States—Relations—Dominican Republic. 5. Haiti—
Relations—United States. 6. United States—Relations—Haiti.
7. Haitians—Dominican Republic. 8. Haitians—United States.
I. Title.
F1938.25.H2W83   1999
303.48'2729307294—dc21   98-25785

The author gratefully acknowledges her gratitude to Catherine Orenstein for preparing the map
on page xix, and to the following sources for permission to quote from copyrighted material:
"Cantos de la Frontera," from *La criatura terrestra*, © 1963 by Manuel Rueda, courtesy of the
author; *They Forged the Signature of God* by Viriato Sencion (Curbstone Press, © 1995), courtesy
of the publisher and the author; "Nueva York 1987: A Julia de Burgos," from *Internamiento*, ©
1992 by Sherezada Vicioso, courtesy of the author; traditional rara lyrics performed by Rara la
Fleur Ginen and recorded by Liza McAlister, 1993, courtesy of Ms. McAlister.

Contents

In Santo Domingo, the mere mention of Haiti provokes passionate reactions.

The woman there who rented me a studio apartment overlooking a garden bursting with yellow blooms and guava trees was of Spanish-Italian background. She treated me like a daughter. Every morning, she brought me a cup of *café con leche*, which she made from instant coffee. She was so proud of the instant crystals, which her daughter brought from Puerto Rico because they were almost impossible to find in Santo Domingo at the time, that I didn't have the heart to tell her I preferred strong, dark Dominican coffee.

When I told her I was doing research on Haiti, she sniffed her nose in a typically Dominican expression of disdain. Then she lifted her long white finger, tapped her freckled forearm, and whispered that Haitians were so black, black as a telephone. "The poor Haitians are like animals. All they can afford to eat are tins of sardines and a little rice," she said. Any time Haiti came up in conversation after that, she changed the subject. Her husband, who had dark olive skin and black wavy hair, was a retired colonel. When he mentioned to me that he was briefly stationed near the border, his wife drew her eyebrows together in worry, as if she wanted to forget even the idea of the western third of Hispaniola.

My landlady's reaction was not unlike that of the middle- and upper-class Dominicans whom I told of my interest in Haiti. "I was just speaking to some people from the United Nations who said Haiti would be better off if someone dropped a bomb on it. And they're right," said the publisher of a newspaper in Santo Domingo.

The names of towns change from Spanish to French along the line marking the border between the Dominican Republic and Haiti. I decided to go to Hispaniola as soon as I saw that feature on the map, which reminded me of the place where my mother was born: Belgium, a small country divided, like the island of Hispaniola, into two languages and cultures. Long before I knew where the Dominican Republic or Haiti was, I spent several weeks in Brussels with my grandmother's family. My French-speaking Tante Mimi's trips to buy bread and cheese at the little markets in the mostly Flemish suburb where she lived usually involved some moments of hesitation over whether she or the merchant would use the other's language. My cousins dodged my questions about why they didn't know more than bits of Flemish and whether they had any Flemish-speaking friends. Political parties were split into factions according to language. After each national census, the government would fall amid Walloon and Flemish squabbling over how to gerrymander political districts by language.

With my Belgian relatives in mind, I applied for and won a grant from Rice University to study the politics of language and culture on Hispaniola. My questions were these: Did different languages make people think in fundamentally incompatible ways? Did culture make it impossible to find political solutions to conflict?

The more time I spent on Hispaniola, the less I believed that the cultural differences were the root of the problem. They were only the mask. The people of both countries are proud of their pumpkin soup. Their music—merengue in Santo Domingo and *konpa* in Haiti—sounds very similar; both styles of music are based on European contredanse infused with a five-beat African rhythm. The main difference between them is the way they are enjoyed: Dominicans dance with a slight hitch while Haitians move symmetrically. The histories of their relationships with the United States were eerily parallel.

Dominicans often asked me about racism in Texas, where I grew up. I usually replied that racism in the American South now was less disturbing to me than that found in the North, in my family's home state of Wisconsin, for instance. In the South, egregious wrongs continued, but at least there was more interracial contact than in the North, where such a wall existed that white people often hushed their voices when talking about other races, religions, or ethnicities, as if they wished that the others would fade out of existence. I also found that, despite the debate over Haiti and constant references to skin color and "good hair" versus "bad hair," Dominicans acknowledged contact between races more openly than Americans did.

I began to realize that the reactions of Dominicans to Haitians closely resembled the way Texans spoke about Mexicans in that illegal immigration, jobs, and land were the real issues behind racist slurs. I began to see the Dominican-Haitian conflicts in terms of immigration as well: more and more Haitians were coming to the Dominican Republic, which couldn't support its own people. Because their skin was darker than that of the mostly mulatto Dominicans, and because they spoke Kreyol instead of Spanish, the Haitians stood out. In Santo Domingo as in Texas, the debate often returned to the theme of jobs, even though the new immigrants were doing work the natives shunned.

Another summer, living in Santo Domingo on a grant from the Tinker Foundation and Columbia University, I spent most of my time in the ghettos and cane fields, where Haitians and Dominicans live and work together closely. These people switched back and forth between Haitian Kreyol and Spanish. They teased each other about their differences but were hardly the bitter enemies the Dominican government depicted. Many people volunteered that they had cousins, aunts, grandparents in the other country. People dealt with racial and cultural boundaries in subtle ways that often contradicted the official picture.

In September 1991, I was reporting in New York City for the Dominican newspaper *Listín USA* when Haitian military forces toppled the government of President Jean-Bertrand Aristide. When I started at the paper, the older, mostly male staff patronized me and resented my assignment to the United Nations. They didn't much trust what a young American woman could do, especially since her written Spanish was still shaky. But in this case, they were unanimous in their support of the publisher's choice of me as the reporter to cover this coup. None of them wanted to go to Haiti. They justified their reluctance by telling me that a Dominican cameraman had been killed in the 1987 election massacre in Port-au-Prince. But behind their excuse, I sensed much deeper fears of the nation next door to the one where they were born. New York is about four hours from Haiti by plane; the flight from Santo Domingo to Port-au-Prince takes just over half an hour. Yet my New York newspaper was the first Dominican publication to send a reporter to Port-au-Prince after Aristide's ouster.

Haitians live in a country on an island poor in material terms but rich in images and symbols. One symbol, the rooster, eclipses all others; it is so ubiquitous that it seems not that the Haitians have chosen it as their symbol but that the rooster has seized them. Haitian Vodou devotees say they do not choose the spirits that govern their religious lives; the spirits choose them. Vodou is a religion that mixes both Roman Catholic and African elements; it is a belief system rooted in right and wrong, in which practitioners serve Bondyè, the Good Lord, who is aided by a coterie of saint-spirits, called *lwa*. Rising from somewhere in the unconscious, the *lwa* come alive in a collective Haitian consciousness.

The cockfight struck me in a similar way as a metaphor for the relationship between the Dominican Republic and Haiti, long before I spent the first of many afternoons watching paired roosters fling themselves at each other. The first time I read about Hispaniola was in the Martinican writer Aimé Césaire's *La Tragédie du roi Christophe*. The play begins with a cockfight in which roosters stand for the two men fighting for control over Haiti after its independence. The rooster is a solitary male symbol, tied to Caribbean machismo and violence. Both the Dominican Republic and Haiti have strongman political traditions in which the word of the man at the top deeply influences how the people act and speak. In Santo Domingo, much of the anti-Haitian rhetoric I heard came from one man, Joaquín Balaguer. Balaguer's political symbol was the rooster. So was that of Jean-Bertrand Aristide, the Haitian President who, for much of the year before Haitian military men deposed him, sharply criticized Balaguer for using Haitians as slaves.

If the symbols that dominate a culture accurately express a nation's character, what kind of a country draws so heavily on images of cockfighting and roosters, birds bred to be aggressive? What does it mean when not one but two countries that are neighbors choose those symbols? Why do the cocks fight, and why do humans watch and glorify them?

My main interest in the sport was not to weigh the morality of breeding and arming birds to fight. Instead, I wanted to understand why sparring roosters aroused so much passion in Haiti and the Dominican Republic. So I went to my first cockfight, at a small arena off Delmas Road in Port-au-Prince. Prone to fainting at scary movies, I was terrified

I'd pass out at the sight of the gore. But as I watched and learned, I was surprised to find myself on the edge of my seat, where I was rooting enthusiastically for a spirited, compact gray bird that lunged and parried with heart until it finally defeated a larger red cock. I was almost ashamed that I identified so much with the fighter, at a level uncomfortably beyond my journalistic interest in the event. What was it about the bloody contest that drew me so?

Today's news coverage of Haiti focuses on violence. The television has brought images of former secret police being "necklaced"—encircled with a gasoline-soaked tire and burned alive—on the streets of Port-au-Prince; soldiers riddling innocent civilians with bullets; U.S. Marines invading, ostensibly to bring order, only to stand by helplessly as they watch police bludgeon a coconut vendor to death in full daylight; and bodies of refugees washing up on shore after their decrepit, overloaded boats sink while they try to flee the island.

Coverage of the Dominican Republic, while less frequent, is in the same vein: footage of immigrants selling drugs or rioting in Manhattan's Washington Heights, boat people braving sharks and waves to cross to Puerto Rico in tiny boats.

Observing Haitians and Dominicans through the lens of American culture is not unlike being a spectator at a blood sport, then. We recoil from the violence but are still somehow fascinated. This mixed reaction is not new; in the fourth century A.D., St. Augustine and a group of friars were drawn against their will to watch the beauty of a cockfight. If we did not watch, the television news people would find other images to fill the screen.

Our culture fixates on violence between men but nonetheless condemns blood sports that pit animals against each other, like the cockfighting that is a Dominican and Haitian tradition. The cockfight is a dramatized combat in which men lay down money on roosters but in reality compete with one another. The two principal cock owners place heavy bets against each other; spectators make smaller side bets. The only risk for the spectators is to their wallets.

Where the Dominican Republic and Haiti are concerned, however, Americans are not just spectators. The stakes are high; what happens in those countries is relevant to the United States, in material and more subtle ways. Our relationship with the island has helped shape the conditions that have resulted in violence and underdevelopment there, and thus the stream of immigrants heading to our shores today. We have invaded each country twice during this century (Haiti in 1915 and 1994; Santo Domingo in 1916 and 1965). As struggles on Hispaniola continue, Dominicans and Haitians flee in search of political and economic security. Over the last two decades, more than two million Haitians and Dominicans (more than one in eight of the total populations) have left Hispaniola to try their luck in the United States. Dominican President Leonel Fernández is one of them; he grew up in Manhattan, where his mother worked at factory and nursing jobs.

Americans' own dream—good jobs at good wages and a fair shot at buying a house and providing for children—is slipping out of reach. The blame for those troubles is often placed on the shoulders of immigrants. We have gone so far as to send troops to Haiti to keep its boat people from flooding our shores. The ongoing debate over immigrants to the United States, like the cockfight that redirects aggression onto birds, now channels voters' frustrations toward foreigners who speak other languages and look different. The roots of the anti-immigrant sentiment in the United States that has grown in the 1990s—and the motives of the politicians who encourage and exploit it—are not so different from the forces that have led to tragedy in the Dominican Republic and Haiti.

If the wealthiest countries of the world claim that their economies cannot support more people, imagine the effect of a massive flow of poor and hungry immigrants from one of the world's most impoverished nations, Haiti, to a country that is not much better off. As vast as the differences are between the United States and Hispaniola, the Dominicans' strategy is the same as ours. The struggles between Dominicans and Haitians are not just theirs. They are ours, too.

Acknowledgments

In Vodou, you do not choose the spirit that is the master of your head, which is to say the one with the most influence over your life. Your *met tet* chooses you. It was that way with this book, something my acquaintance with the rooster spirit Papa Loko made me understand. I am grateful for that, and to the many people who have helped me.

Thanks to Patricia Seed, Bernard Aresu, and Joan Rea, my professors at Rice University, where my contact with Hispaniola started. Lambros Comitas, Frank Moya Pons, and Wilfredo Lozano gave me thoughtful guidance in the initial stages of the research. Facultad Latinoamericana de Ciencias Sociales (FLACSO) provided me with office space in Santo Domingo. Silvio Torres-Saillant and Sara Aponte at the City University of New York's Dominican Studies Institute gave me access to their library and their ongoing speaker series. Rice University's Wiess College Paul F. Bobb Travel Fellowship, the Tinker Foundation (through the Columbia University Latin American and Iberian Studies Institute), and the Open Society Institute (through *World Policy Journal*) provided funding for parts of my research.

For being there in Santo Domingo, many thanks go to Peter Weidlich and his family, Yolanda y Rafael Salazar, Juan Rodríguez y Doña Beatriz, Fernando González Nicolás, Elsie Doñé-Molina y Alejandro Abreu, Wendy Cepeda, Joe and Hannah Ambar, Christina Correa, Solange Saint-Fleur, El Mesón de Bari, the Santo Domingo Little Theatre, and *The Santo Domingo News*. For their wisdom on all things pertaining to roosters, I am indebted to Edgar Jean-Louis, Tina Girouard, Lucas Lendof, Dr. José Martínez, Adriano

Rodríguez, José Then, and all the *galleros caballeros* of the Coliseo Gallístico Alberto Bonetti Burgos.

Many others gave enthusiasm, comments, questions, encouragement, and help of all kinds, and this is only a very short list of them: Jon Anderson, René Aubry, Jr., Gage Averill, Susan Benesch, John Berton, Catherine Brown, Iain Bruce, Chip Carey, Steeve Coupeau, Mary D'Ambrosio, Carol Davis, Sarah Decosse, Santiago Fittipaldi, Patrick Gavigan, José Gonzales, Chris Hunt, Monica Kelly, Jean Leong, Anjanette Levert, Liza McAlister, Gabriel Negretto, Peter Norwood, Bill O'Neill, Katie Orenstein, Steve Phillips, Donna Plotkin, Tim Ryan, Viriato and Milagros Sención, Joel Sendek, Patrick Slavin, Frank Smyth, Louis Spiegler, Les Stone, Katie and Scott Thomson, Laurel Touby, Marie-Claude Toussaint, and Amy Waldman. Thanks to Pierre François for Kreyol tutoring in Milwaukee, and to the late Wilson Désir, whose sonorous voice made his New York radio program a Kreyol lesson as well as a source of information. Bob Corbett's Haiti discussion group raised useful questions and provided helpful leads. Joe Harkins was generous with background on the Sosúa colony and, more important, his friendship. Thanks also to Tom Himmelberg and the whole gang at Technical Data.

This book owes much to Rafael Bonnelly's vision for *Listín USA* and to his wisdom in ignoring my protests that I didn't want to report stories during graduate school. Big thanks also go to my agent, Al Zuckerman, and Christian Finnegan; to my editor, Elisabeth Sifton ("Dominicans and Haitians. Of course!"), for seeing clearly what I wanted this book to be, and her never-tiring assistant, April Lamm. Dr. Jacques Bartoli in Port-au-Prince and Dr. María Elena Muñoz in Santo Domingo provided friendship, contacts, and a place to stay. Thanks to my family, especially my grandparents, John and Mary Wucker and Andrée Buehmann. Above all, my gratitude goes to Melissa Rawlins and Florence Dinerstein, who saw this through.

Author's Note

Reflecting Hispaniola's history as a crossroads, this book is based on interviews and texts in four languages—Spanish, Kreyol, French, and English—a combination that has presented considerable difficulties to its writing. Many of these difficulties stem from the fact that language (like virtually everything else) is political on the island. Many Dominicans still refuse to refer to Haitian Kreyol as a full-fledged language, instead calling it "patois," implying (intentionally or not) that Haitians have not yet managed to speak a "proper" language. For most of Haiti's existence, the language spoken by nearly all Haitians was not considered legitimate, and all government business and elite social interaction were conducted in French. Kreyol was only accepted as a national language and taught in schools in the late 1970s; the result of its recent genesis is that three different systems of transcription developed, and debates still rage over how to spell certain words. More recently, it has become fashionable in certain circles to choose Kreyol over French. (The Haitian band Boukman Eksperyans even has a song about this: *Ayisyen-yo, pito pale Franse—Olye yo pale Kreyol. Se Kreyol Nou Ye!* Haitians don't speak French, we speak Kreyol. We are Kreyol!) Meanwhile, Dominican Spanish often differs in meaning from other Latin American variants of the language. And, to complicate matters further, both Dominicans and Haitians living in the United States and making frequent trips back and forth to the island have added American expressions to the mix.

There are many places in the book where I have used the Spanish or Kreyol original (accompanied by an explanation that makes clear what a word means) instead of fully translating words into English, often because an expression has no exact equivalent. Literal translations would have deprived readers of a sense of the sound of daily life and of the concepts that are part of being Dominican or Haitian. A visitor to Hispaniola will hear these words again and again; a careful listen will reveal the peculiar rhythms and musical sensibility that are part of what makes the place fascinating. To make it easier on the reader who is becoming acquainted with the island for the first time, a glossary follows the body of this book and includes references to the social context of each expression; these are the words that taken together are an abridged linguistic sketch of life on the island.

Etymologies often embody Hispaniola's cultural mix; for example, *fucú*, the word for "jinx," is an African word that has been Hispanicized. Dominican Spanish and Haitian Kreyol imaginatively integrate American terms to produce expressions like *swape* (swab) for mop; *Dominican York* for a Dominican living in New York City; *botpippel* for Haitian refugees; and *delco* for an electric generator, after the brand name.

The transcriptions of Dominican Spanish are fairly straightforward; this is not so for the transcriptions of Haitian Kreyol. The word "Kreyol" itself is the subject of some debate. Its spelling is intended to distinguish the language that Haitians speak, as a freestanding language with its own characteristics, from the family of languages called creoles, similarly structured dialects and pidgins that developed in slave colonies, where speakers of many African languages and dialects had to communicate with one another and with plantation bosses. (Debate continues on whether it should be called "Haitian Kreyol" or simply "Kreyol"; meanwhile, another smaller group insists on referring to Haiti as "Ayiti" and Haitian as "Ayisyen.")

Some Kreyol words have made their way into English, and I have treated these with extra caution. For example, I use the spelling Vodou to reflect more accurately the word's pronunciation, the fact that it belongs to the Kreyol language, and its status as a religion (thus capitalized). More important, I want to distinguish it from Hollywood's "voodoo" creation, a wild distortion that unfortunately is at the root of many Americans' understanding of Haiti's folk religion. In another case, I have adopted the American spelling of a phrase as the most understandable version. Readers of any newspaper story on Haiti in the last two decades are likely already familiar with the *tontons macoutes*, the feared Duvalier private militia. I have adopted the spelling most likely familiar to English-speaking readers, though there were good arguments for using any one of several versions I have seen in Kreyol and French (the Kreyol *tonton makout*, the proper noun Tonton Macoute, and so on).

Doubtless some Dominican and Haitian readers will disagree with some of the spelling choices; but the existence of the debate merely confirms the political power of language on Hispaniola.

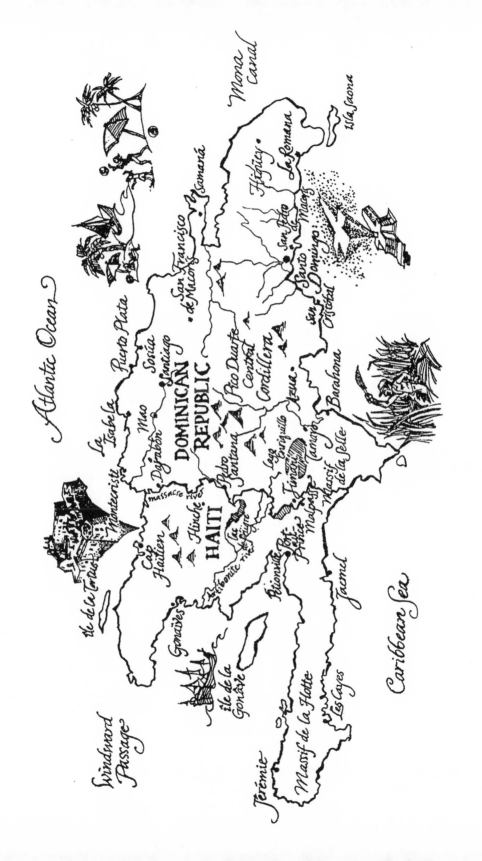

Suddenly we noticed barnyard cocks beginning a bitter fight just in front of the door. We chose to watch . . .

. . . the lowered heads stretched forward, neck-plumage distended, the lusty thrusts, and such wary parryings; and in every motion of the irrational animals, nothing unseemly—precisely because another Reason from on high rules over all things. Finally, the very law of the victor: the proud crowing, the almost perfectly orbed arrangement of the members, as if in haughtiness of supremacy. But the sign of the vanquished: hackles plucked from the neck; in carriage and in cry, all bedraggled—and for that very reason, somehow or other, beautiful and in harmony with nature's laws.

We asked many questions: Why do all cocks behave this way? Why do they fight for the sake of supremacy of the hens subject to them? Why did the very beauty of the fight draw us aside from this higher study for a while, and onto the pleasure of the spectacle?

—St. Augustine
De Ordine (About Order)
A.D. 386

Why the COCKS FIGHT

Roosters
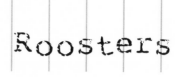

What the cockfight says it says in a vocabulary of sentiment—the
thrill of risk, the despair of loss, the pleasure of triumph. Yet what it
says is not merely that risk is exciting, loss depressing, or triumph
gratifying, but that it is of these emotions, thus exampled, that society
is built and individuals put together.

—*Clifford Geertz*
"Deep Play: Notes on a Balinese Cockfight"

Dangling his dead rooster by its feet, a grizzled
cockfighter shuffles out the gate of the Manoguayabo cockfighting club through the parking lot, past a row of obsolete
but still working hulks of cars, decrepit versions of old Russian models and American gas-guzzlers. He will have a rich
stew tonight, the kind of meal to be eaten with savor and
sadness at once. A *gallero* never wants to have to make dinner
from one of his own roosters, but when he does, the meat
is the best to be had. After all, a fighting cock has been
pampered all its life, fed the best food and exercised daily.
Veteran cockers say the adrenaline the fight releases into the
bird's blood and muscles gives the meat a deep, strong taste.

It is early in the evening to have to go home so sad, so
early that the old crones who lurk around the *gallera* in hopes
of buying the tasty carcass of a fighting rooster have not yet
clustered. The rest of the crowd is only just beginning to
filter through the gate, where a sign is posted in misspelled
letters, PROHIBIDO ENTRAR CON BEVIDAS, warning patrons
not to bring in their own drinks. Inside, the cockfighting
fans navigate past an army of small motorcycles, *pasolas*, on
the way to the arena. Smoke from a diesel electric generator
hangs heavy over the yard. Today, Santo Domingo has suffered a particularly bad bout of blackouts. There has been no

electricity from the bankrupt, broken-down government electricity company since before six this morning. It is after five in the afternoon, just past the normal time when the first fights begin.

Toward the entrance to the ring itself, a dirty cafeteria on the left sells fried plantains and hot dogs. Past the cafeteria, the roosters that have been readied to fight peck impatiently at Plexiglas windows clouded by age and grime. On the near side of the cafeteria, handlers finish preparing birds for the next fight. Seated on rickety, wooden three-legged stools, the men pare the roosters' spurs and tape on artificial ones made of plastic or tortoiseshell. Some use natural spur that has been cut from the legs of special roosters—called *quiquí*—bred not to fight but to produce these weapons for other birds. The whole process ensures that all birds go into the fight with weapons of the same length. Combat between cocks is set up to be fair and equal, even if real life is not so.

The slums of Santo Domingo encroach on the countryside in Manoguayabo, this rough *barrio* on the northwestern edge of the city, and spread past the industrial district of Herrera, all the way to the surrounding sugarcane fields. This is the home of the newest immigrants to the teeming urban capital, coming from rural farms. They wake even before the roosters to catch buses for the long ride to whatever jobs they've managed to swing in town.

Dominicans call the Manoguayabo cockfighting arena the *bajo mundo*, the underworld. The term does not mean "clandestine," since fights are legal here. It means "lower-class." Money, politics, and power are reserved for the sparkling Alberto Bonetti Burgos Cockfighting Coliseum, closer to town, where the elite go to watch fights among prize cocks meticulously bred for generations and brought to the Dominican Republic from as far away as Spain or even the Philippines. The legendary San Francisco Giants pitcher Juan Marichal fights his roosters at the coliseum.

The netherworld is the cockfighting milieu of people only recently risen up from the countryside, who bring with them gritty determination and their fighting cocks. The fans here are men who haven't yet made it to the United States. Over three decades a million other Dominicans have left their farms and family to go north "to find a better life," their stock phrase. Among the younger generation, which is heavily exposed to American culture, baseball and basketball are taking over from cockfights. In the countryside it is enough for a man that his rooster wins battles for him. But now, so many Dominicans are major-league-baseball stars: Jorge Bell of the Toronto Blue Jays; Juan Marichal, Ozzie Virgil, and the Alou brothers (Felipe, Matty, and Jesús) of the San Francisco Giants; Sammy Sosa of the Chicago Cubs. Young Dominicans dream of becoming baseball stars themselves. Even in the countryside, the poorest Dominican boys practice with bats made of tree branches and balls improvised from the pale-blue plastic caps of giant water bottles.

In the United States, cockfighting is still seen as a backward sport. Nobody remembers that George Washington and Thomas Jefferson fought roosters. The sport is illegal in all states but Louisiana, Oklahoma, Arkansas, New Mexico, and Missouri. In Miami and New York City, cockfights are held quietly, in basements and on hidden farms. They are part of a clandestine world, broken up by police from time to time, certainly not a sport where you can dream of fame and millions in earnings.

The entrance fee to the Manoguayabo arena is one hundred Dominican pesos, more than a day's pay at minimum wage. Lucas, a wiry cocker who today has left his birds at home and is here just to watch a couple of matches and chat with friends, stops at the door. He removes the ammunition cartridge from his gun and leaves the firearm in a yellow wooden bin that is quickly filling up. Lucas is a retired policeman (he owns a *colmado*, a convenience store that in Dominican life is also a place where locals hang out, play dominoes, exchange stories), so he could carry the weapon if he wanted to.

"What do people need to bring guns in here for?" he scoffs. "The roosters are the ones fighting. Carrying arms in here isn't necessary and doesn't make anyone more of a man. If you want to fight, let your rooster win for you." Lucas is one of the few cockers who straddles the *bajo mundo* and the world of the coliseum, where his skill in training and raising roosters has won him respect.

His roosters are good enough that he has to worry about their being stolen. Just a few months ago, he lost some of his best birds to a gang of robbers who had been stealing the very best cocks in the Dominican Republic. Before they were caught, the thieves had been smuggling the birds across the border to Haiti. Over there, passions for cockfighting are just as high but the birds, everyone here says with conviction, aren't nearly as good as the Dominican ones. The insult is typical of Dominican sentiment toward Haiti.

At Manoguayabo, the doormen hurry the newcomers in toward their seats to clear an opening for the men who will set up the next fight. Two burly men stride into the green-carpeted arena, which has a diameter the length of three short men lying head to toe and is ringed by a low concrete wall. Each handler carries a canvas sack extended high in front of him to keep a safe distance from the struggling birds inside. The doorway is just wide enough for one at a time, so the spectators must be rushed out of the way. In the three tiers rising above the arena, there is barely enough space to pass through the aisles on the way to plastic seats not really wide enough even for a man as slim as Lucas. Just as the last of the newly arrived fans settle in, the fight begins.

Lucas waves to one owner, who is wearing a pink shirt and sitting ringside a few rows ahead and below along the clean yellow wall keeping the birds in. With a confident smile, the man nods back. "I gave him the father of the white rooster," Lucas says. The combatants here are identified in the fight not by their actual color but by the color of the white or blue tape holding their spurs on their legs. The white rooster, in this case actually speckled brown, is old but good. He's lived four years to the blue rooster's two. In the coliseum, where the best birds fight, it is rare to see a fight between cocks of such different ages; in principle, everything at a fight is equal—weight, age, length of feathers, size of spurs. Weighing the experience and bloodlines of the older bird against the stamina of the younger, Lucas is not willing to wager on either one. The odds are too tight.

The other players think that the white is old and tired and so they bet accordingly, arms and hands flying as they seek partners. Men jump up and wave their arms, holding up fingers to show the odds. "I pay one hundred to twenty" means the gambler gets a hundred pesos if his bird wins but only has to pay twenty if his bird loses. The betting is cacophony, but the players are eloquent in this language. They zero in on a likely partner, make eye contact, flash the bet through shouts and gestures. At the end of the game, they pay promptly. As the match progresses, the odds keep dropping, from seventy to fifty, against the white. But it keeps fighting, on and on, the clock ticking five, ten, fifteen minutes. The young blue can't overcome its older opponent, even after the white bird is blinded and staggers around, lunging by instinct alone.

All of a sudden there is no light. The fluorescent lights over the ring go dead. Santo Domingo's power has come back on and signaled the generator to stop. Natural light has fallen with the dusk and heavy storm clouds hovering over the club. When the lights return and the ceiling fans jerk back into action, the birds are still pecking and lunging, exhausted but persistent. The fight drags on and on, until the twenty-minute bell rings and the judge calls a draw, called a *tabla* or *empate*. The owners take their birds and caress them. The crowd, frustrated, shifts and grumbles. They want a kill, not a slow draw.

Some of the men (for they are, as usual, mostly men here) pour onto the green floor of the ring and out the entrance while the rest wait and debate in their seats. Like politics on Hispaniola, the cockfight is a male ritual. To be sure, the most enduring Dominican legends of strength and redemption are female: the Mirabal sisters, martyred by the thugs of the dictator Rafael Trujillo in 1960 as they returned from visiting their dissident husbands in prison; and the Virgin Mary, who saved the Spanish conquerors from defeat by the Arawak Indians in 1502. In myth as in politics, women are thought of as standing by and supporting, not going into battle.

At Manoguayabo, only two women sit in the stands, no doubt patient girlfriends. They look bored despite their best efforts. Waitresses circulate around the edge of the arena, where they sell drinks out of aqua plastic trays and collect money in Styrofoam cups. Men blow kisses at one waitress, tall, dressed in a tight black dress with silver hearts spattered across the vest. Her hair is slicked back severely into a ponytail of curls. The *gallera* is choked with an onslaught of smells: body odor, cheap cologne, rum hot on the breath of the sweaty men crammed together and dangling their arms into the ring.

After the drinks are served, the handlers reappear, carrying two large blue canvas bags holding the next pair of cocks. They weigh the birds, then shoo the crowd out of the center and begin to taunt the birds, one at a time, with a *mona*, a third bird used exclusively to agitate the combatants. One handler holds the *mona* and thrusts it, beak first, into the face of each rooster about to fight. The birds hop into the air and lunge at the *mona*. The betting begins, a stirring among the spectators around the ring. Men stand up, wave their arms, flash fingers up and down to signal the odds, and shout: "*Blanco! Doy!* . . . *Azul! Ochenta a cien!*" I'm going for the

White! The Blue! Eighty gets a hundred! When the handlers release the cocks, the ruckus dies down and the crowd settles in to watch the fight. This particular combat is uneventful, but only until after it ends.

As the owners take their birds out of the ring, an uproar ensues. The crowd presses toward the entrance, shouting and shoving. A fight. Policemen appear, stern faced, and drag one man out. Half the crowd gathered at the door rushes out after them. A tall man in white pants extracts himself and paces about the ring, gesticulating wildly. Apparently, he was the other party in the fight. His white pants are smeared with blood, though it's not clear whether it is from the passing rooster or from his own fight. A burly man seated at ring's edge points out the smear, and the tall man curses. His pants are ruined. He stalks out.

Word of what happened quickly makes its way around the ring. A man refused to make good on a bet, at odds of a thousand pesos to five hundred, which he had lost to the tall man with white pants. The offender has been thrown out, but the winner never got his money. Small consolation that the entire crowd in the club believes the man in the white pants was in the right. The man who failed to keep his word won't be allowed to show his face here again.

The cockfighter's word of honor, *palabra de gallero*, guaranteeing players' bets, is not to be breached under any circumstances. *Palabra de gallero* means you can make a verbal wager with a person across the ring whom you have never met, establish odds, and trust his word. In the cockfighting arena, any breach of the code of honor is serious enough to ban the violator from the arena forever. In this close-knit circle of men, everyone will remember the one who broke his word and violated the brotherhood of the *gallera*.

It takes a long time for the next fight to begin but far less for it to end. Before even four minutes pass, the fierce-faced victor, a bald *cocolo*, drives his spurs through his opponent's eye and into its brain, killing it immediately. The crowd finally has what it wants and breaks into cheers. The *cocolo*'s owner, ecstatic, retrieves his bird, lifts it, and sucks the blood smeared on the crimson head of the cock.

"In the cockfight, man and beast, good and evil, ego and id, the creative power of aroused masculinity and the destructive power of loosened animality fuse in a bloody drama of hatred, cruelty, violence, and death," the anthropologist Clifford Geertz has written of the cockfights he observed in Bali. As an art form, the cockfight focuses on an aspect of life, aggression, and projects it into a theater where it can be more clearly expressed and understood. Instead of resorting primarily to violence among themselves as a way of answering a base human impulse, the participants translate their urges into a drama of appearances, where they cannot harm the observers or participants in reality.

The cockfight serves the same function in the *bajo mundo* as it does in the coliseum: it allows men to play out aggression through the struggles of their birds. Emotions are displayed in a cathartic microcosm of human interaction, violence released through the flailing spurs, beaks, and feathers in the ring. The cockfight is a "safe" arena for the cockers. A man may lose a few bucks or suffer a blow to his pride for a few days or weeks, but the roosters fight sometimes to the death.

Across the island, on the western, Haitian end of Hispaniola, roosters are all over the walls of the labyrinth of alleys that make up Bel Air, a dust-, smoke-, and exhaust-clogged slum that perches on a hill in downtown Port-au-Prince. It is February 1995, five months after a flock of American helicopters and planes escorted President Jean-Bertrand Aristide back from three years of exile in the United States, the nation he once disparagingly called "that big northern country that casts so many long, dark shadows in our hemisphere."

The residents of Bel Air, in tribute to their returned President, have adorned the walls with paintings of Aristide and his political symbol, the *kòk kalite*, the champion fighting rooster. The variety of renditions seems endless: stenciled red roosters, alone and within circles, paired next to stenciled black-and-tan depictions of the bespectacled President Aristide; speckled blue-and-red roosters painted in the naïve Haitian style; generously plumed roosters bursting with color; crossed American and Haitian flags painted behind a giant, fierce red-and-brown cock. Two brown roosters painted on white cinder block stare each other down across a wall peppered with red-paint splotches that look as if they are meant to depict spatters of blood or bullet holes. A painted Haitian flag, blue on top, red on the bottom, sports a pink-and-blue rooster in the white center instead of the palm tree, cannons, drums, and swords that are on the actual flag. The hand-lettered message below reads, *Vox Aristide, Vox Populi*, above the name "Bob Marley."

The most detailed image, drawn over and over again in varied styles, is that of a hand placing an egg back in a chicken, accompanied by notes declaring, "*Li rantre!*" Yes, it goes back in! After Haiti's military packed Aristide into exile in September 1991, soldiers smugly insisted that once a hen laid an egg you couldn't put the egg back in the chicken. Now Aristide had proved them wrong: he had come back to Haiti, and the murals were celebrating his seemingly impossible feat.

Blood drips from the yellow beak of a proud black-and-red rooster painted on a wall behind a fried-meat-and-plantain stand; below the rooster is a dead gray guinea hen, representing the old Duvalier dictatorship, which had used the guinea hen as its political symbol. One mural reads "*Kòk la ak bib la, se 2 lavalas.*" The rooster and the Bible are both *lavalas*. That is, they are both symbols of Aristide's Lavalas political movement, named for the cleansing flash flood that his backers promised would wash over Haiti with his election.

Things did not end up that way. Aristide lasted barely eight months in office. The powers that be in modern Haiti hadn't much liked him in the first place. When he failed to reassure them that he would protect their privileges and not deter violence against them, they sent him packing to Washington, D.C., via Caracas and returned the country to a military dictatorship. There was nothing new, nothing washed away but hope.

Haiti is a place where reality sometimes seems far away. To explain their world, Haitians often speak in proverbs, translating their daily life into symbols and images rather than attempting the impossible task of dissecting it. Analyses of Haiti's politics, of its shifting alliances and its leaders who change on the surface but nothing more, tend to collapse under their own weight. After Duvalier and before Aristide, five governments came and went.

On one level, the scraggly fighting rooster makes sense as a politician's symbol: politics, after all, is a battle of strategy, endurance, and aggression played out on a national stage. It inspires the same emotion and scheming that the cockfight does in spectators and gamblers. Look closer, however, and the political rooster dissolves into other images with entirely different meanings in religion and daily life. In other contexts, the rooster of aggression becomes a bird of sustenance, a symbol of the dawn and new beginnings, and, most important, a guardian of territory.

In the Bel Air cockfighting arena (*gagè* or *gagaire*, as Haitian cock-fighting arenas are called), tucked among the slum's labyrinthine alleys, a fight begins. The crowd is screaming in Haitian Kreyol. The money men are betting is gourdes, not pesos. The accommodations are poorer than in Santo Domingo, even in the *bajo mundo*. The color of the Haitian cockers' skin is darker. But the game is the same as the one that takes place on the eastern part of the island. Two scruffy roosters face off across a packed-dirt ring a few paces wide. In the dim light, spectators hang over the low circular concrete wall that separates them from the ring; it is painted pale blue, scratched and stained with dirt and dried blood from many past battles.

The birds pace warily around the edge of the circle. The red-brown of their feathers matching the color of the dirt, they eye each other and menacingly raise their neck feathers, then run headlong to the center and jump into the air. The air cracks with the impact of stiffened feathers as each bird tries to push the other to the ground. Around the ring, the Haitian men shout to one another and wave dirty wads of gourdes in the air, seeking bets. A meeting of the eyes, a nod of the head, and a flash of the fingers, a simple code, are enough to cement a wager that will bind both partners till the end of the match.

Soon, the feathers of both cocks are slick with blood and the fight slows to methodical pecks and lunges instead of the more dramatic air-borne jabbing with which it began. The birds here fight with their own spurs instead of the gaffs that cockers across the island attach to roosters' legs. Fights here often last as long as a half hour since it is difficult for a bird to inflict a mortal, or even incapacitating, wound on its enemy. When it appears one bird is gaining the advantage, the pitch of the gambling rises again. Yelling new odds, the wagerers who bet on the losing bird are trying to cover their losses.

The spectators lean forward, a few so close they could touch the birds. A few times, the men jerk back sharply as the cocks rise into the air right in front of them and threaten to hurl themselves over the con-crete barrier into the crowd. Men who are not trying to bet watch in-tently, narrowing their eyes in concentration. A few cover their foreheads with their hands; others gesture, as if to transmit energy and advice across the ring to the birds. The fight slows further as the roosters tire. Finally, the loser walks listlessly away from the stronger bird. The crowd groans in disappointment. The owners pull the blood-soaked animals from the ring, and the spectators step into the circle to settle their wagers before the next match begins.

Combat continues all afternoon, the same ritual over and over: the handlers agitate the birds and place them in the ring, the gamblers line up, and the birds fight. Finally, one man and his cock walk away victorious. The winner has a few extra gourdes in his pocket, and his humiliated opponent will trudge home. When today is over, the cockers will simply wait until tomorrow or a few days from now. The details vary only slightly: different owners, winners, and losers. But the community of cockers and their premise remain the same. Each sends a bird into the arena to do battle for him. The pattern repeats, inevitable as the turning of the days. Yet still the cockers are drawn back to the arena again and again.

The day begins with the cock's crow, for peasants who wake up in the countryside as well as for Dominicans and Haitians who have moved into cities; many rural immigrants have brought their roosters with them to fight in the makeshift cockfighting arenas in Santo Domingo and Port-au-Prince. A community, a brotherhood of sorts, forms around the cockfight, its traditions passed down from father to son and maintained within the family, even with the disapproval of wives and mothers too busy getting on with life to waste so many afternoons at the arena.

Some Dominicans say the merengue, the popular dance of the Dominican middle class, is based on the rooster's courtship of the hen; like the male bird's dance, the merengue has a sideways hitch and shuffle to it. The partners dance in a tight circle, with the man leading on the outside, just like a rooster circling a hen. The rooster has come to represent all aspects of daily life in Hispaniola: politics, home, territory, courtship, healing, sustenance, the passage of time, and brotherhood.

The cockfight is a symbol of both division and community, opposite sides of the same coin. Fascinated by the violence of the cockfight and the combat between men that it symbolizes, Dominicans and Haitians practicing the national sport of their countries also celebrate brotherhood by their unified devotion to the rituals and code of honor without which the sport and betting around it could not take place.

Even the geography of Hispaniola suggests a cockfighting arena. Haiti and the Dominican Republic share an island encircled by the Atlantic Ocean to the north, the Caribbean Sea to the south. The island is situated roughly halfway, 500 miles or so in either direction, between the southern tip of Florida and the northern edge of South America at Venezuela. Cuba lies not 50 miles northwest of Haiti. About a hundred miles north of the Dominican Republic are the Turks and Caicos Islands. Puerto Rico, 50 miles east-southeast, and Jamaica, 120 miles west-southwest, flank Hispaniola. Like the gamecocks, the two nations of Hispaniola share a history of violence that has been compounded by their confinement. Roosters, after all, fight for territory. It is only when they come into too close quarters that fights break out.

Not long after Columbus launched the conquest of the New World from Santo Domingo, the principal settlement on the southern coast of the island, France and Spain wrangled over control of Hispaniola (from the name Columbus chose: La Isla Española, the Spanish island). The European powers resolved the dispute in 1697 by dividing the island in two. The smaller, western end, Haiti, was born in 1804 from a slave revolt inspired by the turmoil of the French Revolution, which took the rooster as its symbol, as Haiti would do many years later.

Competing generals fighting over newly independent Haiti split the country in half. The south, under the rule of Alexandre Pétion, was a republic; the north, Henri Christophe's domain, was a kingdom (he became King Henri I). A century and a half later, Aimé Césaire described the rivalry between the two Haitian leaders as being akin to a cockfight. "Once, the fighting cocks were given names like *Tambour-Maître* or *Becqueté-Zié*, that is, Master Drummer or Peck-out-his-Eyes. Now, we give them the names of politicians: Christophe here, Pétion there," Césaire wrote in his play about the last days of King Henri, crowned Emperor of the north in 1811.

In the very style of the Europeans that Haiti had expelled, Henri Christophe created a spectacular palace modeled and named after the one the Prussian King Frederick the Great had built for himself at Potsdam. At Sans Souci, near Milot, a whole court of black dukes and lords presided over the hamlets nearby, to which Henri Christophe gave names like Marmelade and Limonade. Haitian legend has it that he then worked twenty thousand men to death building the massive Citadelle La Ferrière, a fortress meant to house men and arms that would keep Napoléon's men from ever approaching Haiti again as they had in 1795. (The Citadelle is still there, perched high on a mountain, fully visible only at dawn, before clouds roll down and shroud it by mid-morning.) To prove his men's loyalty, Henri Christophe once ordered troops to march off the edge of the Citadelle; they fell to their deaths below. He fought fiercely to hold on to his territory and to drive his rival, Pétion, out of power. In 1818, Pétion died. Not long afterward, on October 8, 1820, weakened by a stroke and despairing that he had lost his power to rule, Henri Christophe shot a silver bullet through his heart.

In Césaire's play, the king spits in disgust as his efforts fail to unify the north and south under his rule: "Poor Africa! I say poor Haiti! It is the same thing. Over there, tribe, languages, rivers, the castes, forest, village against village, hamlet against hamlet. Here, blacks, mulattos, *griffes, marabouts*, what have you, clan, caste, color, defiance and conspiracy, fights between cocks, between dogs over a bone, combats of fleas!" For Henri Christophe, Haiti is condemned to eternal conflicts, pointless.

His death opened the way for Pétion's successor, Jean-Pierre Boyer, to try to realize Toussaint Louverture's dream of a unified free Haiti over the entire island. In 1822, Boyer conquered Santo Domingo after he promised the people there that Haiti would keep out the Spanish and give the Dominicans the best chance to remain independent from Europe. But Boyer's new subjects chafed under his draconian rule. After twenty-two years, the Dominicans expelled the Haitian rulers in 1844 and established their own nation-state.

Long after the wars over Hispaniola, turmoil continued between the two nations. Dominican and Haitian Presidents sowed plots against each other. Border disputes continued well into this century. The defining moment of conflict came with the massacre that the Dominican dictator Rafael Trujillo ordered of more than twenty-five thousand Haitians along the border in 1937.

Since their country gained its independence from Haiti in 1844, four Dominican Presidents have chosen the rooster as their mascot. General

Manuel Jimenes, elected President of the new Dominican Republic in 1848, practically ran the country from ringside: "His whole time was spent in cleaning, training and fighting cocks, it being frequently necessary to send acts of Congress and other official papers to the cock-pit for his approval and signature," Benjamin Green, U.S. commissioner in the Dominican Republic, complained in a letter to U.S. Secretary of State John Clayton. (The commissioner was the highest representative of the United States in the Dominican Republic at the time; because the United States was considering establishing a protectorate, or at the very least annexing part of the Dominican Republic, formal diplomatic relations were not established until Frederick Douglass arrived in Santo Domingo as chargé d'affaires in February 1890.)

When the Dominican dictator Ulíses Heureaux (better known to Dominicans by his nickname, Lilís) died at the hands of conspirators at the end of the century, the men who followed him adopted the rooster as their symbol. The followers of Horacio Vásquez, who had led the conspiracy to assassinate Heureaux, called themselves *coludos*, the breed of fighting cocks that sports long tail feathers. Men loyal to Juan Isidro Jimenes, who had led a failed expedition against Heureaux aboard the ship *Fanita* a year before the dictator's murder, responded by calling themselves *bolos*, roosters without tail feathers, which weigh down other roosters with vanity.

After Lilís's death, Horacio Vásquez became provisional President but craftily stepped aside to become Vice President, handing the Presidency to Jimenes only as a way to bide his time before forcing him out in 1902. Vásquez lasted not even a year in his new administration before loyalists of the old *caudillo* Lilís pushed him out of office in turn. Several political convolutions later, another group of dissidents plotted against a *coludo* President, Ramón Cáceres, a cousin of Vásquez. The new plotters, a military group, went by the name *bolos pata prieto*, black-legged tail-featherless roosters, while their onetime allies in the civilian and intellectual leadership called themselves *bolos pata blanca*, white-legged roosters. The latter wanted to lie low and support the government, but the military men in the black-legged group lost patience: the *bolos pata prieto* prevailed. In November 1911, they attempted to kidnap Cáceres and killed him when he tried to fight back.

Joaquín Balaguer, the man who virtually personified the Dominican

Republic during his seven terms as President, also chose the rooster as his symbol. Puppet president when Trujillo was assassinated in 1961, Balaguer was deposed not long after; he founded his own party, with the rooster as mascot, while he was in exile in New York in 1964. In 1965, Dominicans fought a civil war that ended when Lyndon Johnson sent in twenty-two thousand combat troops. A year later, Balaguer returned to Santo Domingo and became President, with the support of the United States. He spent twenty-two of the next thirty years in the Dominican Republic's highest office.

To enter politics on Hispaniola is, in effect, to enter a fighting ring. The metaphor works both ways: the cockfight represents men's fight for power, but at some point the ritual of the cockfight goes beyond just representing the way politics and society are structured. In Césaire's play about Haiti, the cocks are given names of men. In reality, the leaders on both sides of the island have themselves taken on the identity of the fighting cock so intimately that the rooster is man and the man rooster. Politics begins to imitate the cockfight instead of the other way around.

Santo Domingo's Alberto Bonetti Burgos Cockfighting Coliseum is hosting an international three-day tournament. There are fans from Panama, Peru, Cuba, Haiti, Puerto Rico, and Miami. In the coliseum, the *galleros* drink scotch, wear freshly starched and pressed linen, and relax in wide, comfortable theater chairs. It is a whole world away from Manoguayabo, though only fifteen minutes by car. In the coliseum, the waitresses are plump and uniformed, asexual and quiet; they move easily along the aisle between the feet of the *galleros* and the padded edge of the ring. In the clean, air-conditioned air, there are hardly any smells except from the antiseptic used to wipe down the edge of the ring at the end of each fight. It hardly seems a place where roosters will be goaded to attack each other to the death.

In the early 1970s, cockfighting was in a state of disarray. There were no controls, laments Dr. Angel Contreras, president of the coliseum. You never knew whether a fighting rooster was pumped full of drugs or had poison on its spur tips. The coliseum was born when a group of Dominican businessmen, cockfighting fans all, sat down to plan a place that would help "separate the good from the bad," as Contreras puts it. "At first, the other cockfighting clubs were jealous. But we slowly convinced them that the coliseum would raise the level of the sport and thus would attract more people to it." Along with a group of core investors, another hundred fans each put up a thousand dollars. In 1973, the founders broke ground for the building, which was completed two years later. Contreras himself picked out a microscope to use in the antidrug lab; he asked the police what they used and bought a more advanced model of the same microscope. President Balaguer inaugurated the coliseum.

The founding members of the club sit in reserved seats ringside, while visitors are up in the balcony. As in the *bajo mundo*, the audience is nearly all men. (Today, one of the few women visiting is a nun.) The spectators seated above are darker than the members and owners down at the edge of the ring, though in the excitement of the fights this is largely ignored or forgotten. In theory, everyone is equal at the cockfights, where political disputes and class distinctions are left aside.

The international tournament's first two fighters appear, caged in a Plexiglas cable car at the end of a mechanical trolley above the balcony. When the cab reaches the end of the metal track, it lowers slowly down to the center of the ring. The handlers lift from the top a handheld blackboard identifying the contestants and center bet, and insert the board into another cart that holds a time clock. "Each match will be fifteen minutes," the judge announces. All the trappings of the fight are formal, official. This is the big league.

The handlers pull out the birds, stuff them into bags (one blue, one white, matching the identifying tape on the roosters' legs; one bird has an extra thin blue tape along the white tape that holds its spurs on), and weigh them on a scale attached to the bottom of the cage that brought the birds down from the preparation area. After the judge is satisfied that the birds are equal in weight and plumage, the cage and time clock are hoisted away from the ring and the handlers begin agitating the animals. The handlers thrust a *mona* rooster into the faces of the cocks, whistle at and blow on them, ruffle their feathers, clap beside their heads, lift and drop them rapidly, anything that will serve to rile them. The birds lift their neck plumage and lunge at the hands that torment them.

Betting begins. Though the owners of the two combatants have put up 3,000 pesos against each other, they now make additional bets with the spectators, and all the participants seek partners for other side bets. The stakes, counted in both money and honor, are high. For that reason, a breach of the code of honor is far less likely here than in places like Manoguayabo, in the underworld. José Brito, the *juez de valla*—"referee" seems too lowly a translation to express his true status; this man is indeed a judge—can't remember the last time he had to throw someone out for failing to make good on a bet.

The more you know about the owners, the better you can tell how a fight will go. "The owner is more important than the rooster itself," Dr. Contreras explains between matches. "If you know the owner, you know his style, his birds' reputation, the skills of his trainers. You may even know a bit about his strategy: whether he puts up his better birds earlier or later in a tournament."

The second match ends quickly when the winner jumps into the air and drives its spurs deep into his opponent. This is a mortal wound, a *golpe de sangre*. "He split that one's breast in half. He's a criminal, that one," says Dr. Contreras, guffawing. He enjoys applying his medical knowledge to the excitement of this fight, the best one of the day.

Most matches aren't determined so quickly. As a match progresses, the odds rise and fall as the apparent advantage switches back and forth. You can tell sometimes by the amount of blood on the tape holding the spurs to a rooster's legs. The more blood, the higher the number of successful stabs the bird has made at his adversary.

If a rooster appears to be a sure loser, the owner may begin to bet against himself. In Santo Domingo, to hedge this way is called *cubrirse*, to cover oneself. But if you are a *criador* who has bred, brought up, and overseen the training of a rooster, you never do that. The real *criador* will never sell his rooster short. That would reduce the match to a business transaction and the *gallero* to a mere player of the odds, not unlike investors who buy options or make short sales to hedge against losses in the stock market. There would be little emotion involved, only the cold thrill of cash.

Though a rooster may appear seriously wounded, sometimes it recovers a half hour later. Other times, if a cock has been hurt too badly to win but will not die and does not run away, the owner may ask to have him pulled. That way, his life can be saved and he can fight again a year later. There is nothing dishonorable in making such a decision.

In the third match, one bird falters early on. The owner, in a striped shirt, sits glum and silent several chairs away from us. As the opponent batters him, the losing cock crows pitifully. The favorite keeps attacking. Finally, the loser picks himself up, runs, and flings himself against the padded edge of the ring. He scrambles up and over and tumbles into the aisle, where spectators haul him up and back into the ring. The *juez de valla* cuts the tail feathers of the rooster who turned tail and ran. The bird has dishonored its owner and the sport and does not deserve to fight again.

The matches continue for hours. When Puerto Rican or Cuban birds fight and foreign players spring into action, the Dominicans slow their betting; they don't know these birds or owners so well. They also lose interest because they know that the Miami and Puerto Rican contestants haven't brought their best fighters; U.S. law requires them to keep the birds for forty days in quarantine when they go back home, and they won't do that with their champions. The matches are disappointing. One drags on for thirteen minutes and forty-two seconds, until the birds are too tired to fight and simply circle each other making halfhearted pecks.

Near the end of the evening, a tired-looking Dominican—fortyish, balding, with glasses—sits down just in time to see one of his own birds fight. Federico "Quique" Antún Batlle, who has been fighting roosters since he was practically a child, says the first rooster of his very own was a gift from Modesto Díaz, two weeks before Díaz and a handful of other Dominican men assassinated the hated dictator Rafael Trujillo on May 30, 1961. (When another conspirator, Salvador Estrella, returned from the killing, he told Díaz's young nephew that the blood spattered all over his shirt was from the cockfights, according to the journalist Bernard Diederich's account of the assassination.) Díaz and nearly all his co-conspirators died horrible deaths at the hands of Trujillo's associates not long after. The rooster Modesto Díaz gave Quique Antún fought only once and lost.

Thirty-four years later, in the late winter of 1995, Quique Antún is secretary-general of the ruling Reformist Social Christian Party, whose symbol is the fighting red rooster. Antún still keeps a large *traba*, a farm where fighting cocks are raised and trained, and regularly gives gamecocks to regional Reformista political organizers as gifts. "The roosters aren't only a hobby; they are political," Antún says. The ongoing election campaign is why he looks so tired. President Balaguer, who must step down at the end of this term, is not throwing his support behind his party's candidate, Jacinto Peynado, whose campaign is Quique Antún's responsibility, and Peynado is running a distant third in the polls. Earlier in the week, newspapers quoted Antún's saying his party would have to seek alliances going into the election in May, not even two months away. The stress is clearly wearing on him.

When Antún's rooster, wearing the white tape, is lowered into the ring, weighed, and inspected, the judge clips ever so little from the feathers at the back of its neck. According to coliseum rules, the birds must have equal plumage so that one does not gain an unfair advantage by being able to grab on to more of the other bird's feathers. Antún, watching the fight, seems vaguely distracted. Before long, it is clear that the other bird is stronger, though Antún's bird has heart and tries hard to defend itself. As the odds shift strongly in favor of the blue, Antún slides back in his chair, subdued. The white cock's spurs have split, leaving him defenseless. There is no hope for him. Shortly after the match ends, Antún leaves, politely excusing himself and pleading exhaustion.

The next fight, the last of the day, is a disaster. The losing cock runs madly from the aggressor, jumping out of the ring onto spectators' laps. Each time, the handlers grab him and set him in the middle of the ring facing his opponent. As soon as they release him, he runs again. The fiasco is over in almost no time. As the judge snips the cock's tail feathers, spectators mill toward the exit. It is as if they are embarrassed for the owner, who has been humiliated by the rooster with no heart in this sport that celebrates honor, courage, and the fight to the death.

Fifteen employees care for the hundred roosters, hens, and chicks at Rafael Perelló's *traba*, where he raises and trains his birds. An agricultural businessman, Perelló comes by here once or twice a day to check on the birds. Some of his roosters come directly from Spain at $200 or more apiece. The rest are *criollos*, Dominican descendants of Spanish birds, just as sixteenth-century Dominicans were the offspring of Spaniards come to the New World. As Perelló gives a tour of the *traba*, one can see that each cage where hens bring up their chicks is marked with the numbers, not names, of the mother and father.

One cage holds four chicks: one gray and taller than the others, and three smaller brown ones. The tall gray chick, despite his advantage in size, is edging to the corner of the cage away from the others; his head is red with pecks from the other birds. Perelló is disgusted: "Look, bigger than all the others, and look what he lets them do to him."

Perelló knows from their ancestry which chicks will grow up to be the strongest roosters. "These," he says, stopping in front of a cage marked "536, 1889." It seems so impersonal, yet he remembers exactly which numbers are the best. Some *galleros* don't believe in naming their cocks, because doing so makes it harder when the birds lose, and those who fight many birds don't have the time or energy to put into it. The really famous birds have names: the most renowned of all was Carioca, a Dominican cock who fought in Puerto Rico in the 1950s.

Only one of Perelló's roosters merits a name instead of a number: Dinamita (Dynamite). The bird is nearly nine years old and has never fought. Perelló knows he is good because of his blood. The birds raised on this *traba* will never fight in the *bajo mundo*; they have been bred for the highest level of cockfighting, at the coliseum. Cockfighters gather in cliques, frequenting the same arenas and becoming fiercely territorial about where they bring their birds and whom they fight. Just like Dominican society, the cockfight is sharply stratified, with the elite separated and far away from the humble peasant cockers.

The cockfight is a family affair, passed down from one generation to the next. Perelló's father had a *gallera* in the Trujillo era, back in the days when cockers still had to practice their sport clandestinely. Trujillo knew well that the cockfight was a political arena. He discouraged cockfighting: not by decree or formal law, but he simply "made it known." That was his way: to govern by suggestion and innuendo, letting fear and suspicion alongside an unspoken code do his work for him. Making his wishes known so subtly, Trujillo could arbitrarily enforce them. Though he was said to feel that cockfighting discouraged good work habits, it could just as well have been that he disliked the fighting rooster that represented Horacio Vásquez, the President that Trujillo had forced from power. Or it could be that Trujillo opposed the image of the Dominican Republic as a country in turmoil, caught between two fighting parties. For his own political symbol, Trujillo chose the royal palm, erect, phallic, steadfast, hardly scrabbling for power.

Trujillo allowed neither enlisted men nor high civil officials to engage in cockfighting. Nonetheless, he was politically astute and in 1947 allowed a key adviser, Dr. Rafael Vidal of Santiago, to convince him to declare cockfighting a national sport. In the stylish, sedate old Hotel Jaragua (the predecessor to the present one, a pink Las Vegas–style monstrosity where Robert Redford stayed while filming *Havana* here in 1989), two rooms were converted into cockfighting arenas. Even Amable "Pipí" Romero, an associate of Trujillo's family, went to the cockfights. The night Trujillo was assassinated, Pipí went to the house of Juan Tomás Díaz, one of the men in on the plot to kill the dictator, to drop off a pair of spurs.

Rafael Perelló laughs when asked if there are any notorious rivals among the *galleros* at the coliseum. "Those things come and go," he says. "It depends on who has been winning a lot lately." The game becomes one of knocking the recent winner out of the top position. Over the last few months, the birds of a cocker named José Then have been winning consistently. Then's champion rooster, Bacundú, killed six rivals in eighteen minutes and earned his owner the title Gallero of the Month. Perelló won't say explicitly that he and Then are rivals, but he hints at it.

José Then looks at his watch: it is nearly eleven. "Seven minutes to feeding time," he says. His roosters eat punctually at 11:00 and 3:30 each day, and disrupting the schedule is bad for their constitutions. The only change ever made in their routine is on days before a fight, when the portion of food is reduced so the birds won't be sluggish. The roosters begin clamoring; their sensitivity to time is part of what has made them heralds of the dawn. José picks up a bucket of corn one of the assistants has brought for him. As he walks around the cages, the bucket held over his head, the roosters crow even louder, drowning his words.

Feeding time is an almost religious ritual. José Then spends his whole day at the *traba* and lives for the birds. Every time one goes out to fight, it is as if he is in the ring, too. His wife despairs at the time he spends with the birds. She sighs at the trophies and stuffed roosters that clutter the cabinets in their dining room and living room. But she accompanies him on each of his many trips to Santo Domingo and waits patiently during the hours he spends with his roosters.

José Then lives in New York. His little diner in Brooklyn makes New York's best *morir soñando*, "to die dreaming," a concoction of orange juice and milk poured and drunk right away before the milk curdles. His daughters live there. But his heart is here in Santo Domingo, where he

spends half the year, passing the afternoon training his cocks and preparing for the battles his birds fight for him. His business in his native
country is real estate, but when he writes down his work phone number,
it is that of the *traba*.

Unlike Rafael Perelló, José Then belongs to the school of cockers
who believe in naming their roosters. He rolls off from memory the
names of his very favorites: Blanco Ajitici, named after a very hot pepper;
Pingamosa, after a poisonous plant; El Zombi; Mal Amigo (The Bad
Friend); La Muleta; El Chicle (Gum), *porque pega el que llega*, because
it sticks to you if you step in it; Madonna; and El Cielo (The Sky),
because it always looked up at him when he went to inspect it.

His favorite, naturally, is Bacundú. Santo Domingo's weekly cockfighting newspaper, *El Gallístico*, bills Bacundú as *El Rey del Coliseo*, King
of the Coliseum. "Eagle-headed, his chest as broad as the sword of Attila,
with robust muscles as red as the desire to sin and feathers as white as
the purity of good souls," the paper gushed. Bacundú's name itself is
simply a mix of letters José Then chose from the family tree, though
several cockfighting fans have suggested that the name evokes some long-
lost African spirit that gives the bird his extraordinary power. Bacundú's
father was named El Loco (Crazy One). His mother was a daughter of
another of Then's best roosters, Enrique Blanco. *Galleros* will brag about
the siring powers of their famous cocks, but only a few (Then is one of
them) will tell you that the real power to pass on strength and endurance
lies in the hen.

Bacundú was born twenty-two months ago in back of the barn next
to a tree that had a giant Dominican yam, a *ñame*, growing underneath
it. José Then was planning to pull out the yam soon and weigh it; the
yam, he believed, might have had something to do with Bacundú's special
strength and skill. Openly and proudly superstitious, Then has decided
never to wear a name tag if his cocks are fighting, because last Saturday
he had to wear a name tag and all his roosters lost. Another day, on the
way to the cockfights his car hit a dog and killed it; all his roosters won,
and he thanked the dog for the good luck it brought. Then there was
the time he reluctantly lent money to a friend the day before a fight;
when the fights went well, he went looking for another friend who
wanted to borrow money.

The *ñame* is part of the mystical world José Then has constructed around his roosters. When champion roosters tire, they go to an *asilo de viejos* (retirement home), where he sends the old champions to live out their lives in peace. In the *colegio de niños*, the children's school, young roosters exercise and grow. When a rooster is ready to mate, he goes, naturally, to a cabaret. The *colegio* and cabaret rest along the foot of a gentle hill he calls La Lomita de la Suerte, the Good-Luck Hill.

In the nursery, the hens and chicks are speckled light and dark under the shadow pattern cast by a row of shade trees alongside their cages. Next to the cages, there it is: the famous yam, or at least the tip of it. José summons one of the workers to dig out the yam so it doesn't damage the tree next to it. The digging lasts nearly half an hour, and by the time it is finished there is a crater in the ground. The worker, with the help of another, hauls out the giant yam; when weighed, it turns out to be more than eighty pounds.

"This is where Bacundú was born, in the middle of all these trees and with the luck of the yam. Nature is with him," José Then says proudly. This yam is large and round, feminine, like the Spanish slang meaning of "yam," not at all like the English slang, which figures the yam as phallic and makes the word synonymous with "cock."

The fight is not just about the birds. It is about José Then and his way of life. His recipe for cooking a fighting rooster is as follows: First stew the meat in water. Then strain the broth from the carcass; you can use it for soup. Pull the meat from the bones and shred it. Place it in *escabeche*, a traditional Dominican marinade of vinegar, garlic, and onion. On the side, serve white rice. But Then won't eat the dish himself if the rooster was one of his most prized fighting cocks. He will give away the carcass of a rooster that had real heart.

In cockfighting as in life, José Then is philosophical about the times his birds lose: "They say that women and roosters have something in common. One day, they will fail you. Any rooster, even the best one, will lose one day."

This morning, Bacundú is staring fiercely out of his cage. Though he has killed six opponents, he hasn't escaped unscathed. The champion rooster has only one eye; one of his more valiant victims took one successful stab before expiring. Bacundú has been resting and recovering and is almost ready to go to his next fight. Though it's hard to imagine on this cool spring morning, it will be his last.

When Bacundú arrives at the coliseum a few days later, the opponent he draws is one of Rafael Perelló's roosters. It is the final day of the three-day international tournament, and all the *galleros* have been waiting. Everyone wants to see if Bacundú will win again.

The fight starts badly, very badly, for the famous rooster. Almost immediately, Rafael Perelló's cock slashes out Bacundú's remaining eye, then continues to attack. He hits Bacundú so hard in the chest that it looks as if the match might be over then and there. But Bacundú picks himself up and, guided by a sixth sense, for he is completely blind now, flings himself at his opponent. When Bacundú pulls back, the other bird is dead.

When judging time comes, the outcome is almost unbelievable. The match is declared a draw. When the handlers had presented the dead bird to Bacundú again, the champion rooster had not continued pecking at his limp opponent. The *juez de valla*'s word is law. There is nothing José Then can (or would) do. He and the many spectators who agree that Bacundú had won are stunned. How could this champion who had killed the other bird be said to have only tied?

All José Then will say is that something very strange went on. He will not stoop to criticize the judge or to behave in a way that even remotely appears to be that of a sore loser. It would be against the code of the *gallero*, a breach of honor. Bacundú will go into retirement in the *asilo de viejos*, along the side of the barn not far from the trees and the giant yam where he was born. And José Then is left wondering if, by pulling the lucky yam out of the ground, he gave Bacundú the strength to overcome his final opponent or if he doomed the prize rooster to lose his sight and his fighting career.

"An image, a fiction, a model, a metaphor, the cockfight is a means of expression," Clifford Geertz has written about the sport in Bali. On the farms where the birds are raised, in the arenas themselves, and among the men who fight cocks, cockfighting is part of the ritual and imagery of life, but it has gone beyond that to become a metaphor for politics and society. This elaborately constructed fiction is not only about roosters.

The cockfight is a drama not just between the owners of the two roosters in any given match but also for those who watch as mere spectators. For José Then, the cockfight is a test of his philosophy of life and the rituals with which he surrounds his chosen sport. For the true *gallero*, the fight is a drama in which he can act out the passions of life. It deflects his aggression and frustration into the ring, where the roosters release emotions that men are not allowed to display.

The cockfight is not about the roosters. It is about the men. That is the essence of the symbol of Hispaniola's two countries, where cockfighting and life imitate each other. The confrontations between the Dominican Republic and Haiti, trapped and fighting for limited territory, have been dramatic and tragic.

The conflict between the two countries sharing one island, like the cockfight, also masks something else; clever observers and players can profit from the fight, and, more important, those who identify themselves closely with the combatants can play out a shadow game that redirects conflict away from themselves.

The Massacre River

Medias montañas,
Medios rios,
y hasta la muerte compartida.

Between them mountains,
Between them rivers,
And even a shared death.

—*Manuel Rueda*
"Cantos de la frontera" (Songs of the border)

The Artibonite River begins high in the Dominican Republic's Cordillera Central mountain range. It runs west, then curves south, parallel to the Carretera Internacional, the highway along the north-south border dividing the island of Hispaniola into east and west. The road is an international highway in the sense that it is the only direct route through the very center of the island, right along the Dominican-Haitian border. Rather than the grand thoroughfare its name suggests, the International Highway is a maze of rocks, crevasses, and quicksand strung together through the mountains that helped give Haiti its name, from an indigenous Taino word meaning "high place" or "mountain." It can take a whole day to travel, though it is less than two hundred kilometers long, beginning in the south at San Juan de la Maguana and ending in the north at Dajabón, by another river, the Massacre.

The Artibonite River links the two countries. The Massacre River, and the terrible events that occurred in 1937 along the border formed by its waters, separates them. At the Pedro Santana military fortress, just north of the midpoint, the Artibonite twists, slows to a trickle, and crosses the highway and the border. It snakes west into Haiti past the Lac de Peligre, the Lake of Danger, then twists its way down the mountains and pours into the sea far away at the scruffy western town of Gonaïves.

For the short time the river tracks the International Highway, it gurgles far, far below it, straight down a sheer precipice. From the edge of the road, you can see the river only if you stop your vehicle and climb through the grass that covers the very few yards separating the road from the drop. Every few mountaintops apart, an outpost bearing a tattered Dominican flag pierces the mist. Each station is staffed by a lone soldier, who, if he is lucky, might have his family living in a shack at the foot of the lookout tower.

The mail truck comes by each Monday and Thursday. Some of the days in between, no vehicles pass at all. If your Jeep breaks down, as many do on this rough terrain, you could be stuck for days. During that time, you might be carried away forever. The mountains are haunted by the spirits of runaway slaves and Indians who lived and died here centuries ago but still inhabit the terrain of trees, rocks, and rivers in the form of mythical beings tormented by the horrors of the past. Naked and mute, tragic, savage creatures called *bien-bienes* live in the trees. These ghosts of runaway slaves rob the peasants' mountainside gardens by night. If humans disturb their forest retreats, the *bien-bienes* shriek and moan with such grief that the intruder will be overcome by sadness for the rest of his life.

Sitting on boulders along the mountain streams, beautiful, tiny women with golden skin comb their long, supple tresses. These are the *ciguapas*: mountain sirens, spirits of the Taino Indian women who fled here from the Spaniards centuries ago. Insanely jealous and mostly mute, *ciguapas* make chirping and trilling sounds like birdsongs to lure men into their river caves forever. No one can ever trace their tracks to rescue the lost men, because the *ciguapas'* feet are attached backward and their footsteps always lead in the wrong direction. The people who live in the mountains are afraid of them, because if a *ciguapa* falls in love with a mountain youth, she will kill his human lover. There are tales, too, of male *ciguapas*, who are just as dangerous.

Even more fearsome than the *ciguapa* is the *baka*, the Dominican werewolf, cousin to the Haitian *loup-garou*, a creature so dreadful that the very sight of it is enough to kill or paralyze anyone unfortunate enough to cross its path. Often, the monster disguises itself as a black dog or goat, so it can watch quietly and attack when it has the best advantage. The only way to convince a *baka* not to attack is to offer it a human sacrifice, ideally a family member. Such a sacrifice enters a property owner into a pact with the *baka*, which will then protect all the owner's belongings. But one sacrifice is not enough. To satisfy the monster, its master must keep supplying it with human flesh, or the *baka* will turn in revenge and devour the master. There are two ways to acquire a *baka*. The simplest is to go to Gonâve Island, in the Haitian bay west of Port-au-Prince, and find one. The other is to grow one from an egg buried under a crucifix on Holy Friday. After nine days, the egg will hatch a *baka* in the form of a black chicken.

If the perilous monsters of local legend fail to discourage most Dominicans from venturing into these mountains, tales of real-life dangers succeed. Rumors in the capital have it that gangs of roving bandits lie in wait along the International Highway to ambush unsuspecting travelers. For this reason, the soldiers at Pedro Santana check each vehicle passing through. In the laborious handwriting of men with hardly a grade-school education, they impress the numbers of the vehicle registration and the identification of the driver into the moist pages of a dog-eared ledger. The sentinels then copy the numbers again onto an official piece of paper and stamp it in blue to give to travelers before allowing them to proceed.

Rain starts slowly in the mountains. You can see clouds wrapping around the next ridge over, throwing wisps of mist through the pine trees. When the cloud envelops your peak, you don't even notice the first drops of rain; thirty minutes later, you realize that it has been raining for half an hour. By that time the rain has become persistent and threatens never to end. The rain falls in loud silence, a rush of white noise that does not muffle but instead accentuates other sounds: the crash of a tree, the plop of a rock in a stream of water. The depth of the potholes on the International Highway becomes a mystery measurable no longer by sight but by faith.

The people who live here appear as surreptitiously as the mountain rain. Stopped as you wonder how best to navigate a patch of quicksand that has devoured the road, you hear a mango dropping into the soft earth, loud in the rain. When you look up, a family of Haitian peasants has appeared under the trees. The father, leaning on his machete, stares. His children peek out from behind a tree. An old man stands nearby watching. Later, he will ask if you have any medicine to stop the pus oozing from his ear.

The peasants shuffle down the hill. They point to a shallow spot at the side of the quicksand pool. A car could pass here if it went forward without stopping. The Haitians guide you past, with a wave, then tread back up the hill into the trees and the silence. It is two hours at a turtle's pace to the next town.

Hard to reach and far from the commerce of the coasts, the desolate, mountainous center of Hispaniola for centuries has been a no-man's-land, neither Spanish nor French, Dominican nor Haitian. Abandoned during most of Hispaniola's history, the mountains are the defining physical feature of an island whose geography is, in effect, its story. Their peaks are shrouded by mists that surge early in the day and then travel down the slopes, embracing and obscuring the sheer heights, then penetrating the chasms between them. The drama of the landscape obscures the few people who live here, at the focal point of an island enclosed by its shores, divided by mountains, and crossed by rivers.

Soon after Columbus landed on the shores of Hispaniola, the mountains became a refuge for the native Taino Indians, who fled rather than let the Spaniards work them to death mining in vain for gold. Many African slaves, brought in later in the sixteenth century, after the Indians died of European illnesses or were killed off, followed the same escape path high into the wilderness. Out of the reach of their European masters, these runaway slaves—called *cimarrones* by the Spanish and *marrons* by the French—established colonies high up in the Cordillera Central. Decades later, the mountains buffered the European powers vying for control of Hispaniola.

Not long after they arrived, the Spanish realized little gold was to be found there. So when the explorers Alonso de Ojeda, Vasco Núñez de Balboa, and Hernán Cortés discovered gold and silver deposits in South America and Mexico in the early sixteenth century, the Spanish quickly abandoned their Santo Domingo settlement in favor of the more promising precious-metal deposits elsewhere in the New World. Their exodus opened the way for the island to become a surrogate battleground for the European powers racing to dominate the New World.

As the Spanish colony dwindled, France and England saw gold in Hispaniola in the form of agriculture: coffee, tobacco, mahogany, sugar, and molasses. In the early seventeenth century, adventurous buccaneers and enterprising tobacco farmers set up outposts on the western end of the island, in particular on the tiny but strategically placed Île de la Tortue, Turtle Island, at the far western end of the north coast. In 1618, when the Thirty Years' War broke out in Europe, the French incursions into Hispaniola became symbolically more important, and the island became an arena where aggressions between France and Spain were played out. Meanwhile, England tried repeatedly to wrest parts of Hispaniola from its European rivals. The colonists who remained in Santo Domingo suffered what is still called the Hundred Years' Misery.

Repeated military threats from France forced the skeletal Spanish colonial government on Hispaniola to recognize that it could not enforce its claim to the western end if it did not establish its presence there and, indeed, across the entire island. Trying to regain its footing, it granted land to any Spanish subjects who would brave life in the interior. The infant settlements soon succumbed to isolation and disease. Meanwhile, Spain tried time and again to expel the French from La Tortue and western Hispaniola.

After Sir Francis Drake and his band of pirates sacked Santo Domingo in 1586, the colonial government called on the Spanish settlers to ally with the African slaves to fend off attacks by such marauders, who were often supported by foreign governments eager for a bigger share of the riches of the New World. Desperate to keep up the dwindling Spanish population as a last defense against French and English aspirations to shrink Spain's territory on Hispaniola, the colonial government went so far as to encourage white colonists to marry the former slaves. These mixed-race children were treated as Spanish and white and brought up with a strong sense of Roman Catholic identity to strengthen their resolve in fighting off Protestant invaders.

Ironically, this early racial mixing in Santo Domingo continued in part because Spain wanted to subdue the colonists, not to strengthen their numbers. In the early sixteenth century, even before the Africans arrived, when a strong-arm Spanish colonial governor, Nicolás de Ovando, had forced many of the colonists to marry Indians, his main aim had been to subdue a group of rebel settlers who wanted freedom from the Spanish government. Many of the men, according to the Dominican historian Roberto Cassá, were already living with Taino women because the relationships gave them authority within the Indian communities whose help they enlisted against the Spanish government. When the rebels were coerced into marrying formally the Taino women, Ovando seized their property to punish them for having mixed with the local population. Their offspring were considered half-breeds with no legitimate claims to property.

In the end, Spain failed to hold on to the island. By 1655, France won western Hispaniola from Spain permanently, though it did not wrest a formal concession until the 1697 Treaty of Ryswick, which sealed the truce in the Nine Years' War in Europe and split Hispaniola into two colonies, the much larger Spanish Santo Domingo and the smaller French Saint-Domingue.

The colonies were as different topographically as they were in terms of language and European ties. The lay of the land was to create sharply different economies, which in turn shaped race relations. With its broad open lands, the eastern, Spanish Santo Domingo was suited to cattle, on which the colony came to depend; though sugar cultivation was begun in the sixteenth century, it was not to become a significant industry until the twentieth century. By contrast, the western, French Saint-Domingue relied on labor-intensive tobacco and sugar cultivation carried out on its mountains and low coastal plantations. As the Dominican historian Frank Moya Pons points out, cattle herding cannot work without cooperation between the owners of land and the men who work it; by contrast, plantation farming requires a strict hierarchy of powerful landowners as masters of the masses who work the land. The result was that the free European and the enslaved African populations remained separate in Saint-Domingue but mixed in Santo Domingo.

Over the centuries, the racial lines within Dominican society blurred, and it became, as it still largely is, mulatto, where color divisions are still important but movable. As early as 1549, according to the Dominican historian Franklin J. Franco, Santo Domingo's colonial government defined seven racial types: black, or *negro*, slaves brought from Africa and their children; white, pure-race Spaniards; mulatto, offspring of black and white; mestizo, descended from Indian and white; *tercerón*, child of a mulatto and white; *cuarterón*, child of a *terceròn* and white; and *grifo*, mixed Indian and black. Over the years, the residents of Hispaniola refined those categories. *Blancos de la tierra*, Dominicans later called themselves, whites of the earth.

In the Dominican heartland, the Cibao valley, the Dominican sociologist Daysi Josefina Guzmán in the early 1970s identified nine hair colors and fifteen main kinds of hair texture on a spectrum between *bueno* (good) for soft Caucasian hair and *malo* (bad) for kinky Negroid hair; *lacio*, straight and smooth; *achinado* for straight stiff hair; *espeso*, thick, abundant, and very slightly wavy; *macho*, thick and strong, abundant, but without luster; *rizado*, thick and fine with small waves, but dull; *muerto*, thin and greasy; *ondulado*, wavy; *vivo*, thick, dry, and out of control; *variable*, of any type, indescribable; *crespo*, thick and frizzy; *de pimienta*, peppery, growing slow and tight to the skull in small balls; *motica*, like peppery hair but thin, wavy; *pegaíto*, so close to the skull that it is impossible to comb.

She identified twelve skin colors: *lechoso*, too white, like milk; *blanco*, white; *cenizo*, ashen; *descolorido*, without color; *pálido*, so pale as to appear sick; *desteñido*, jaundiced; *pecoso*, freckled; *pinto*, mostly light but with large freckles or moles; *trigueño*, light with a very slight dark touch; *manchado*, dark with white streaks; *negro*, very dark; *morado*, so black as to be almost purple. In addition, there were ten facial structures, six physical types, and five general racial types. Each category could, practically, be used as a guide to where any Dominican stood on the social scale.

There is another racial category that Guzmán did not mention in her study: Haitian. In the Dominican Republic, calling someone Haitian is on the surface synonymous with describing them as *negro* or *morado* but with an added psychological weight of fear and hatred. Haitians are generally darker than Dominicans. The best guess is that more than two-thirds of Dominicans are mixed race (mostly African and European, but possibly with a tiny portion of Taino blood) in the middle of the color spectrum. The remaining population is split more or less evenly between the black and white ends. In Haiti, by contrast, a small elite with light skin counts for no more than a tenth of the population; the vast majority of Haitians occupy the darkest end of the color spectrum.

The early French colonists in Saint-Domingue identified 128 different racial types defined quite precisely along a mathematical scale determined by simple calculations of ancestral contributions. They ranged from the "true" mulatto (half white, half black), through the spectrum of *marabou, sacatra, quarteron,* all the way to the *sang-mêlé* (mixed blood: 127 parts white, 1 part black). The celebrated writer and historian C.L.R. James attributes the precise naming to the whites' fear of the slaves and to the desire to keep the black and mixed populations subject to the whites: "The mothers of the Mulattoes were in the slave gangs, they had half-brothers there, and however much the Mulatto himself might despise this half of his origin, he was at home among the slaves and, in addition to his wealth and education, could have an influence among them which a white man could never have," James wrote in *The Black Jacobins,* his classic work on the Haitian Revolution.

The sociologist Micheline Labelle has counted twenty-two main racial categories and ninety-eight subcategories (for varying hair types, facial structures, color, and other distinguishing factors) used among Haiti's middle class in Port-au-Prince in the 1970s. Within each category, the words are often as imaginative as they are descriptive: *café au lait, bonbon siro* (candy syrup), *ti canel* (little cinnamon), *ravet blanch* (white cockroach), *soley levan* (rising sun), *banane mûre* (ripe banana), *brun pistache* (peanut brown), *mulâtre dix-huit carats* (18-carat mulatto). Their levity belies the dramatic history behind the gradations of color and the color-class system that persists in Haiti centuries after the white French planters set up a system of slavery so brutal that the black slaves rebelled and forced the whites away from the land.

Today, Haiti's main (if movable) dividing line separates blacks and mulattoes in a distinction that depends on class as much as color. A rich black man is a mulatto, a poor mulatto is black, Haitians say. The Kreyol word *nèg* has a broader sense than does the English "Negro": *nèg* means "man." Likewise, the word *blan* means not "white" but "foreigner" of any color. Dark-skinned Americans, even Haitian-Americans, are *blan.*

As Spanish Santo Domingo declined in the seventeenth century, French Saint-Domingue prospered. When the first settlers established themselves on the west of the island, there were few white women in Saint-Domingue, so the male planters availed themselves of their female slaves. At first, the children of those unions enjoyed more rights than did their black half sisters and brothers. In 1685, Louis XIV's *Code Noir* tried to ensure that the slaves would be treated humanely. That code allowed whites to marry the slaves who bore them children; those children, like free Negroes, were equal with whites under the code. As the years progressed, however, the number of mulattoes grew, approaching the number of whites and becoming a minority no longer. By that time, the French population had expanded and the Spanish dwindled enough that the white French made their priority regaining control over the masses of slaves who worked the cane and coffee plantations.

In 1759, the planters forbade the mulattoes to carry swords. James writes that the mulattoes could not wear European-style clothes, play European games, or gather in groups, even for weddings and feasts. They had to seek permission to purchase ammunition. By 1781, the mulattoes no longer enjoyed the privilege of calling themselves "Monsieur" or "Madame." They could not sit at meals with white men, even in their own homes. By the end of the century, Saint-Domingue had ten times more blacks than whites. Divisions between the two groups, exploited by an angry mulatto class stripped of the rights it had once known, soon tore the colony apart.

Events in Europe deepened the colony's race and class cleavages. By 1789, merchants were selling forty thousand African slaves a year to Saint-Domingue to fill the demand for labor in France's richest colony. As the century drew to a close, Saint-Domingue was growing 60 percent of the coffee sold in Europe, and more sugar and coffee than any other place in the world. Yet the colonists of Saint-Domingue, chafing under the taxes they had to pay to the mother country, believed they were not being compensated properly.

When the Revolution broke out in France, the emboldened colonists saw their chance to win the rights to the profits they felt were theirs. As the colonists directed their energy toward breaking the yoke of France, the mulattoes and slaves sought ways to win their independence as well. They were an attentive audience when the French Assembly declared in 1791 that all men were free and equal, helping to begin a revolution that would once again redraw the racial and geographical borders dividing

Hispaniola. The slaves of Saint-Domingue rebelled in 1793, led by a former slave coachman named Toussaint Louverture. With the slaves given new hope of freedom, the mulattoes offered to ally with them to overthrow the white plantation owners.

The chaos also gave an opening to foreign powers, whose designs on the rebellious but wealthy colony were by no means extinguished. By the spring of 1793, France and Britain were at war over Saint-Domingue. Meanwhile, France and Spain went to war the same year, making Britain a Spanish ally, temporarily at least.

Though Spain still controlled Santo Domingo, the eastern two-thirds of the island was only a shadow of Saint-Domingue. The total population of the Spanish part, including 15,000 slaves, was barely more than 100,000, only about a fourth that of the French colony, where there were as many as half a million slaves living under the control of perhaps 30,000 whites and 35,000 mulattoes. And, in contrast to the agricultural riches of Saint-Domingue, Santo Domingo was producing little sugar and even had to import tobacco and coffee to fill its own needs. Spain, eager to regain the western half of Hispaniola, set its hopes on Britain's driving out the French government.

Spain also saw the benefit to be gained by allying with the rebellious slave army, which it hoped would be able to control the rest of the island once France was defeated. In July 1793, the Secretary for Colonial Affairs in Madrid urged the Santo Domingo governor to offer land, freedom, and Spanish citizenship to Toussaint and his troops, who, lured by that promise, briefly allied with Spain. Despite proclaimed Spanish intentions and the strength of the British abolition movement, it was only a matter of months until it became obvious that neither government had any intention of freeing the slaves. Thus, weeks after the French commander Sonthonax decreed a partial end to slavery in August 1793, Toussaint switched his allegiance to France in a move that guaranteed the colonial power success in expelling English and Spanish troops. Then, with fervent rhetoric praising human dignity, the French Assembly in February 1794 abolished slavery, over the protests of indignant planters.

Toussaint's power was growing. By 1798, he had driven British troops out of Hispaniola. In 1801, Toussaint's army invaded Santo Domingo in hopes of unifying the island and abolishing slavery in the eastern, Spanish end. He ran up the French flag instead of the Spanish one there. But later that year, France betrayed him when he tried to negotiate independence for the colony under his control; with the help of the turncoat former slave Henri Christophe, the French sent a chained Toussaint away from Saint-Domingue to die in a mountain prison. Napoléon Bonaparte's troops replaced Toussaint's in Santo Domingo, which remained under French control for eight more turbulent years.

In 1804, the victorious former slaves established Haiti, the first free black republic in the world and the second independent nation in the Americas. After twelve years of war, they had driven the French, Spanish, and British out of Saint-Domingue, and in the process weakened the hold of all three European nations on Latin America. Meanwhile, Napoléon's war in Europe left Spain without a credible king, with the result that soon it would have no choice but to cede its colonies in the Western Hemisphere to newly established independent governments.

Jean-Jacques Dessalines, the general who declared Haiti's victory over the French and then became the new nation's first emperor (Jacques I), ordered that all the French who remained in Haiti be killed. Some of the colonists tried to pass as Creoles who had grown up on the island and had African blood. Dessalines devised a test to weed out the ones who had not spoken Kreyol all their lives; they had to sing, "*Nanett alé nan fontain, cheche dlo, crich-a li cassé*" (Nanette went to the fountain, looking for water, but her jug broke). The French gave themselves away when they could not properly pronounce the Kreyol or duplicate the African cadences of the melody. Their lie uncovered, they met the bayonets of Dessalines's men. (More than a century later, black Haitians would die for failing a similar test in the Dominican Republic.)

Again in 1805, troops under Dessalines tried to take Spanish Santo Domingo but failed and retreated. Despite the euphoria of having defeated Napoléon's army, Haiti's new leaders could not agree on who would guide the infant nation, which split at first between rival generals in the north and south. In 1820, after Henri Christophe's suicide in the north, the country united under the leadership of Jean-Pierre Boyer. Toussaint's dream of one undivided island nation revived. Rumors flew that the French were launching boats from Martinique, an island slave colony that remained under French control, with troops who would attack Haiti from the Spanish end of Hispaniola. France and Spain were forming an alliance, making the rumors even more dangerous if they were, as seemed likely, true.

Boyer realized that Haiti's chances for continued freedom depended on securing Spanish Hispaniola. He knew also that the colonists in Santo Domingo were chafing under continued European rule. For decades, the colonies had been struggling to loosen European control over trade in the Americas, and Haitian independence had crystallized the drive for commercial independence into early successes as the hemisphere pushed for political independence as well. The Dominican elite shared the other Spanish colonists' sympathies for the revolutionary Simón Bolívar, who called for a new Western Hemisphere federation controlled not by Europe but by *criollos*, the descendants of the original European settlers. (Bolívar, who had promised he would end slavery in the former Spanish colonies, received arms and money from Alexandre Pétion's government to help his independence movement; he later reneged on his pledge to free Spanish slaves and acceded to pressure from the United States to isolate Haiti diplomatically.)

In November 1821, the Dominicans declared their independence from Spain, and President José Núñez de Cáceres aspired to attach Santo Domingo to Bolívar's Great Colombia federation. But Boyer planted another idea in the minds of the governors of the outlying Dominican states: one by one, he convinced the leaders of Cotuí, La Vega, Macorís, Azua, San Juan, Neiba, Santiago, and Puerto Plata that joining Haiti was the only way to ensure that Spain would not again take over Santo Domingo. With their support, Boyer went to Núñez de Cáceres and "offered" to send twelve thousand troops to defend the island. The Dominican President saw that he had no choice. At 7 a.m. on February 9, 1822, the Dominicans met Boyer and his troops at the Puerta del Conde, the massive gate that now marks the entrance to Santo Domingo's commercial and tourist district, and handed the Haitian leader the keys to the city. Boyer's first act was to declare an end to slavery across the entire island.

Santo Domingo was not only the Haitians' protection against invasion from the European powers but also a cash box holding part of the ransom for Haitian independence. In 1825, desperate to regain access to

European markets, Boyer agreed to pay France an indemnity as restitu-
tion for property lost by its colonists during the Haitian Revolution.
Incredible as it was that the Haitian victors had to compensate the *losers*
in their war for independence, the sum agreed upon was even more amazing: 150 million francs. Under Boyer's plan, Dominican sweat would raise
the funds to pay the debt.

Boyer's men appropriated former Spanish government and Church
property in Santo Domingo. Because much of the land still in the name
of the old authorities had long since been handed over de facto to the
criollos, the Haitians were in effect seizing private property. That immediately angered the Church and even the independence-minded elites
who had once favored the Dominican-Haitian alliance. To quell rebel-
lion, Boyer banned political meetings; in 1830, he went so far as even to
restrict cockfights, which he knew were the perfect mask for assemblies
of men who wished to agitate and which also took Dominicans away
from work.

Resentment simmered. The lives of the *criollos* and former slaves only
worsened under Boyer; this so-called independence did little good. Soon,
both the eastern and western sides of Hispaniola were clamoring against
Boyer. Worse, drought was hurting the island's crucial coffee harvest.
Financial troubles abroad pushed down prices for Hispaniola's already
shrunken crops—that is, in the places where Haiti still had markets. Its
trade relationship with the United States was tenuous after Boyer, re-
sponding angrily to continued U.S. congressional refusal to recognize
Haiti's independence (which would have angered the slave-owning
South), declined welcome to a U.S. commercial agent to Port-au-Prince.
Finally, his nation bankrupt, Boyer crawled begging to the French government in 1838 to ask it to reduce the indemnity Haiti had agreed to
pay thirteen years earlier.

On May 7, 1842, the entire island shook from the force of an earthquake. In the eastern part, most of the north-central city of Santiago de
los Caballeros collapsed. When the Bishop of Santiago proclaimed that
the tremor was a divine warning, the residents fled the city in fear and
left it to looters. In the western end, the port town of Cap-Haïtien fell
in on itself. Sans Souci, the palace built by King Henri Christophe,
crumbled to the ground. The earthquake marked the beginning of the

end for Boyer, who had already foiled a number of attacks on his life
and his government. Opposition groups now claimed he failed to give
support to the citizens whose homes were destroyed.

A blue-eyed Dominican businessman named Juan Pablo Duarte had
been meeting since 1838 with a rebel group he founded, La Trinitaria.
In the months after the earthquake, Duarte and his men plotted to oust
Boyer, then free Santo Domingo from Haitian rule. In January 1843, a
Dominican freedom fighter, Ramón Mella, arrived in the southwestern
port town of Les Cayes to collaborate with Haitian conspirators
there. On January 27, military officers back in Santo Domingo began a
revolt, just as Haitian opponents of Boyer prepared to unseat him. By
March 8, the rebels held Les Cayes and were marching on the Haitian
capital, Port-au-Prince. Five days later, Boyer was forced from office,
and he and his family boarded a British ship, which carried them into
exile.

The new Haitian government was determined, however, to hang on
to Santo Domingo. During the next year, Haitian General Charles He-
rard hunted down the Dominican revolutionaries, but they continued
plotting clandestinely. Duarte fled to St. Thomas on August 2, but the
remaining Trinitarios pulled back together. A young mulatto, Francisco
del Rosario Sánchez, met in secret with Mella for months to plan a new
assault. While in exile, Duarte procured arms and money from Venezuela
and Curaçao. On February 27, 1844, the Trinitarios marched on the
Puerta del Conde, where they declared the liberty of Santo Domingo
from Haiti at the very site where Núñez de Cáceres had given it up
twenty-two years earlier.

Unlike Haiti and other countries of Latin America, the Dominican
Republic does not celebrate the anniversaries of independence from a
European colonial power. Every February 27, it reminds itself that it
fought off its neighbor, Haiti, to become an independent nation.

In reality, independence from Haiti did not mean freedom at all.
The Dominican economy was in a shambles, and the Haitians were
threatening a new invasion. The United States, eyeing the strategic Samaná Peninsula that formed Hispaniola's northeastern coastline, was
hinting at the possibility of annexing the Dominican Republic as a way
to "protect" the nation from Haiti's continued threats. (Ironically, Hai-

tian President Boyer's efforts to maintain a presence across the island had heightened U.S. interest in Samaná, where black Americans from Philadelphia had responded to Boyer's 1824 invitation to establish a small community on the peninsula; their descendants still speak English.) But repeated U.S. commissions sent to Hispaniola failed to come up with an arrangement that satisfied Washington or Santo Domingo. Meanwhile, the Haitian incursions continued over the next decade and a half.

Clearly, the infant Dominican Republic could not go it alone. In 1859, General Pedro Santana, who had established military rule in Santo Domingo, began negotiations with Spain in the hopes that it might protect its former colony. By March 1861, Dominicans were again Spanish subjects at their own request. But almost immediately, the new Spanish administrators, shocked by the dark skin of their new citizens, began to exclude Dominicans from army, government, and social positions in their own land. Adding insult to injury, they refused to exchange Dominican money at face value, seized livestock and goods, imposed new rules on the local clergy, and hampered trade that was not with Spain.

Within only a few years, the Dominican general Santiago Rodríguez was rallying the peasants in the central Cibao valley in preparation for an uprising to expel the Spaniards. Haiti's President, Fabré Nicolas Geffrard, also anxious to rid Hispaniola of the Spanish presence, gave the Dominican rebels arms and shelter. On announcing Spain's annexation of Santo Domingo to Haitians on April 18, 1861, Geffrard had made clear that unless Santo Domingo was independent Haiti could not consider itself free of threats to its own sovereignty: "You know that this flag authorizes and protects enslavement of the children of Africa . . . The Fatherland is in danger, our nationhood threatened, our liberty compromised. To arms, Haitians! . . . It is necessary to end Spanish domination of America. We will expel [the Spaniards] from Santo Domingo and this defeat will be precursor of their definitive expulsion from the Gulf of Mexico." Haiti's stance became even firmer in 1862, when Spain announced its intention to win back land Toussaint Louverture had taken from it in 1794 and Spanish troops evicted Haitians from Dajabón and Capotillo, at the border.

Ironically, among the Dominican exiles who received help from Haiti were Francisco del Rosario Sánchez, one of the Trinitarios who had fought for Dominican independence from Haiti in 1844, and José María Cabral, who soon would try to replace Spanish with American protection. For two years, the island was consumed in warfare as the Haitian-supported rebels battled the Spanish occupiers. Ultimately, Spain had no chance at winning the island, which, in any case, had already proved to be more trouble than it was worth. Defeated, Spain on March 3, 1865, annulled its reannexation of Santo Domingo. By the end of July, its troops were gone. The town of Restauración, on the border just south of Dajabón, received its name as testimony to the Haitians' help in the War of Restoration to free the Dominicans from Spain.

Yet the Dominican rulers had not learned their lesson from the Spanish experience. In 1868, shortly before returning to his third Presidential term (after two turbulent turns at the Presidency before the Spanish annexation), a *caudillo* named Buenaventura Báez offered the United States the strategic northeastern Samaná Peninsula for one million dollars in gold, another hundred thousand dollars' worth of arms, and military support in the form of three warships. But the U.S. Senate, showing uncharacteristic prudence in the face of discord on the island, in 1871 turned down the deal.

Meanwhile, Santo Domingo and Haiti had returned to wrangling over the border. Between 1874 and 1912, no fewer than eight efforts failed to define where Dominican territory stopped and Haitian territory began. By 1916, the point was moot: both countries were again occupied by a foreign power. This time, it was no longer a European power that claimed dominion over the former colonies: it was the United States. Hispaniola had become one more place where the Americans proved that they, not the Europeans, were the power in the hemisphere. In the Spanish-American War of 1898, Spain had lost Cuba and Puerto Rico; the 1901 Platt Amendment gave Washington the permanent "right" to intervene in Cuban affairs. The United States encouraged Panama to break away from Colombia so the Panama Canal could be built. Teddy Roosevelt, wielding his Big Stick, was laying claim to Central America and the Caribbean, establishing a naval base in Cuba's Guantánamo Bay, using the Marines to force the setting up of a pro-American government and customs receivership in Nicaragua. In 1905, Roosevelt's boys took over Dominican customs operations under a fifty-year mandate (which ultimately would be shortened by special arrangement in 1941).

American troops invaded Haiti in 1915. ("Dear me, think of it! Niggers speaking French," Secretary of State William Jennings Bryan is often quoted as having said in 1912.) A year later, they occupied the Dominican Republic as well. What need was there to keep separate two countries that were both under the control of the same foreign power? When they invaded, the Americans cited the need for political stability. In reality, they wanted to force the Dominicans and Haitians to repay their huge debts to mostly French and English creditors, whose governments had now stationed warships off the coast of Hispaniola. Under the Monroe Doctrine, first enunciated in 1823, when the new country had been threatened by Spain in the south and Russia in the northwest, the U.S. government had declared it national policy to prevent Europe from considering the Western Hemisphere territories as "subjects for future colonization." The doctrine insisted that European intervention would be considered "as the manifestation of an unfriendly disposition toward the United States."

In 1904, the Roosevelt corollary to the Monroe Doctrine committed the United States to forcing debtor nations to honor their foreign obligations. As tensions in Europe grew, forcing Haiti to make good on its debts, too, became even more important, because France and England needed the funds for their war efforts, and Germany especially could not be allowed an excuse to interfere in Haitian affairs. Located along the Windward Passage, Haiti was of strategic military importance as well, a point that soon became crucial as the Wilson Administration fretted over the possibility of Germany's establishing a Caribbean naval base and bringing the Great War to the Western Hemisphere.

Busy administrators of occupied Hispaniola set out to put in place a new economic strategy to get customs revenues flowing in and then out again to foreign creditors. In the Dominican Republic, American multinationals laid out vast new sugar plantations, which needed more workers than Santo Domingo could provide. Haiti, with the same population but half the land, was a natural source, so the companies moved thousands of people across the border, establishing a steady flow from west to east.

Despite the mountains between them, the two former colonies were being pulled together far more quickly than they were prepared to handle. For the first time, roads reached into the center of Hispaniola, to tiny hamlets that before had been accessible only by days' or weeks' journey on mule back. In 1924, as the Marines prepared to leave the Dominican Republic, Hispaniola was once again home to two countries with governments of their own; though Marines were still stationed in Haiti, the nation had its own functioning government. (When Franklin Roosevelt took office in 1933, arrangements were made to terminate the American presence in Haiti; the occupation ended in 1934.) It was time to decide once and for all the border question. Prompted by the United States, the Dominican Republic and Haiti on January 1, 1929, drew a new line, the one that still stands. Under the accord, negotiated under watchful American eyes, Haiti ceded land, allowing Dominicans to build the International Highway, while the Dominican Republic gave up a two-hundred-meter-wide swath for another highway to be built by Haiti in the south.

The border along the International Highway, tracked for a short time by the Artibonite before that river pierces the center of Hispaniola, marks the geographical division of the island. But the psychological border is another river, the Massacre, flowing south from the Atlantic Ocean, marking the northernmost part of the frontier between the two countries. The memory of what happened at the Massacre River in 1937 is still vivid in the minds of the islanders. Even now, it is nearly impossible for Dominicans and Haitians to think of each other without some trace of the tragedy of their mutual history that took place that year.

The Massacre River looks innocent. Children play and women do laundry at the foot of the green bridge spanning its shallows at the northern Dominican town of Dajabón. The river lost its original Taino Indian name, Guatapana, in 1728, when Spanish soldiers slaughtered thirty pirate buccaneers seized there. In honor of the slaughter, the river was christened in blood as the Río Masacre. The Massacre earned its macabre name a second time in 1937, when Rafael Trujillo ordered the slaughter of Haitians who had crossed over to the Dominican side or who had always lived there. The death toll reached into the tens of thousands as the blood of innocent Haitians flowed freely into the water and transformed the border from a place that had once been a refuge from persecution and slavery into a memory to forget, to flee.

Trujillo was in a way another legacy of the U.S. occupation, which had left behind newly trained military officers in both Haiti and the Dominican Republic. Occupying troops had recruited the young Trujillo into the National Guard in 1918, then groomed the clever young officer for leadership. When the Americans left in 1924, and President Horacio Vásquez was running the country, Trujillo was head of the revamped armed forces. Overconfident in the Americans' willingness to protect him and boost his power, Vásquez failed to realize that Trujillo was a serious threat. When, in late 1929, the aging President traveled to Baltimore for an emergency medical operation, it was just the opening Trujillo had been waiting for. Taking advantage of Vásquez's absence, he lined up allies to support him in a military coup. A few months later, on February 23, 1930, he forced the still frail Vásquez to resign; after sham elections held on May 15, Trujillo became President.

However great his power, Trujillo, a military man who openly preyed on the country's most beautiful young women, was not immediately accepted by the Dominican elite. What use had they for a man, born out of wedlock, who had once been a humble sugar weigher, then a plantation guard? They knew he was a petty thief, forger, and sometime blackmailer. Aware of their scorn, Trujillo dreamed up and ordered carried out one absurdity after another to show the society snobs that, however much they looked down on him, he remained the most powerful man in their country. In 1936, he rechristened the capital Ciudad Trujillo. He even changed the name of Duarte Peak to Trujillo Peak. (At 10,128 feet, this apex in the Dominican Cordillera Central is the Caribbean's highest mountain; it is about a third the height of Mount Everest and surpasses the measurement of any North American mountain east of the Mississippi. Legend has it that a geographer laboring under Trujillo feared that even the peak's impressive height would not be enough to please the President, so he recorded its height at 3,175 meters—10,417 feet—instead.)

Trujillo was an accomplished dancer and womanizer (though the success of his romantic exploits apparently was attributable more to coercion than to charm) and put his own cultural stamp on Dominican merengue music. He brought it into society ballrooms, to the dismay of the elite, who looked down on its humble origins, but to the delight of the peasants, whose lives revolved around the music. A mix of European contredanse horn- and accordion-based tunes and essentially African rhythms, merengue had first been popular in the countryside. Its instruments spoke to the music's rural origin: the *tambora* (a small double-headed drum made of hollowed logs) and *guïro* (now made of tin, but fashioned in the nineteenth century from a hollowed gourd with holes bored into it and scraped with a metal fork). Couples danced the merengue at gatherings after cockfights, peasant towns' central social activity. Trujillo also commissioned endless songs to be composed in his honor: "Faith in Trujillo," "Trujillo Is Great and Immortal," "Trujillo, the Great Architect."

The greatest tribute he planned for himself did not involve building or creating. It was an act of destruction designed to erase any doubt that he was the leader of the Dominican nation and that, though African rhythms may have pulsed in the merengue he popularized, dark blood did not run in his veins.

Smooth, sweet Dominican rum was poured liberally at the festivities in the border town of Dajabón on the night of October 2, 1937. Doña Isabel Mayer, a wealthy Dominican who owned much of the surrounding land, was giving a banquet at her home in honor of the President himself, Generalissimo Rafael Leónidas Trujillo Molina, Great Benefactor of the Nation and Father of the New Dominion. For Trujillo, the trip was a break from the headaches of the capital. He had just received reports that opponents of his regime were plotting against him. In his own sinister way, Trujillo had sent out his spies and gunmen to satisfy himself that he was not materially threatened. Still, the incidents troubled him. This trip was his second to the remote northwest border. It took place just two months after he had gone there in August to inspect the beginnings of the new International Highway, the center point of his grand plan to link the north and south and to fortify the Dominican presence on the border. So little work had been accomplished on the highway that he and his entourage had had to ride in on mule back to get to the project that drew a line between two points through nowhere.

The border itself was officially only eight years old. When President Vásquez and Haiti's President, Louis Borno, in 1929 drew a permanent border, the strokes of their pens had created a large foreign population on Dominican land. After so many years of ambiguity, the people who lived in the central regions and who were now arbitrarily assigned a new country were not about to move just so they could live on Haitian or Dominican territory. Haitians did not stop speaking Kreyol, even though the land they lived on now happened to be Dominican. With time, the people might have begun to match the nationalities the new boundary assigned them. But for Trujillo, later was not soon enough.

A decade earlier, waves of Haitians had crossed into the Dominican Republic to find work cutting cane on the vast sugar plantations, which were pushing to export more and more to a market that paid more than twenty cents a pound for the sweet white stuff. But in 1929, when Black Monday hit, catapulting world markets into the Great Depression, sugar fell immediately to just four cents a pound, then later to two. With the market all but destroyed for Dominicans' biggest export, Haitian workers were no longer needed. Throughout the 1930s, therefore, Dominicans had been seeking ways to send the Haitians packing. In July 1937, a new law forced foreigners to register with migration officials. Later that summer, Dominican authorities deported eight thousand Haitians who did not have proper papers. But these deportations barely assuaged the Dominicans, who were angry about the country's economic straits. For six years, Trujillo had ordered local military posts to submit to him thrice-monthly reports of the results of their patrols of the Dominican-Haitian border.

On his first trip to the border in August, Trujillo was surprised to see so many Haitians around, even though a thousand or more had been coerced into working on the new highway. It also struck him as strange that there were no cattle on the grassy expanses in the valley around Pedro Santana. Peasants and town officials at each little town along the new highway responded that Haitians had stolen their livestock. Trujillo called Lieutenant Colonel Manuel Emilio "Niñí" Castillo, chief military official of the north of the Dominican Republic, to meet him in Dajabón to discuss the alleged Haitian incursions across the border.

By October, rumors were flying about "incidents" concerning Haitians. A few days before Trujillo's visit, the Montecristi provincial governor had complained that three hundred deported Haitians had returned to the hills around Montecristi. In response, the Interior Ministry had been alerted and the army mobilized. Whispers passed that just south of Dajabón, Dominican soldiers had killed a group of Haitians. In Sabaneta, it was said, Haitians had died. Other reports circulated of deaths in confrontations between Dominican soldiers and Haitians awaiting deportation from barbed-wire detention camps.

The tension did not dampen the festivities surrounding Trujillo's visit; indeed, they seemed to heighten the revelry. Amid the jovial atmosphere at Doña Isabel's banquet for him, Trujillo assured the guests: "I have learned here that the Haitians have been robbing food and cattle from the ranchers. To you, Dominicans, who have complained of this pillaging committed by the Haitians who live among you, I answer: I will solve the problem. Indeed, we have already begun. Around three hundred Haitians were killed in Bánica. The solution must continue." For emphasis, the drunken dictator banged his fist on the table.

In the wee hours of October 3, the formal killing of Haitians began. No longer a series of isolated incidents, the confrontation on the border became a massacre. "That day, such horrors took place under the torrential rain that your mouth tasted of ashes, that the air was bitter to breathe, that shame weighed down on your heart, and the flavor of all life indeed was repugnant. You would never have imagined that such things could come to pass on Dominican soil," the Haitian author Jacques Stephen Alexis wrote later in his novel about the massacre, *Compère Général Soleil*. (Alexis himself became a martyr in 1961, stoned to death in Haiti for his efforts to unseat François Duvalier.)

Trujillo's soldiers used their guns to intimidate but not to kill. For that, they used machetes, knives, picks, and shovels so as not to leave bullets in the corpses. Bullet-riddled bodies would have made it obvious that the murderers were government soldiers, who unlike most Dominicans had guns. But death by machete can be blamed on peasants, on simple men of the countryside rising up to defend their cattle and lands. Even a bayonet leaves wounds enough like those of a simple knife that the true authors of the crime can be masked. This elaborate façade left out one crucial detail: if the massacre was, indeed, the result of a Dominican peasant uprising against the Haitians, why were there no casualties on the Dominican side? And why did a number of Dominicans, at a great risk to their own lives and livelihoods, hide Haitians in efforts to protect them from Trujillo's murderers?

In the early fall of 1937, the border patrols were heightened; yet reports that came in every ten days failed to mention their sinister achievements at Manzanillo Bay, Tierra Sucia, Capotillo, El Aguacate, La Peñita, El Cajuil, Santiago de la Cruz. But the tales of survivors brought out the truth. Trujillo's men searched the houses and estates of the region one by one, rounded up Haitians, and initiated deportation proceedings against them; once the paperwork was done, the Dominican government had "proof" that the Haitians had been sent back to Haiti. The Haitians then were transported like cattle to isolated killing grounds, where the soldiers slaughtered them at night, carried the corpses to the Atlantic port at Montecristi, and threw the bodies to the sharks. For days, the waves carried uneaten body parts back onto Hispaniola's beaches.

Often, the soldiers did not even bother with the charade of covering up their crimes. Entire families were mutilated in their homes. For Haitians not actually in their homes—in the streets or in the fields—the soldiers applied a simple test. They would accost any person with dark skin. Holding up sprigs of parsley, Trujillo's men would query their prospective victims: "*¿Cómo se llama ésto?*" What is this thing called? The terrified victim's fate lay in the pronunciation of the answer. Haitians, whose Kreyol uses a wide, flat *r*, find it difficult to pronounce the trilled *r* in the Spanish word for parsley, *perejil*. If the word came out as the Haitian *pe'sil*, or a bastardized Spanish *pewehi*, the victim was condemned to die. The Dominicans would later nickname the massacre *El Corte*, the Harvest: so many human beings cut down like mere stalks of sugarcane at harvest time.

Yet the Haitians who lived from cane cutting escaped the blades of the bayonets and machetes. Trujillo, having gauged just how far he could take his maniacal plan, stayed clear of the plantations owned by the Americans, as Robert Crassweller has recounted; these owners refused to hand over their workers. Even so, strange things happened on the sugar-cane fields, which had drawn Haitians to the eastern end of the island in the first place. In late September, Ingenio Porvenir, near the southeastern coastal town of San Pedro de Macorís, had requested and received permission to import Haitian workers for the 1937–38 harvest. But in the first week of October, while Trujillo's henchmen were carrying out the massacre, the sugar mill mysteriously had its permit revoked.

For Haitians who had worked their way to professions more lucrative than cane cutting, *El Corte* showed no mercy. The few who managed to

escape to safety in Haiti arrived across the border in the town of Ouanaminthe (pronounced Wahna-ment) with grisly reports of their ordeals.
(The name Ouaminthe, ironically, was a phonetic version of Juana
Méndez, the name of a Dominican woman who had helped the Haitian
revolutionary leader Toussaint Louverture during one of his forays into
Santo Domingo.) A man named Cime Jean fled to Ouanaminthe from
El Fundo during the massacre, barely escaping the hands of the Dominican soldiers. After an early morning of work, he reported, he had returned home to see Dominican soldiers entering his back yard. Thinking
their presence had to do with an arrest, he fled before they saw him.
When he returned hours later, he found slain on the ground outside
his house nearly all his family: his forty-year-old wife, his parents-in-
law, his three children, his nephew and the nephew's six children, two
cousins, his daughter-in-law and her two children. Cime Jean's son escaped with his life but not his mind, tormented by the horrors he had
seen. When Cime Jean passed by his neighbors' homes, he saw the same
brutality repeated. Telling Haitian authorities at Ouanaminthe about
what he had seen, he estimated the dead at sixty. His story was just one
of tens of thousands.

Loyal servants of Dominicans were not spared, nor were Haitian
husbands and wives of Dominicans. Sometimes, if they were lucky, the
victims convinced their murderers to let their children flee to Haiti. "The
children cry in Spanish now. Who will understand them in Haiti?"
the Dominican Freddy Prestol Castillo wrote in his novel about the massacre, *El masacre se pasa a pie* (You can cross the Massacre by foot).

As the killing progressed, reports of the carnage leaked out of the
Dominican Republic. Not wanting to bother with criticism from the
world, Trujillo finally, after the massacre had gone on for more than a
week, ordered an end on October 8. The worst excesses ceased, though
some of Trujillo's men took an additional week or so to finish off the
remaining details, giving up the fiction of machetes and kitchen knives
and resorting to rifles to complete their vicious assignment more efficiently.

By the time *El Corte* was finished, Trujillo's men had the blood of
at least 15,000 Haitians on their hands. Haitian President Elie Lescot
put the death toll at 12,168; in 1953, the Haitian historian Jean Price-
Mars cited 12,136 deaths and 2,419 injuries. In 1975, Joaquín Balaguer,

the Dominican Republic's interim Foreign Minister at the time of the massacre, put the number of dead at 17,000. Other estimates compiled by the Dominican historian Bernardo Vega were as high as 35,000.

When the American journalist Quentin Reynolds traveled through Santo Domingo and Haiti for *Collier's* magazine shortly after the massacre, he saw hundreds of victims who had survived. At hospitals, he stared horrified at machete wounds, deep, jagged, crude caverns in the flesh of children with mangled hands and disfigured heads. From Haiti's hospitals, Reynolds flew to Santo Domingo to hear President Trujillo's side of the story. Over the finest champagne Reynolds had ever tasted, the unctuous dictator insisted that the incident had been exaggerated. It had merely been an uprising of Dominican farmers against Haitians trying to steal their livelihood. "It was a truly lamentable incident, and nobody feels worse about it than I do," he cooed. Trujillo maintained the fiction that his soldiers could not have done the killing, since the victims died under thrusts of knives and machetes, and everyone knew that the Dominican army used rifles and revolvers in situations where force was necessary. It was a stunning performance, Reynolds noted, a show of disdain for the mutilated bodies the massacre had left behind and of the facts of life in a country where very little happened without Trujillo's blessing.

In the Museum of Dominican History and Geography, the personal effects of Rafael Leónidas Trujillo Molina are on display. Among them is a small shiny case containing light pancake makeup, which he used every day to smooth and lighten his complexion. The general, so proud of his looks, with every hair in place, was denying the one aspect of his appearance he could not change: a skin color darker than what he believed would have won him acceptance among the upper classes of Dominican society. Trujillo's grandmother was Haitian; his family was a lower-middle-class one, making their home in the town of San Cristóbal, half an hour west of Santo Domingo. The fiction he maintained in his personal appearance was bizarre. Even more bizarre, and more sinister, were his elaborate schemes to disguise his macabre achievements and blame the Haitians for the fate he had inflicted on them, for it was his obsession with race that was behind the massacre.

In the months leading up to the horrible deed, Trujillo had tightened his ties with Nazi Germany. He publicly accepted a gift of Hitler's *Mein Kampf*, whose racial theories it was quite clear he agreed with. On September 24, 1937, the newspaper *Listín Diario* carried an editorial rhapsodizing about the attentions paid to Trujillo by two visiting Nazis at the opening that day of the Dominican-German Institute of Science: "Long live our illustrious leaders, the Honorable President, Doctor Trujillo, and the Führer of the German Reich, Adolf Hitler."

After the massacre, Trujillo went to extreme lengths to maintain the fiction that the October 1937 slaughter at the Massacre River erupted from a real threat from the west and from popular frustration with Haitians on the Dominican border. He invoked history in the name of the Dominican nation, so as to hide the horror of what he had ordered. With the help of a coterie of nationalist, racist, and particularly anti-Haitian intellectuals, he launched a massive propaganda campaign to portray himself as the savior of Dominican nationhood: Catholic, white, and oriented to Europe.

In mid-October, Justice Minister Julio Ortega Frier confided to an American diplomat over dinner in Santo Domingo that if nothing had been done to slow the immigration of Haitians, the Dominican part of Hispaniola would be black within three generations. Official Dominican policy toward the Haitians was not only one of deportation, he said frankly; it was to no small extent intended to be one of extermination. If deportation failed, the government would have to find "other ways" of dealing with the problem. Dead or alive, he told the American diplomat calmly, the Haitians would leave Dominican soil.

Interim Foreign Minister Joaquín Balaguer responded to international queries: but of course the Dominican government was trying to force the Haitians out, he said. In many areas, the Haitians were stripping the land into a desert and cutting down Dominican forests:

> The events of 1937, which the enemies of the Dominican government have tried to depict as a massacre of innocent Haitians, were instead the crystallization in the heart of our country of a sentiment of protest and defense against four centuries of Haitian depredations . . . The work of nationalization, initiated under Trujillo, continues apace . . . In addition to creating special schools and churches to promote our language and religion, it

has become indispensable to the effort to maintain an army on the border in order to protect the integrity of our territory and out of respect for our inalienable patrimony.

Decades later, after Balaguer ascended to the Presidency, he was still repeating these anti-Haitian arguments. "The country is becoming Haitianized; Dominicans are leaving work so that the Haitians can substitute for them in the hardest jobs, which require the most effort. This is a form of spiritually dissolving the country. All the moral resources of the Dominican citizen are being relaxed. They are being lost because we are allowing Haitians to take over ownership of our country," he wrote in *La isla al revés*, the title of which translates literally as "the island inside out" but connotes an image in reverse, as if in a mirror. The title page shows white letters on a dark background reflected from dark letters on a light background.

Balaguer originally wrote this book shortly after the massacre under the title *La realidad dominicana* (Dominican reality). The book is openly racist, warning that "the vegetation-like increase of the African race" was a dire threat to Dominican culture and values. Dominican political analysts believe that Balaguer reissued the book with its new title in 1983 to counter the political ambitions of another man whose personal history was linked to the massacre: at the time, José Francisco Peña Gómez, a leader in the Dominican Revolutionary Party (PRD), was a likely candidate to run for President. Peña's very black skin and childhood near the border made him vulnerable to accusations that he was of Haitian ancestry, which were fueled by the fact that he was born a few months before the massacre, was orphaned, and was brought up by white Dominican parents.

Balaguer's book summarizes the official Dominican discourse that for many years shaped how citizens were supposed to think of race and Haiti: "The black man, abandoned to his instincts and without the brake that a relatively high living standard in any country places on reproduction, multiplies with a speed almost like that of plant species," Balaguer wrote. "Santo Domingo has been able and is required to serve as the seat of the race that is spiritually the most chosen and physically the most homogeneous in the Americas."

With the aid of cronies like Balaguer, Trujillo tried to charm his way out of a mountain of evidence that the carnage was his own doing. If he could not cleanse the smears of evil from his soul, he would at the very least try to remove the dark pigment from Dominicans' skin. Trujillo embarked on a crusade of "Dominicanization"; through his own cultural revolution, he defined as anti-Dominican any actions that could be construed as anti-Trujillo. The Great Benefactor of the Nation redoubled efforts to finish the International Highway, build Dominican military outposts on the Haitian border, and teach every single Dominican child that Haitians were a threat to everything true and right in Santo Domingo.

The Haitian government's reaction to the massacre was oddly muted. The best explanation is that for some time before, Trujillo had supported Haitian President Sténio Vincent. If he had not gone along with Trujillo's efforts to mask what really happened at the border, Vincent risked having his relationship with the Dominican dictator come out into the open, which would have destroyed him politically. On October 15, Haiti's ambassador in Santo Domingo, Evremont Carrie, and Balaguer issued an accord celebrating that

> the cordial relationship in existence between the Dominican Republic and the Republic of Haiti has not suffered the slightest damage . . . Let the friendship that has always existed and does exist between the honorable President Trujillo and the honorable President Vincent constitute the strongest and most effective force to prevent the destruction of the harmony of their two peoples and the patriotic works of these two illustrious leaders, works which, for their elevated spirit of morality and justice, have merited the applause of all the nations of the Civilized World.

In early 1938, Trujillo and Vincent drew up and had their representatives sign in Washington an agreement to "resolve" the conflict. In return for the removal of the right of the wounded and the families of the dead to seek damages, the Dominican government agreed to pay $750,000 to the Haitian government, which in theory would distribute the money among the survivors of the massacre. If fifteen thousand people had died, then each survivor would have received fifty dollars. The money was to have been paid in several installments, beginning with an immediate lump-sum payment of $250,000. The accord also obligated both governments (but was clearly directed at Haiti) to adopt "the necessary measures to prevent their nationals from entering the territory of the other state, without the corresponding permit from its competent authorities." Between the words, the Dominicans were blaming the Haitian government for the events that led to the massacre: they implied that it had been simply a migratory-control problem.

In Haiti, Vincent's astonishingly lax response to the massacre earned him the scorn of his countrymen. While Trujillo only strengthened himself as events unfolded, the weak Haitian President, who stood by helplessly as the countrymen he had undertaken to lead were slaughtered like livestock, became weaker still. In November 1937, a plot to unseat Vincent (one hatched even before the massacre) was in full motion. The plotters intended to replace Vincent with Colonel Demosthène P. Calixte, a soldier who had nurtured close ties with Santo Domingo. Trujillo even went so far as to confer upon Calixte the highest military decoration, the order of Juan Pablo Duarte, the father of Dominican independence from Haiti. On December 13, the conspirators tried but failed to pull off their coup. Vincent decreed martial law and ordered sweeping arrests. Meanwhile, Trujillo coddled the former Haitian ambassador to Santo Domingo, Elie Lescot, who would defeat Vincent to become President in 1941; a light-skinned mulatto, Lescot shared Trujillo's racial biases and would place color favoritism above all other factors in his Administration.

Though pressure from Haiti was not a problem for Trujillo, the rest of the world continued to be troublesome. Hamilton Fish, the Republican chairman of the Committee on Foreign Affairs, demanded that the United States break off relations with Trujillo's government. (He later reversed his position after a visit to Santo Domingo, during which, *The Washington Post* reported, he received a check from Trujillo.)

The dictator's plan was to create a ceremonial Presidency and mock elections, tools to deflect attention from himself. In 1938, he named Jacinto Peynado his candidate for President. Peynado easily won. Though there was no real competition, Peynado added a glib politician's touch to his "Presidency" by excoriating the United States for its meddling: "In the world of the chicken, the cockroach has no rights," he said.

But power remained in Trujillo's hands. In fact, the U.S. condemnation of the Dominican dictator simply fed into the new nationalist campaign Trujillo conceived to whip up loyalty among his subjects and erase any misgivings Dominicans might have had about the Haitian massacre. The crowning glory of his efforts to soothe international uneasiness was a solution of extreme irony. As his cronies were dutifully blasting foreigners—whether the black Haitians who had been killed or the international community criticizing the massacre—Trujillo offered to bring into the Dominican Republic many new foreigners, who would solve two problems at once: they would infuse new light blood into the Dominican nation; and they would give the United States a solution to its own "foreigners" problem.

The people Trujillo planned to bring to the Dominican Republic were Jewish refugees from Germany under Hitler, and he now offered one hundred thousand visas to them. The United States supported Trujillo's offer. Trujillo's solution, offered at the 1938 Evian conference, provided a way to get some refugees to safety without causing political problems for President Franklin Delano Roosevelt, who faced intense pressure to stay out of the conflict. It also, naturally, provided a way for the Dominican dictator to rehabilitate himself, at least enough to keep negotiations smooth toward the eventual freeing of Dominican customs from the U.S. administration that had been in place since 1905.

So it was set. Trujillo reserved twenty-six thousand acres of his own land along the north coast (which, conveniently enough, he had appropriated in the preceding years) at Sosúa. Strict limits on the number of married immigrants allowed suggested Trujillo's real intention: to encourage Jews to marry Dominicans and continue "whitening" the country. Trujillo's offer of land to the refugees was no olive branch at all.

The strongest Dominican protests had to come from abroad, because speaking inside the country was too dangerous. In a letter published in the Dominican newspaper *La Opinion* in 1943, the exiled Dominican politician Juan Bosch addressed the intellectuals Emilio Rodriguez Demorizi, Hector Inchaustegui Cabral, and Ramon Marrero Aristy:

> I have heard you speak—especially Emilio and Marrero—almost with hate toward Haitians. And I have asked myself how it is possible to love your own people and make less of the other, how it is possible to love children who are your own, while at the

same time hating the children of your neighbor, simply because they are the children of someone else . . . I believe you have not thought deeply about the right of a human being, whether they be Haitian or Chinese, to live with the minimum well-being so that life is not an unbearable burden; that you consider Haitians somewhat less than animals, because to pigs, to cows, to dogs you would not deny the right to live.

The protest was of little avail. And, sadly, Bosch himself would later give Dominicans cause to believe that he, too, was deeply anti-Haitian.

Decades later, Dominican children are still told that Haitians eat babies. The Jewish colony at Sosúa has become a resort. Sunburned, overweight German and Canadian tourists on budgets crowd the small beach and flirt with brown-skinned Dominicans; teenage gigolos called *sanky-pankys* accompany over-tanned foreign divorcées. Nearly all the Jewish settlers left within a few years of arriving, though a dairy company and a small synagogue remain as reminders of their brief presence.

Hours away, the border is as desolate as it has always been.

More than fifty years after the massacre, the market in the Dominican border town of Elías Piña fills on Tuesdays and Saturdays, when the guards let in Haitian merchants from the hamlet of Belladère, five kilometers across the border, to buy and sell goods. A long line of Haitians, some on burros, some on foot, stretches from the market, back through the arch of the customshouse, and out of sight down a dusty road. Feet crunching on chalky gravel, the Haitians pass by two customshouses: a newer warehouse on the Haitian side, and, a kilometer down, an old, abandoned one near the Dominican end of the road. Chatter mixes with the sound of motorcycles without mufflers, chickens squawking, donkeys braying. Phrases of Kreyol mix with Spanish as merchants exchange gossip, talk politics, cut business deals.

A stocky, jowly sergeant watches over the line of Haitian peasants making its way to market from the muddy river that is the border. He pauses to stop a young Haitian woman and her mother walking up the hill to Elías Piña. "*Doña*, lend me your daughter so I can marry her," he says to the old woman. Neither she nor her daughter is fooled by the nice face he puts on. The two women stiffen, and the daughter says firmly, "No, *señor*." The sergeant's smile hardens. "What do you mean you don't want to marry me?" The young woman is trying to be polite to avoid trouble, but she can't hide her anger. Finally deciding the young woman isn't worth the bother, the sergeant allows her and her mother to pass.

A clean-cut official of Cedopex, the Dominican export agency that handles customs, chases after an old woman who has slapped the side of her donkey to hurry it past him in an attempt to avoid a customs search. A soldier stops the donkey, and the official carefully pulls out a long, crooked metal rod with which he pierces the edges of the sugar-sack bags hanging on each side of the animal's belly. The Haitians are not permitted to take home any goods that the Dominicans have bought with dollars. That means even sugar, which is being imported right now, because all the domestically produced sugar is exported to meet the quota in the United States, where it fetches three times the world price. The Haitians suspect the customs officers' diligence in monitoring the border crossing has less to do with international law or economics than with the possibilities for enriching the officers' own pockets.

The commanding lieutenant has been resting inside the new customshouse. Ready to stretch his legs, he comes out for a moment to survey the morning's proceedings as Haitians cross a muddy stream and clamber up the hill on the Dominican side. "You know there isn't anything worth seeing there," says the lieutenant. "You want to know what's over there? From here, there are two roads. The one to the south goes to Haiti. To the north, the route continues through the Dominican Republic." In the middle, the lieutenant explains, "*Esta no es tierra de nadie.*" It's a no-man's-land. He means it in every sense of the word.

"Over there." The lieutenant dismisses Haiti with a wave of his hand. "They are brutal, savage." With a broad wave of his other hand toward the green hills of the Dominican Republic, his voice softens. "We Dominicans are a people who have more morals, more discipline, more courtesy than those people. The Haitians are too violent, too brutal." The lieutenant spits and shakes his head. "Even the educated ones are that way."

Miles away, along the International Highway, a mango thuds into the soft earth. The rain has started again. For twelve years on this tiny steep slope on the Dominican side of the border, the Haitian peasant Senesant has grown mangoes and flowers. Each August, he makes the long trip to the market in the capital to sell his harvest. Today, his four small children watch as their mild-mannered father navigates his way down the hill to help pull a stranded car out of the road; the mist and splashing puddles have soaked the battery of the car, which was too small for the treacherous route, and it has died on the front edge of a puddle that may well be quicksand. The car has to wait for a while to dry out before it can attempt to cross the giant puddle at the foot of Senesant's hill.

In Kreyol-accented Spanish, Senesant says he is from a town called Ti Lorey, the Little Ear, in Haiti. It has been many years, more than he can remember, since he has lived there. There is not enough to eat there, where the barren hills support little life.

These days, many Haitians like Senesant have followed the way to the Dominican Republic. Another government has fallen, a small group of soldiers is running Haiti, and the world has cut off supplies to the country in efforts to force the soldiers out. People are starving. To try to escape, they once again are running to the center of Hispaniola, fleeing across the border in hopes of finding a means to survive. Senesant has nothing much of his own, but he gives what help he can when Haitians cross through his little patch of mountain. All he has to give are directions, maybe a bite to eat, a soft place to sleep in his tiny shack, out of the rain as much as it is possible to be in the mountains, where rain clouds seem to come up from under you and sideways. Senesant offers his mangoes, rich, dripping with juice, to the passing travelers.

The Land Columbus Loved Best

*In overthrowing me, you have done no more than cut the trunk of
the tree of black liberty in Saint-Domingue. It will spring back from
the roots, for they are numerous and deep.*
—Toussaint Louverture

Cry tears for me, those of you who have charity, truth, and justice.
—Christopher Columbus
Inscription on the Columbus Lighthouse in Santo Domingo

Tourist brochures boast of Hispaniola as the island
where tobacco was discovered, the home of the first university,
the first cathedral, the first colonial city—a near-endless string
of superlatives about the New World. Most of the foreign
travelers who come to the Dominican Republic are oblivious
to this image of Santo Domingo as the glorious footprint of
Spain in the Americas: they want to lounge on the beaches,
drink rum, and enjoy everything but history. Outside the resorts, however, Dominicans live in a state of hyperconscious-
ness of the past, as if permanently suspended in the days of the
Spanish conquest. This is not an accident but the result of
many decades of efforts carried out at the highest levels of government to insist on one version of who the Dominican people
are; sadly, this official story is more about who they are not.

Their history is rooted in the ideology of the *caudillo*:
literally, the strongman on a horse. He is the great leader
under whom the masses toil. Hispaniola is split between
strongmen and weak masses, whom the leaders have considered needed to be led or exterminated. The world is divided
into men to be glorified and people who are less than human
and thus to be forgotten. Men at the top, surrounded by elite
groups living in symbiosis with them, bestow paternal lar-
gesse on the masses below.

chapter

3

The *caudillo* has been embodied in real men throughout Dominican history: Ovando, Santana, Báez, Heureaux, Trujillo. Because Dominicans have believed in the image of the strongman, they accepted Trujillo's recast image of the past and his idea of a present that required his presence. To Trujillo, nationhood was not a lifting up of the people but the fortification of his own glory. And, because the past remains so much a part of the present, retelling history after Trujillo is still a battle about him.

Two legends compete for dominance over the story of Hispaniola: in Santo Domingo, the government retells the myth of Columbus, representing the domination of the Spanish over the Indians and Africans; in Haiti, the legend children grow up with is that of Toussaint Louverture, who won freedom for the island's former slaves. Both men achieved their goals: Columbus, the discovery of the New World; Toussaint, the independence of Haiti and the end of slavery. But, ultimately, both failed. Columbus lost control of his new colony, which would languish for many years, and died in poverty. Toussaint, betrayed by the French with the help of his once-trusted generals, ended his days in prison; and the people of the Haiti he left behind could hardly be called free.

When the crews of the *Niña*, the *Pinta*, and the *Santa María* set foot for the first time in the West Indies, Columbus recorded in his log that the Taino natives he found there were timid, unwarlike, and "good to be ordered about, to work and sow, and do all that may be necessary." From Hispaniola, he wrote to the Spanish monarchs Ferdinand and Isabella that they were unarmed, timid, friendly, and fearful. He also told of his encounter with another tribe, the Caribs, on the Samaná Peninsula, in the northeastern corner of Hispaniola, at a place now named Las Flechas (the Arrows), after an early battle between the Spanish and the Indians. By the time Columbus encountered them, the Caribs had exterminated or assimilated other indigenous groups throughout the Lesser Antilles and launched periodic attacks on the Caribbean's larger islands. At Las Flechas, they met with Spaniards instead of the fearful Taino. The Caribs, said to eat human flesh, were "a wild people fit for any work, well proportioned, and very intelligent, and who, when they have got rid of their cruel habits to which they have been accustomed, will be better than any other kind of slaves," Columbus wrote.

In his letters back to his financiers, he described the natives as having two sets of qualities he thought the Spanish Crown wanted to hear about. One group offered strength, the other submission: both included able-bodied people to help find the gold and silver Columbus had promised he would bring back from his travels. The Taino, he suggested, would work for Spain because timidity and submissiveness were their nature; the Caribs, he insinuated, practically deserved to be made slaves because of their barbarism.

In April 1494, Spanish Captain Alonso de Ojeda headed an expedition to the inner reaches of Hispaniola, where he demanded gold of the Indians he met. When one proud Indian chieftain, or *cacique*, refused his demands, Ojeda set his men on the village, seizing prisoners and carrying them back to Columbus at La Isabela, the settlement he had founded on the north coast. Several of the Indians were hanged, as the first of many "examples." The Indians soon revolted.

By the next year, the Spaniards had sent their artillery, cavalry, and trained dogs out to quiet the Indians. They took 1600 prisoners and sent 550 to Spain for sale in the slave market of Seville. The Indians left behind either fled to the hills or were forced into labor in the gold mines and required to hand over a piece of gold every three months. If they did not pay, the Spaniards cut off the Indians' hands. Over time, the Spanish developed even crueler punishments. The Dominican historian Frank Moya Pons recounts the story of one guard who complained that roasting Indians alive made too much noise. A more practical colleague shoved sticks of wood into their mouths so they would stop screaming.

One *cacique*, Guarionex, who failed to meet the gold quota, thought he could reason with the colonizers. The real wealth of the Taino, he argued, was their agricultural skill, which could be used to raise crops in the fertile valleys. (French plantation owners later proved him right when they made their colony Europe's treasure.) His people, Guarionex offered, could pay with harvests of *yuca*, the sustaining root of the yucca plant. (Boiled *yuca* remains a staple of the Dominican diet.) The gold-crazed Spaniards refused to accept this idea and cracked down even harder on the Indians who failed to meet their quotas. Many of the Indians hiding in the central mountains starved to death. Those who could not escape enslavement in the mines killed themselves by eating raw *yuca*. Cooked, the root was a life-giving staple; raw, it was poison.

Columbus and his men extended their reach south, establishing a new capital, Santo Domingo de Guzmán, on the southern coast of Hispaniola, at the mouth of the Ozama River. A wanderer and explorer, not an administrator, Columbus failed colossally during his seven years as governor there. When he left for Spain in 1496 to seek funds for a new expedition farther into the New World, the colony was impoverished and divided. With Columbus away, a Spanish rebel, Roldán, defied the temporary government left in charge. But in July 1498, Columbus returned to Santo Domingo and subdued the revolt by granting the Roldanistas masses of Indian slaves and large tracts of land he had claimed for the Spanish Crown.

When word reached Europe that Columbus had lost control, the Spanish government sent a replacement in the form of the cruel commander Francisco de Bobadilla. In July 1500, Bobadilla sent Columbus in chains back to Spain. Nicolás de Ovando, an administrator as brutal as he was capable, succeeded Bobadilla in 1501. The conditions for the Indians steadily worsened.

Columbus shortly afterward returned to favor in Spain and set out on a new voyage of exploration. Intending to stop in Santo Domingo to change ships on his way, he hoped, to new discoveries in the New World, he found that Ovando had barred the harbor to him, and he waited out an impending storm in the Bay of Ocoa. But he had put much of his property onto ships going back to Spain. Their captains ignored his warning of the storm and headed off: the ships were lost at sea with the bulk of Columbus's wealth.

The Great Discoverer died a pauper, discredited. Beyond his single-minded goal of finding and exploring new lands, he was not a leader. He understood maps and compasses but not men. Like nearly all the Spaniards, Columbus did not grasp that the Indians he encountered were anything beyond a potential workforce to extract gold from the hills. Nor did he comprehend Spanish ambitions in Santo Domingo.

Under Ovando, efforts to subdue the Indians continued. Caonabo, the *cacique* of Maguana in the south center of the island, organized a group of men to fight the Spaniards. When the invaders hunted him down and threw him in jail, the other *caciques* continued fighting. After several months, the combatants came to a showdown in 1502 at Santo Cerro, the Holy Hill, at what is now Higüey, in eastern Hispaniola. When the Spaniards were on the verge of defeat, their leaders knelt at the base of an orange tree and prayed. Nuestra Señora de las Mercedes (Our Lady of Mercy) appeared above the tree and said their pleas would be answered; as she promised, the Spaniards emerged victorious over the *caciques*. Another strong image of a female who blessed Spanish dominion over the island, La Virgen de la Altagracia (the Virgin of Highest Grace) became the protectress of the Dominican people, who still make pilgrimages each January 21 and August 16 to visit her at the cathedral at Higüey. Altars are set up in many homes to honor La Virgen de la Altagracia, who listens to millions of daily pleas to *la Virgencita* to intercede.

Though Spain briefly entertained its stated goal of evangelization of the Americas, declaring any Indians who converted to Roman Catholicism "free vassals," Ovando convinced the Crown in December 1503 that the need for labor exceeded the Church's concerns for saving souls. In the name of gold, he obtained a decree authorizing him to enslave even the evangelized Indians. Then he ordered his troops to hunt down the *caciques* Higüey and Xaragua and destroy any Indians who crossed their paths.

Before long, religious men who had established themselves in the colony began to speak out against the cruelty. Even invocation of divine blessing could not hide the atrocities the Spaniards were perpetrating on the Taino. Besides, if the colonial government continued to enslave Indians who had converted to Christianity, the Church would lose followers. "Are these not men?" Friar Antón de Montesinos asked a Santo Domingo congregation on the last Sunday before Christmas in 1511. "Do they not have rational souls? Are you not bound to love them as you love yourselves? Do you not understand this? Don't you feel this? Why are you sleeping in such a profound and lethargic slumber? Be assured that in your present state you can no more be saved than the Moors or Turks, who lack the faith of Jesus Christ and do not desire it."

For a time after the celebrated friar Bartolomé de Las Casas arrived at Hispaniola in 1502, Indian slaves worked the tract of land the government had granted him. But reading Ecclesiasticus 34:18—"Tainted his gifts who offers in sacrifice ill-gotten goods!"—the friar gave up his land and slaves and threw himself into defending the Indians in the New World. In 1516, the Spanish government formally appointed him their protector. In fiery pamphlets, most prominently *Brevísima relación de la destrucción de las Indias* (Very brief account of the destruction of the Indies), the priest set about documenting the "atrocious and unnatural cruelties" the colonizers were committing.

Equally as impassioned in defense of the pursuit of profit and the justification of abuse, the jurist Pedro de Sepulveda argued that the Indians were not truly human, but rather "little men" who were neither worthy nor capable of being baptized. Like beasts of burden, they merited the cruel treatment that was their lot in life, according to his argument.

Las Casas prevailed. Already in 1513, the Crown had rescinded the right of colonizers to seize Indians, though by then it was almost too late. Even if the settlers had wanted to keep enslaving the Taino, far too few were left on Hispaniola to satisfy the need for labor in the sugar mills, which began operating in 1515. Of the more than 300,000 Taino estimated to be on Hispaniola before Columbus landed in 1492, only 60,000 were still alive by the time the Spaniards carried out the first census in 1508; by 1511, only 33,000; six years after that, not even 12,000.

In 1517, Las Casas proposed that Hispaniola import slaves from Africa to work on the sugar plantations, arguing that "the labor of one Negro was more valuable than that of four Indians." The Africans, he reasoned, were incapable of accepting the Christian faith and thus did not possess human qualities. Years later, Las Casas realized he was wrong. "In the old days, before there were any *ingenios*, we used to think in this island that, if a Negro were not hanged, he would never die, because we had never seen one die of illness, and we were sure that, like oranges, they had found their habitat, this island being more natural to them than Guinea. But after they were put to work in the *ingenios*, on account of the excessive labor they had to endure, and the drinks they take made from cane syrup, death and pestilence were the result, and many of them died," he wrote in his *Historia de las Indias* (History of the Indies). His regrets came too late, however, to prevent the sad history of the African slaves.

As the Spaniards brought into Hispaniola fresh supplies of African slaves and forty thousand Indian slaves captured elsewhere in the West Indies, an Indian called Enriquillo led the last effort to free the remaining Indians of Hispaniola. Rescued from the troops of Governor Nicolás de Ovando as a child, Enriquillo had been educated by Franciscan monks and baptized. He began his war on the Spanish in 1519 in the western half of the central mountain range, in territory that is now Haiti. Enriquillo and his band of five hundred rebels established mountain hideouts that were virtually inaccessible to the Spanish troops, and, after each attack, the band retreated and regrouped, guerrilla-style. His men attacked messengers; they made repeated incursions into colonizers' villages and plantations. They took arms, money, and provisions and freed any Indian slaves. For fourteen years, Enriquillo frustrated Spanish attempts to defeat him. Finally, tired of fighting, Enriquillo in 1533 signed a peace treaty. In return for a pledge that the Spaniards would leave the Indians in peace, Hispaniola's last *cacique* gave his word to drive escaped African slaves back to their plantations.

The Dominican writer Manuel de Jesús Galván immortalized Enriquillo in his 1882 historical novel, *Enriquillo*, and, more broadly, set the foundation for the noble Taino as a focal point of Dominican heritage. Mourning his demise and celebrating his legacy, Dominicans resurrected the past and constructed a Taino-influenced ancestry to explain their color. Today, mulatto and black Dominicans call themselves *indio*, and they say that their color is dark like that of Indians but different in quality from African skins. They can identify with Enriquillo because he was Christian. Enriquillo redeemed at once the unconverted Indians and the Spanish for the sin of exterminating them. In the far west of the Dominican Republic, near the Haitian border where Enriquillo and his men fought, alligators swim and flamingos feed in a giant inland saltwater lake named after the Indian chief. His story is stamped on that of Hispaniola. A heroic Indian who put peace with Spain above alliance with the black slaves, Enriquillo fed the Dominican myth of the Great Man. He became the counterpart to Columbus.

By day, the concrete-and-marble hulk of the Columbus Lighthouse looms over the easternmost edge of Santo Domingo. Longer and wider than a football field and set in the center of a giant expanse of grass, the monument is built of giant concrete slabs impressed with crosses. It lies flat on the ground instead of reaching into the sky as most lighthouses do. From the outside and inside, the structure looks more like a spaceship or a twenty-first-century tomb than a beacon.

By night, the concrete colossus traces in the sky two ghostly beams of light, one many times the length of the other, visible for miles and miles. Sometimes, if there is no cloud cover, the light all but vanishes, leaving a vertical glow reaching up into nothing. But if the night is overcast, the two beams intersect just above downtown Santo Domingo and create a giant cross of light. Around the edges, the cross blurs, scalloping where the clouds collapse into themselves and reflecting onto the haze around. The effect is beautiful enough that it is possible to forget the ugly structure supporting the intense round glow that at night creates the light.

Along the vast park surrounding the monument, a sweeping avenue marks the final approach to Santo Domingo from the airport. A coral wall, with cross-shaped spikes impaled on the top to keep out the people living in the nearby slums, which the government could not finish razing before the inauguration of the monument honoring the quincentennial of Columbus's arrival in the New World, lines the far edge of the road. The government warned residents not to improve their meager homes because they soon would be torn down. The wood and aluminum shacks still standing in the shadow of the lighthouse have numbers chalked on their walls to indicate when they will be destroyed.

When technicians first started testing the beacon, lights went out all over Santo Domingo: the monument had sucked out all the power that the dilapidated Dominican generators could pump. The giant beam was all the light to be had in the shacks, where the monument's impoverished neighbors could only peer over the coral wall and the spiked row of crosses. They called it the Wall of Shame, a modern barrier between people to be glorified and those to be forgotten.

"You shall put up crosses on all roads and pathways, for as God be praised, this land belongs to all Christians, the remembrance of it must be preserved to all time," Columbus had told his men. The cross is supposed to be a blessing in memory of a man who loved others so much he gave his own life for them by dying on a cross two thousand years ago. In some hands, the cross of Jesus Christ gives hope and salvation.

But when invoked in vain and wrongly, the cross is a dividing line, separating the world into Christian versus infidel, souls that can be saved versus those that cannot, human versus animal, Old World versus New.

The lighthouse and its ubiquitous crosses do preserve the memory of the early Christian settlement on Hispaniola, as Columbus predicted. But this lighthouse—intended as a monument to great human achievement, to conquest, evangelization, and discovery—with its engraved marble and concrete testifies to aspirations to greatness gone wrong. More than a hundred years in the planning, the monument cost tens of millions of dollars at a time when the average income was less than a thousand dollars a year. The government that built the lighthouse insisted on maintaining a glorious Spanish version of history but stamped out the memory of the horrors of colonial times and the stories of the lives the Spaniards trampled.

A Dominican historian originally conceived of building a lighthouse in Columbus's honor in 1878. Hemispheric leaders at the Fifth International American Conference in Santiago, Chile, in 1923 resolved to build it "with the cooperation of the governments and peoples of America." In Madrid in 1931, a year after Trujillo seized the Dominican Presidency from the ailing Horacio Vásquez, an international panel of judges chose the unwieldy concrete design of a British architecture student, J. L. Gleave, as the best among 455 entries from forty-eight countries. But funds were slow to come in.

In Dominican folklore, the very name of Christopher Columbus carries a jinx, the *fucú de Colón*. Rather than bring bad luck, journalists refer to Columbus as "the Discoverer," "the Great Admiral," "the Genoese sailor." Any Dominican who inadvertently speaks the name of the leader of the expedition of the *Niña*, the *Pinta*, and the *Santa María* immediately cries out *"Zafa!"* to deactivate the jinx.

Rafael Trujillo believed in the curse. When he honored a Mexican ambassador with the medal of the Royal Order of Columbus, the pin used to attach the medal pricked the diplomat through his suit; days later, the man was dead of tetanus. After that, whenever Trujillo wanted to move an adviser from his preferred circle to the list of those out of favor, he would decorate the unfortunate subject with the dubious honor of the Royal Order of Columbus. Even before the first stone was laid in the Columbus Lighthouse, it was clear the structure was cursed, too.

When the project's proponents finally coordinated an international air show to collect funds, the *fucú* struck. On Columbus Day in 1937, as Trujillo's massacre of Haitians on the Dominican border ended, three Cuban planes crashed while on tour to promote the lighthouse. A fourth plane, the *Columbus*, survived.

Financial troubles and the curse notwithstanding, Trujillo chose a plot of land for the Columbus Lighthouse in 1946 and broke ground in 1948. Once listed in the *Guinness Book of World Records* as the world leader who built the most statues in his own honor, Trujillo was a master of the monument. To such a man, the idea of building a veritable Eighth Wonder of the World was so appealing that he brushed aside the Columbus superstition. But even Trujillo eventually abandoned the project as too expensive, especially after other Latin American governments stopped giving money because they suspected he was pocketing it.

When Trujillo was assassinated at the hands of disgruntled former loyalists in May 1961, Dominicans' first response was to tear down the many monuments he had built to himself. They changed the name of the capital back to Santo Domingo from Ciudad Trujillo. Years later, at the very spot on the renamed 30th of May Highway where the dictator died, they erected a memorial of concrete and twisted, rusted steel—a tribute to the pain he had inflicted and to his fitting death, rather than to the glory Trujillo had envisioned.

The lighthouse came back to life as the dream of Trujillo's protégé, Joaquín Balaguer, a man even more obsessed than his mentor had been with creating a personal mythology and cementing his place in history as the man who defined Dominican nationhood. Balaguer was a child when the U.S. Marines invaded the Dominican Republic in 1915. As an adolescent, he joined the Nationalist Party and participated in demonstrations against the continued U.S. presence in the Dominican Republic. Soon after he graduated from law school, the pale, bespectacled young Balaguer made an impression on Trujillo. He wrote speeches for him, held a diplomatic post in Spain for some time, and rose easily through the government. Near the end of the Trujillo era, Balaguer was named Vice President and, in 1959, replaced the puppet President, Trujillo's brother Hector, who had to resign after the dictator's failed plot to kill Venezuela's President, Rómulo Betancourt, was revealed.

Trujillo's downfall came not long after he ordered the brutal murder of three sisters, Minerva, Patria, and María Teresa Mirabal, who were married to dissidents working to bring down his dictatorship. The Mirabal sisters were returning from a visit to their imprisoned husbands on November 25, 1960, when Trujillo's thugs forced their car off the road, killed the women, and pushed their car off a ledge to make it appear that they had died in a crash. The Mirabal sisters became martyrs, the center of a new legend that overshadowed Trujillo's, their death uniting the country in disgust. The Roman Catholic Church, which had thus far gone along with Trujillo's rule, now distanced itself from the dictator.

When Trujillo was assassinated, the Dominican Republic was without a leader for the first time in thirty years. None of the conspirators had planned to take power himself, but without the protection of a new leader, the men who killed Trujillo had nowhere to turn. Even though they were national heroes, nobody was willing to protect them. The men had begun their plot with the covert support of the U.S. government, but at the crucial last moment, this support was withdrawn. The general whom the plotters had enlisted to ensure a smooth transfer of power also backed out. Within weeks, all of the conspirators but one lost their lives.

At Trujillo's beach home, west of San Cristóbal, his son Ramfis and friends tied several of the conspirators to palm trees and spent an afternoon binging on alcohol and taking turns shooting at the men. Dominicans called these slow murders *"una tarde de tiros y tragos,"* loosely translated as "an afternoon of taking potshots while drinking shots." Today, only poor Dominicans with children who play at water's edge in tattered underwear go to that beach, which lies far from the foreign tourist hotels in the north and east.

One by one, Trujillo's brothers, then his sons, gave up their claims to the dictator's legacy and fled the country. Balaguer was forced into exile. Without a clear leader, the Dominican Republic descended into chaos. An elected President, a coup, a handful of provisional governments, a civil war, and a U.S. invasion later, Balaguer returned to the Presidency in 1966 as the favored candidate of the United States and the Roman Catholic Church. A group of thugs called *La Banda Colorá'*, the Crimson Gang, kept Dominicans in line by killing suspected leftist sympathizers or driving them out of the country; Balaguer intimidated or disgusted most opposition parties out of running against him. The political scientist Jan Knippers Black and others have called the repression under the first six years of that regime even bloodier than the worst excesses under Trujillo.

But as the end of the decade approached, the U.S. government had begun to pressure Latin American leaders to respect human rights, in a shift that had profound implications for the Dominican Republic. When Antonio Guzmán of the Dominican Revolutionary Party (PRD) won the 1978 election, Balaguer at first showed no intention of stepping down; the army tried to seize the ballots and declare him the winner, but President Jimmy Carter refused to turn a blind eye to yet another stolen election, and Balaguer reluctantly sent the military back to its barracks.

Over the next eight years, poor Dominicans erected shantytowns on the land near where the lighthouse was planned. But by 1986, Dominicans had tired of Guzmán's PRD and its weak, incompetent, and corruption-riddled government. Facing fraud allegations and having failed to convince his party to agree to his choice of a successor, Guzmán killed himself forty-three days before his term ended. The second PRD President, Salvador Jorge Blanco, openly absconded with considerable sums of money from the national accounts. Balaguer might have been corrupt as well, but at least he was discreet about it. And he got things done. In 1986, Dominicans voted him back into office, even though he was blind and well into his eighties.

One of Balaguer's first moves early in his fifth term as President was to announce that construction would begin on the Columbus Lighthouse. The monument of light was to be the grand legacy of an aging blind President to his impoverished country. It would honor Spain, the Roman Catholic Church, and the quincentennial of Christopher Columbus's landing in the New World. Pope John Paul II himself was to come to Santo Domingo to officiate a Mass at the lighthouse to inaugurate a hemisphere-wide ecumenical gathering on October 12. It went unsaid that the lighthouse would pay homage not to one man but to two: Christopher Columbus and Joaquín Balaguer. The Columbus quincentennial, the Balaguer government hoped, would be the biggest tourism draw in the history of the country. Five hundred years after Columbus landed in the New World, Balaguer was obsessed with retelling the legend of the explorer, to make up for Columbus's sad end and his failure to hold on to the world he had found for Spain. Balaguer had written dozens of books about the history of Hispaniola. He knew that many of the island's leaders, like Columbus, had abandoned their subjects to pursue personal obsessions. After nearly thirty years in power, he considered himself one of the men who defined the Dominican nation. He did not want to be one of those who were betrayed and assassinated or exiled.

Yet the closer the monument came to being finished, the more apparent it became that it was still cursed. Shudders ran through Santo Domingo in July, when Pope John Paul II fell ill and it was announced that he had colon cancer. His October visit suddenly was in doubt. Dominicans remembered the Columbus curse. Had the *fucú* hit? What if their President was responsible for the Pope's illness?

The grand inaugural celebration, originally planned to feature entertainers Julio Iglesias and Frank Sinatra, lost its luster. Then, the whole spectacle fell through when government bureaucrats blundered the arrangements by offering "exclusive" promotion rights to several different companies, all of which withdrew when they realized they were being conned.

The structure itself did not seem to want to cooperate. When the thing was nearly finished in 1992, *Vogue* magazine suggested the monstrosity looked less like a lighthouse than like a housing project in Ceauşescu's Bucharest. ("Perhaps it is a good thing he cannot see it," Dominicans joked about their blind President.) Nor was it tourist-friendly. The 1931 blueprint for the lighthouse had not included air-conditioning. Small air conditioners were now installed in some of the exhibits, but most of them lacked climate control, and visitors sweltered in the tropical heat rather than marveling at the monument. Then authorities discovered, almost too late, that the building left exposed to the wind, sun, and sea air the ornate structure containing Columbus's bones. At the last minute, Japanese backers agreed to finance massive fiberglass plates to shield the bones.

As if there was not enough trouble, Spain and Cuba both insisted that Santo Domingo's claim that the bones were Columbus's was false, that his remains rested with them. Since the Dominicans planned to move the admiral's alleged bones from the Cathedral of Santa María la Menor into the lighthouse, in a location that would have been in full view as Pope John Paul II spoke, the Vatican fretted about the political implications of a papal appearance next to the bones: would this appear to endorse the Dominican bones as the real ones? At the Vatican's insistence, the Dominicans grudgingly moved the Pope's place to the plaza behind the monument, from which point the bones were hidden by the long tail of the lighthouse.

The weight of history was crashing down around the Columbus Lighthouse. As the Wall of Shame rose to protect it from the slums, a clamor of voices lifted around the world asserting that the quincentennial was glorifying Spain and the Church and once again trampling on the stories of the indigenous people of the Americas and on the African slaves who were brought to the New World. The international pop star Juan Luis Guerra, a Dominican *merenguero* whose band 4:40 has sold millions of records, condemned the lavish celebrations. Columbus's arrival in the New World, he said, represented the beginning of nothing less than the decimation of the indigenous peoples who lived on Hispaniola and throughout the Americas. Even Roman Catholic representatives split over the event. The conservative Archbishop of Santo Domingo, Nicolás de Jesus López Rodríguez, was heading the government's preparations for the celebration of the quincentennial of the beginning of the evangelization of the Americas. But the clergy's lower ranks, especially liberation theologians, protested. Priests speaking at an alternative ceremony commemorating five hundred years of indigenous resistance scoffed at the official version of events and remembered instead the friars who had fought Spanish Catholic cruelty to the Indians.

In the spring of 1992, when commemorative replicas of Columbus's ships sailed into Santo Domingo's harbor on the Ozama River, a group of protesters organized by the radical painter Silvano Lora dressed up as Indians and rowed out to meet them, shooting arrows at the ships. The *fucú de Colón* hit again: the small boat of protesters capsized, sending the disheveled group paddling back to the shore.

The louder the protests sounded, the more determined the Dominican government became that its celebration would dominate October 12. Then disaster struck. Just two weeks before the Pope was to arrive, opponents of the quincentennial hoopla streamed into the streets of Santo Domingo to protest the lavish lighthouse and Balaguer's neglect of Dominicans' African and Indian heritage. At the head of the demonstration, the young Dominican human-rights lawyer Rafael Efraín Ortiz sang out loud, "*Colón, fucú, aquí no cabes tú,*" marching and repeating, "Columbus, fucú, there's no room here for you." His good intentions did not protect him from the curse. Video cameras recording the event zoomed in on his open defiance of Balaguer's version of his country's history. As the cameras aimed, so did the guns of the security police. Gunfire rang out. The bullets entered Ortiz's brain while he stood at the center of the camera lenses and the crowd. For days afterward, television stations played and replayed the video clip of the murder.

The armed forces declared that "terrorist" activities had been planned to coincide with alternative celebrations of the event. Defense Minister Hector García Tejada warned those who wanted to protest the Pope's visit or the lighthouse: "Anyone who dares to attack or disrupt the public peace will have to pay with his own life." By the time President Balaguer remonstrated with the army to respect the rights of Dominicans, it was too late. At protests after the funeral for the twenty-six-year-old Ortiz in his hometown of Azua, a seventeen-year-old boy was killed in the confusion. The monument to the past had been deemed more important than two Dominican lives in the present.

The protests so shocked Vatican officials that they insisted the Dominican government move the inauguration of the lighthouse forward six days so that it would not coincide with the Pope's visit. The glorious inauguration on October 12 was not to be.

The *fucú* hit one more time. For the inauguration, Balaguer's beloved sister Emma, the Dominicans' surrogate First Lady to the bachelor President, made the half-hour trip out to the monument her brother had built, but when she returned home a few hours later, her heart stopped. Her death, superstitious Dominicans whispered, was punishment for President Balaguer's audacity in invoking the name of Columbus. Balaguer blamed her death on the best-selling novel *They Forged the Signature of God*, written in the Bronx by Viriato Sención, a self-exiled former intimate of the Balaguer family who had worked on a state charity with Doña Emma. In retaliation for Sención's easily recognizable depiction in the novel of the excesses of Balaguer and Trujillo, Balaguer refused to allow the book to receive the country's highest award for literature.

History, especially one that repeats itself as Hispaniola's does, is hard to rewrite. But in building the Columbus Lighthouse, that is what Balaguer was doing: he was insisting that the country tell a story of victory. That is why the myth of the man Columbus, of Spain's achievement through him, had to be the one that prevailed over the story of failure and betrayal. Columbus was the man who had brought the cross to Enriquillo, who had allowed him to become a hero.

Columbus's legacy, reinforced by that of Enriquillo, was also what protected the Dominican Republic from Haiti. "There are today, as in earlier times, those who hold dear the idea of the unification of the island, to make it once again what it was in its early days, one of the most beautiful islands in the Caribbean Basin," Balaguer pronounced in official publications promoting the quincentennial celebrations. "The idea in itself is infantile and even ridiculous. Water and oil can coexist for many years, but cannot be mixed together without losing their organic composition or giving up their identities." He still defined his country in terms of Europe, Africa, and Haiti. In his version, the Dominican Republic was tied to its European past, not broken from it, as Haiti was; its people were Spanish, not French or African; their skin was white, not black. "The Dominican Republic, then, will continue being, for centuries upon centuries, a nation with her own flag, an addict to Iberian culture, not like Haiti to Afro-French culture. She will continue for centuries on centuries a nation proud of her traditions, her origin, guardian of Spain in the New World, guardian of her immortal nature and jealous of the radiance with which Spanish character projects its star in the American territory."

In insisting so strongly on what Dominican was not, Balaguer failed to say what Dominican was. "Spanish" was only partly the truth, as anyone could tell from Dominicans' skin. In the early days of Santo Domingo, when the Spanish colonial government needed to increase the population, the practice of calling mixed-race residents white and Spanish had been the best way to gain their loyalty. But even 150 years after their independence, there was still no official story of who the Dominicans were. And when the people who lived in the Dominican Republic tried to articulate their idea—that they were a mix—the old man silenced them, as he quieted the lawyer Ortiz at the protest against the Columbus Lighthouse.

"Cry tears for me, those of you who have charity, truth, and justice," read Columbus's words now engraved on the lighthouse in his honor. The inscription is a cruel irony.

Haiti's commemoration of Columbus seemed more appropriate. In 1986, a military coup overthrew Haitian President for Life Jean-Claude "Baby Doc" Duvalier after thirty years of Duvalier family dictatorship and graft. Jubilant Haitians stormed the houses of the *tontons macoutes,* the family's personal thugs. Then they marched to downtown Port-au-Prince and mobbed the statue of Christopher Columbus that the Italian government had helped erect years before. Throngs of exuberant protesters tore the bronze Columbus off his base and cast him into the ocean that had brought him to Hispaniola.

Haitians had their own legend and leader, Toussaint Louverture, who like Columbus died tragically in Europe. But Toussaint's legacy, a nation of freed slaves, stood, though like Columbus, he probably would have wept at seeing the results of his dream of liberty.

"Saint-Domingue is a second Sodom, which will be consumed by the wrath of God," wrote the Count d'Ennery, an eighteenth-century governor of the colony who witnessed the barbarities that the French colonists were practicing against their African slaves. They doubtless fancied witty the names they dreamed up for the tortures they applied to their slaves for the slightest infraction of their masters' rules: "the four-post" (tying hands and legs to posts impaled in the earth); "the torture of the ladder" (lashing a slave to a ladder); "the hammock" (suspending the slave upside down by four limbs); "the thousand refinements" (torture by whipping); and "to burn a little powder in the arse of a nigger" (blowing up a slave by inserting gunpowder into his orifice). The *Code Noir* (Black Code), guidelines established late in the previous century to limit owners' rights to abuse their slaves, was little more than paper protection. In 1788, a group of slaves attempted to sue the planter Lejeune for having his female slaves beaten to death. The local court absolved him, and Lejeune then punished his slaves for having sued him.

As time passed, however, black men began to stand up to the French. In 1752, a sugar mill chewed up and spat out the arm of a Guinean slave named Mackandal. The disfigured man ran from the plantation at Limbé to the hills, where he studied the herbs that grew there. Safe in the mountains of the Massif Central, Mackandal mastered the art of elaborating medicines that healed and poisons that took life away. One by one, other mountain exiles came to him for help curing their illnesses and injuries. Word of his mystical powers spread, for Mackandal's power came not only from his knowledge of which herbs could heal but also from his intense contact with the African *lwa*, spirits. Mackandal, they said, could see the future and was immortal.

Mackandal intended to use his arsenal of herbs to free others from abuse at the hands of the planters. He prepared potions to carry out an elaborate plan. On January 26, 1758, his followers put it into action, poisoning their white masters. Six years after Mackandal took refuge in the hills, he and his followers sounded the first call for freedom. Terror spread among the colonists. Mackandal's revolt, however, was short-lived. His prowess as lover as well as healer doomed him. He had seduced a woman whose lover betrayed Mackandal to the French planters. They tracked him down and tried to burn him at the stake. As the flames licked up around his chest, the slaves who watched marveled as they saw his soul leap out, transformed into a fly, and escape high into the air to seek followers again. Later, the slaves believed, he came back in the form of a horde of mosquitoes bringing yellow fever to the French. "Fire killed Mackandal, and fire will destroy the riches of Haiti," the slaves repeated, as Martin Ros recounts in *Night of Fire*, his account of the Haitian Revolution.

Others would heed the call, made louder by the cries for freedom begun by the French Revolution. In the woods of Bois Caïman, Alligator Forest, on August 14, 1791, the Jamaican-born slave and Vodou priest Boukman ceremonially slaughtered a black suckling pig belonging to a French plantation owner: "Throw away the symbol of the god of the whites who has so often caused us to weep, and listen to the voice of liberty, which speaks in the hearts of us all," Boukman said, urging them to cast away the crosses around their necks, as C.L.R. James recounts. The offering of the animal's blood and songs to the spirits who had come from Africa set drumbeats of revolution throbbing all through the north of Saint-Domingue. The spirits heard the slaves' supplications and answered: Guede, master of the dead; Ogou, the spirit of war and flames; Simbi, the clairvoyant one and the guardian of water; Gran Bwa, governor of the forest; and a host of their companions. All around, thunder crashed and the wind howled as a hurricane pelted rain on the island.

On the night of August 22, Boukman and his men set fire to the plantations of the region. They killed 2,000 whites and destroyed 180 sugar plantations and 900 coffee plantations. The Haitian Revolution had begun. Fire, as Mackandal's devotees predicted, was destroying Haiti's riches.

As they had after Mackandal's attack, the whites took revenge, slaughtering as many as twenty thousand slaves. Among them was Boukman, martyred in the cause of freedom. The whites did not risk the chance that he would escape from the fire as Mackandal had. After they executed Boukman, they impaled his head on a spike and exhibited it on the gates of the city Cap-Français, today Cap-Haïtien.

Not far from the Cap, the freedman Toussaint Louverture saw revolution coming; he resolved to join it as soon as his family and master were safe. Born in 1743 on the Breda plantation, to slave parents descended from a minor African ruler, Pierre Dominique was so frail as a boy that his nickname was Fatras-Bâton (Little Stick). Out of pity, the priest Simon Baptiste took him under his care and gave him a Roman Catholic education, teaching him to read and write, and later Latin and the classics. When Pierre Dominique grew to adulthood, they called him Toussaint (All Saints), because he had been born on African All Saints' Day, May 20.

He was fortunate to live on a plantation where the manager, Bayon de Libertas, was known for his kindliness and wisdom. Overcoming the physical weakness of his childhood, Toussaint became a skilled horseman and was Libertas's personal coachman for many years. Libertas, impressed by Toussaint's loyalty, education, and skill, granted him liberty and put him in charge of forty acres and thirteen slaves. To celebrate his new status, Toussaint took a new last name, Louverture (the Opening), for his goal of opening the doors to freedom for the slaves. He listened to the news of men like Mackandal and Boukman who shared that dream.

As Boukman's flames consumed the north of Saint-Domingue in the 1791 revolt, Toussaint returned Bayon de Libertas his kindness: he drove his former master and family to safety so they could sail, unharmed, for the United States. (His brother Paul took Toussaint's own family to Spanish Santo Domingo.) When Toussaint returned to the ashes of the plantation where he had grown up, he was ready to leave behind his old life as a plantation worker. With his own family safe in Spanish Santo Domingo, he joined the slave revolution. His education, perseverance, and skill would make him the man who personified the coming revolution. Before long, he headed an army of former slaves.

By the time French revolutionaries executed King Louis XVI in 1793, Toussaint Louverture agreed to bring six hundred trained men under his command as colonel to an alliance with Spain, controlling Santo Domingo, in the east of Hispaniola. The anti-French alliance did not last long, for it soon became clear that the Spaniards had no intention of granting Toussaint his demand to end slavery. But Toussaint had fought on the Spanish side long enough to make the French fear they would lose the island, and they knew the only way they could keep Hispaniola was with Toussaint on their side. By August 29, 1793, the French general Sonthonax had no choice but to abolish slavery. It was France's last chance to convince the rebellious slaves to put down their arms.

As the French were pleading with Toussaint to rejoin them, the black soldier marched his men west, taking one town after another: Dondon, Marmelade, Ennery, Gonaïves, Plaisance. By early 1794, he held all of what is now northwest Haiti. Ringed in by Toussaint to the north and the threat of an English invasion from Jamaica to the southeast, the desperate French promised Toussaint the governorship of Saint-Domingue. He accepted. His days as a slave coachman behind, Toussaint Louverture then drove back the British, who in 1798 gave up any remaining hopes of seizing Saint-Domingue.

In 1801, Governor Toussaint drew up a constitution that prohibited slavery forever and gave the colony the power to make its own laws without consulting France. Napoléon, infuriated that his men had in effect turned over Saint-Domingue to former slaves, dispatched his most able troops, headed by his brother-in-law Leclerc, to Saint-Domingue to unseat "that gilded African" Toussaint. Leclerc came with orders to make the generals of Saint-Domingue declare allegiance to France, then to deport them, and, if they did not concede, to kill them.

Unwilling to give in, Toussaint's forces, especially those led by the former slave Jean-Jacques Dessalines, burned down the northern port city of Cap-Français and then Port-Republicain (as the capital had been temporarily rechristened). Where the French had hoped to claim Saint-Domingue's riches, they found only burnt-out shells of cities.

But without the support of the French, Toussaint's dream of building a newly prosperous island for the slaves could not come true. For one thing, he needed a market for Saint-Domingue's crops. For another, peace depended on bringing back into the fold the mulatto class, whose leaders had now allied themselves with the French. These lofty goals made him willing to trust. He began secret talks with the French, which he hoped would end the war and preserve the liberty of the former slaves. But history would prove his goodwill to be misplaced. In the end, Henri Christophe, the soldier whom Toussaint had charged with negotiating on behalf of the slaves, accepted the bribes the French offered. He defected to the French, then carried Leclerc's three false promises to Toussaint: France would uphold the liberty granted the former slaves, allow Toussaint's officers to retain their ranks and duties, and let Toussaint keep his staff and retire as he liked in the colony. Trusting them, Toussaint retired to his plantation.

On June 7, 1802, Leclerc summoned Toussaint to a meeting at his military headquarters. There, French soldiers arrested and bound him; others went to his home, arrested his family, and stole or destroyed his assets. They piled him and his family aboard the frigate *Héros,* which carried Toussaint away from his homeland forever. Deprived of medical care and heat during the following winter, isolated from his family, and fed only meager rations, the Haitian leader's health and spirit broke down. Starved and weakened by tuberculosis, Toussaint died in 1803 behind the bars of Fort Joux prison high in the Jura Mountains. But back in Saint-Domingue, the echoes of his last words to the island reverberated: "In overthrowing me, you have cut down in Saint-Domingue only the trunk of the tree of liberty. It will spring up again by its roots, for they are numerous and deep!"

As Leclerc attempted to disarm the former slaves in Saint-Domingue, rumors spread that Napoléon intended to restore slavery, repeating what France had done in the rest of the Caribbean under its dominion. The traitor who betrayed Toussaint, Henri Christophe, now returned to the side of the slaves. Repentant and vengeful, he joined Jean-Jacques Dessalines to fight the French. This time, the slaves won the war.

The former slaves, once considered incapable of human thought and feeling, in a single battle reduced 60,000 French troops to almost nothing. Over the course of the war, from 1791 through 1803, at the cost of 350,000 lives, the slaves drove out the men of the mighty Napoléon. "But what men these blacks are! How they fight and how they die! One has to make war against them to know their reckless courage in braving danger when they can no longer have recourse to stratagem," Lemmonier-Delafosse, a French officer, wrote five decades later.

On November 28, 1803, the French conceded; on November 29, the generals Dessalines, Christophe, and Clairveaux pronounced the former colony independent. On December 31, they read a formal declaration naming their new land Haiti after the Taino word for "mountains." The victorious Haitians ripped the white center stripe from the French tricolor and joined together the blue and red to create a new flag.

In October 1804, Jean-Jacques Dessalines crowned himself Emperor Jacques I and ruled a nation isolated from the world. Crippled by the cost of the war, France was forced to sell the Louisiana Territory to the United States. The U.S. government, which had the land thanks to Haiti but did not want to send the wrong message to its own slave plantations, waited fifty-eight years after Haiti won its liberty before recognizing the world's second independent constitutional republic. President Abraham Lincoln, fittingly, finally accepted Haiti's sovereignty in 1862.

A year after independence, Dessalines ordered his soldiers to kill every last one of the whites who remained on Hispaniola. His subjects hesitated, but only until the threat of a return to slavery under France reappeared. When, in March, French squadrons appeared off the coast of Haiti, the former slaves rose to the call of Dessalines: "*Kaze tet. Brule kay.*" Crack heads, burn houses. They massacred those who had once tormented them, sending thousands of whites to horrible deaths like those their forefathers had suffered.

But Haiti never rose above its tragic earlier history. The revolution had been so embodied in a single man that no one could follow him. Dreams of revolution gave way to infighting and to a series of men who fancied themselves leaders but were in reality only despots. Nearly two hundred years after their country became the first free republic of former slaves and the second free nation in the Western Hemisphere, most Haitians can do little better than leave it. They go to places they call *lòt bò*, the other side—New York, Miami, or Santo Domingo.

Linking Europe, the Americas, and Africa, Hispaniola has always mediated between arrival and departure. The Spaniards and French came to the island to extract profit, bringing enslaved Africans to make the island rich through their labor. The old triangle of trade was thus: slaves from Africa were bought with European goods; their work in the New World enabled Europeans to sell sugar and tobacco back in Europe. The new triangle is also one of labor but around a much smaller axis: Haiti, Santo Domingo, the United States. German, British, and Canadian tourists arrive on package tours, and their leisure leaves dollars behind. Dominicans leave to work at low-income jobs in the United States and send money back to their country, and so do able Haitians; other Haitians go to Santo Domingo to earn wages to send back to Haiti.

Tucked behind the tourist-filled Colonial Zone and spreading up to the Duarte shopping and sex district, Little Haiti in Santo Domingo lies at the new crossroads between the Dominican Republic and Haiti. It clusters around the Modelo market, whose massive arched roof spreads over a labyrinth of stalls where Dominicans sell jewelry, handicrafts, naïve Haitian artwork, vanilla, cheese, carved wood, leather goods, and candy. Strung along the front entrance, at the top of a staircase leading down to the street, are bottles of rum filled with herbs and spices, a Dominican medicinal and allegedly aphrodisiac concoction called *Mama Juana*. At the back of the covered market are the stinking fish vendors. Down the back steps and outside is a great shed where fruit and vegetable sellers hawk their goods and where poultry merchants pile squawking chicken cages into pyramids next to their butcher blocks in the open air filled with flies.

You hear more Kreyol than Spanish on the streets here. Many of the Haitians are passing only a few days, long enough to sell the truckloads of canned goods they bring from Port-au-Prince and to buy enough food to load up again and make the trip back—one day of driving and two more days to clear customs at the border. A life-size statue of St. Lazarus peers out of a little *botánica*. The store sells religious articles honoring the spirits of Vodou disguised as Roman Catholic saints who can answer the prayers of the faithful. When colonial plantation owners forbade their African slaves from worshipping the spirits of their motherland, the slaves used the names of Christian saints to conceal the identities of their African spirits. St. Lazarus is really Papa Legba, the Afro-Caribbean god of crossroads who protects travelers who wander in and out of Little Haiti. Next to him, merchants sell bright little bottles of magic bathwater that trucks have brought from Haiti. The bottles carry their own magical promises: they will make you young, restore your health, enhance your beauty, bring you money, strengthen your virility. The potion called *Vini vini* will convince a lover to come to you. *Ven acá* will do the same. You can believe in the powers of the magic water if you want. In a world where reality is something less than what you'd like it to be, seizing on a myth is often the only way to survive.

At the edges of the market, the loading docks and parking lots are filled with tap-taps—giant Haitian trucks painted like circus wagons— waiting to be loaded with goods. *Esperance, Travail, Christ Capable*— Hope, Work, Christ Can Do It—read the slogans painted in bright red, yellow, and blue on the front. Past the loading docks, the streets spoking out from the market are filled with shops where merchants peddle cloth, pots and pans, grains and sugar in massive bags threatening to burst, spare auto parts piled on greasy tables. In luxury Rocky and Montero jeeps, the Dominican owners of the shops drive past the tap-taps to survey the scene.

By day, the glaring sun beats down on the cooks frying food in the street, on the vendors selling oranges and coconuts from their wooden carts, on the men who simply stand around. In the cool of the night, or in the dark corners of certain tenement hotels in the afternoon, drug dealers peddle their goods, aware that in any place where people come to buy there is a market for the products of night as well as of day. Drug authorities raid this neighborhood often, hauling off either suspects or bribes. The Haitians are easy prey. Caught between worlds, their home is no longer Haiti. Nor is it the Dominican Republic, which does not welcome them. If they do not go along with the police, they can be deported or simply thrown in jail and forgotten.

Down the street and around the corner from the Modelo market, the walls are covered with graffiti: *Abajo Haiti! Fuera los Haitianos!* Down with Haiti! Haitians Get Out! These slogans are scribbled all around town, on the Haitian embassy, not far from the American embassy and the Dominican President's house, and on the walls around the Feria market in southwestern Santo Domingo. Under the scrawls are letters spelling ORDEN (ORDER), the name of an anti-Haitian group. The Haitians make easy scapegoats.

Spanish schooners no longer arrive at Hispaniola from the Old World. Instead, airplanes and tiny, creaky fishing boats called *yolas* carry Hispaniola's people away to the United States. Most Dominicans have little sympathy for the Haitians who appear in their midst fleeing hunger and poverty. Tens of thousands of Dominicans, like the Haitians, are leaving their island each year to seek their fortune in the United States.

The Haitians come to Santo Domingo to escape the hunger and violence wrought by decades of brutal and corrupt dictators who have bled Haiti dry. Their countrymen who can, board airplanes for the United States. Others set sail on ramshackle boats headed, they hope, for Miami. Some make it. More die or are turned back by the U.S. Coast Guard. Little Haiti's promise is not the glitter of Miami and New York. Santo Domingo puts only mountains, not an ocean, in the Haitians' way. It offers merely the chance to eat rather than starve.

In Santo Domingo, the Haitians live in buildings they call "hotels," a name that is accurate only in the sense that people pay to sleep there. The hotels are filled with rickety rooms built of pieces of scrap wood loosely nailed together to create living spaces of six by eight feet at most. Whole families sleep away the heat in these tiny rooms. Inside the worst of the hotels, Haitians cook over open wood fires. On the balconies, four or five Haitians may bathe and sponge themselves in aluminum tubs. Men play dominoes, keeping score using bright-colored laundry pegs pinned to their faces. The better hotels, still small and dirty, are comfortable enough so that market women can use their rooms as little stores from which to sell clothes and perfume.

The cool mornings in Little Haiti begin in gray and violet before dawn. Out of the pink hallways of the Hotel Santome emerge sleepy travelers, recently arrived to sell clothes or else hastily packing to begin the twelve-hour journey back to Port-au-Prince. The Santome is one of the better hotels in Little Haiti. It does well enough to dedicate space to a lobby at its entrance, rather than having guests knock on the door of the owners' quarters to make arrangements.

"Get up!" the burly manager orders the blanket-covered men sleeping on the couch and on a pile of rags on the lobby floor. The blankets pitch and heave, then collapse on themselves and lie empty. Their occupants shuffle off to begin their days. Taking their places and filling the lobby are giant burlap sacks of underwear, slippers, bras, and little-girl dresses, which the owner has hauled out from a back room. He will sell them to other merchants who come to buy from him before their own business day begins and they have to shuffle back to their own tiny rooms in nearby hotels. Dominicans come from all over the country to buy what the Haitians are selling here.

The little merchants, *ti comersants*, come and go, to Haiti and back. They trade frilly underwear and shampoo they brought in suitcases from Curaçao and Panama, and toiletries from Miami and Puerto Rico. Some of them do well enough to bring their families here and start homes. Others must send what they can back to Haiti and go there to visit when they cannot endure being away and the money is good enough to return for a few weeks. Meanwhile, they stay with their strange new family of little merchants, selling goods from the tiny rooms they rent for ten dollars a week in the crowded hotels and guest houses.

From the balcony of the Hotel Santome, you can see merchants peel the tarpaulins away from the masses of fruits and vegetables that fill huge tables under the tents of the market. A heavyset woman heaves along a burlap bag almost as big as she is. After each step, she balances herself by leaning on the bag. In the drowsy morning, it's not clear if she is carrying the sack or if it is holding her upright. She finally comes to rest next to the flower women. A row of sunflowers towers above them as they wait for dawn, when the market will open. A man comes up to bargain for his day's wares.

"No, *doña*, I can't do that. How can I pay that much?" he argues. The deal falls through. She can do better selling during the day, to people who will pay her price.

"*Café! Cigarillos!*" shouts a grizzled man balancing a box of coffee and cigarettes on the handle of his bicycle. The man who wanted the flowers chases him to get some coffee, poured searing hot from a thermos into a tiny plastic cup, one peso, eight cents.

A red pickup truck drives slowly under the red-and-white Hotel Santome sign. In the truck bed lie long blue fish, their bodies crisscross. Behind it comes a duck truck, the birds still quiet in the halfway light. Once the sun is up, business will be lively and the streets full. While some of the day's business will be done inside the yawning Modelo market and on the docks around it, just as much commerce will be transacted within the cool, humid halls of the hotels lining Delmonte y Tejada Street, the main strip of the neighborhood.

The merchants who do the best business work out of a huge street-front room filled with tables. Store owners stream in and out the wide doors as they look for wholesale clothes. From a table in a corner of the room, Ferdinand Alexy sells shirts and shoes. He walks with God: the wooden pendant he wears around his neck guarantees it; on the round disc is painted a Christ in agony, with blood dripping from the crown of thorns. Ferdinand, now twenty-eight years old, came to Santo Domingo's market in 1981, when his mother decided that life was better here than in Haiti. She traded clothes, and her son followed her path. Business is good enough to support Ferdinand's three children, ages one, two, and nine. He even can send some money back to his uncle, sister, and brother who still live in Haiti's Artibonite Valley. The family itself earns enough for food, but the fifty dollars a month Ferdinand can send back helps them get extras. He doesn't want to live in Haiti. "There's no security there," he says.

After four years in Little Haiti, Ferdinand's wife, Antoine, won't return even though she misses her family in Port-de-Paix. She waits anxiously for news of them in letters or through friends who arrive every day on the tap-taps that come from Haiti. "I'm not happy here," she says. "The Dominicans don't want us here." She learned a little Spanish, but it is hard because she has little contact with Dominicans: "I stay at home, I keep to myself." The Haitians here have learned to become invisible in order to survive.

Down the street, through a tiny door and up a slanted staircase, a room opens up. Hanging crooked on one wall is a dim etching of the faces of Duarte, Sánchez, and Mella, the three fathers of the Dominican Republic. The Haitians here do not note the irony of this small tribute to the men who liberated the Dominican Republic from Haiti in 1844. Below it, a young Haitian woman lounges on top of a pile of green-and-white tennis shoes. In another corner of the room, an older woman, Marie, sits with her calculator amid piles of brassieres, underwear, shirts, and dozens of maroon bottles of Placenta Shampoo. A bottle is worth about 50 pesos in Port-au-Prince. The rumbling tap-taps carry the loads on the ninety-minute trip to the border, where they wait for days until the military customs officials allow them through after charging them another 50 pesos, "tax," to allow the shampoo through. By the time it arrives in Santo Domingo, the bottle costs 125 pesos.

Down Delmonte y Tejada Street, at the top of the stairs to another merchants' hotel, letters as tall and stern as the American Old West warn, NO DRINKING OR SMOKING IN THIS COMMERCIAL ESTABLISHMENT. Sister Boyer's room is the first one on the corridor. Two mornings a week, she leaves before dawn to buy clothes in the market or farther away at the industrial free-trade zones at the edge of the capital. (The industrial parks, by law only for export, are not supposed to sell clothes locally, but the little merchants can get seconds from them.) Then she hurries back before her own customers begin to arrive. Sister Boyer is a sharp bargainer, not one to let a customer get the better of her, and has gained a loyal following of Dominican shop owners who come here for her goods. Sister Boyer can read just a little, but she is a whiz at the calculator. She does a brisk business selling clothes and perfume from her tiny room.

Haitians call such merchants "Madam Sara," after the black finch, the *madansara*, whose cackles and trills sound like the shrill calls of women selling their wares. The birds work themselves to death gathering food for their young; Sister Boyer works hard here so she can earn enough money to support her grown daughter, Micheline, and two grandchildren, who live in Haiti in a concrete-block house on the dusty streets of Delmas, on the outskirts of Port-au-Prince. Sister Boyer strings together her years between visits home. In Santo Domingo, she has accumulated a substitute family. "We call her Padre Billini, after the Dominican saint who took care of everyone. She watches out for all of us, if someone is sick or has a problem," José, the brother-in-law of the hotel's owner, Doña Julia, says respectfully of Sister Boyer.

Propped above Sister Boyer's door is a small suitcase, which holds, among other necessary things, a photo album. Along with the pictures of her daughter and grandchildren is a browned photo of Sister Boyer when she was twenty, a beautiful young woman with loose hair and eyes turned up, full of hope. Could it have been nearly thirty years ago that this photo was taken? The eyes are still the same but now creased with wrinkles. Her hair has been tied back under a black net.

Today, Sister Boyer doesn't seem as intent as usual on holding her customers to the price she sets. As the Dominican shop owners come through to inspect her clothes and perfume, she seems distracted. In her eyes is the concern of a mother. There are problems in her little family here. The police came on Thursday and arrested three Haitians and four Dominicans. One of them was Sister Boyer's nephew. Along with the seven suspects, the police hauled off a plastic bag of cocaine, divided into forty-two portions for sale. They said they found the cocaine packets behind the street-front door, where merchant women sell underwear.

Middle- and upper-class Dominicans in the party scene know this area for the tiny houses where they can get drugs. In the first three months of 1992, authorities arrested more than seventy people in Barrio San Carlos, as Little Haiti is officially named. The area with the next highest number of arrests had only twenty-six. Narcotics police come through on frequent raids, making sweeping arrests. Often, those arrested sit for days in jail before they are charged or released, and then it takes some money to grease the lock before the prisoner is freed.

Today is Monday. Sister Boyer was to have left for Haiti this morning to see her daughter and grandchildren. But now she has this problem to deal with. She refuses to believe that her nephew was involved. When the police come, it is hard to tell who is or isn't guilty. The police have the power to arrest without warrants if they say someone is part of an "investigation." Sometimes, there really is a reason. But often, the reason is merely to line a policeman's pockets. Dominicans call the practice *macuteo*, from Duvalier's personal thugs, the *tontons macoutes*. The *macuteros* line their wallets with a little extra money here, a little there: justified, they say, because their government salaries are so low.

Yesterday was supposed to have been a festival for Sister Boyer. It was the activity day for the Missionary Baptist Church of Little Haiti, where she sings each Sunday night. But Sister Boyer had to go to the jail to take food to her nephew. She doesn't know if he got the plate of rice, beans, and sweet plantains she left with the guard. They wouldn't let her see him.

Sister Boyer wasn't the only one who was worried. The police came to Little Haiti again on Sunday night. Men who identified themselves as migration officials had been there in the morning at what is known as the painters' hotel, across the street from the church. When it was dark out, they went back and threatened to arrest five of the Haitians living there. Fifty pesos from each man solved the problem.

Around the corner and down the street, two other men were at work, two *vagabons, vagabundos*: good-for-nothings ready to take advantage of whomever they could, Dominican or Haitian. They saw Marcelo Pérez in the street cleaning up after a day of selling *fritay*, the fried plantains and meat, rice, and beans he cooks to earn 150 to 200 pesos a day. They said they were police and demanded his money. Marcelo has lived in Santo Domingo for fourteen years. He opened his wallet to show his identification proving he is a legal resident of the Dominican Republic. Lighter than many of the Haitians who live here, he speaks Spanish without the slight lisp most Haitians have. But he handed over the money. Better to avoid trouble.

The *vagabons* went to another hotel filled with Haitians. In the street, they told a resident they were police and demanded money. Around the corner, the real police discovered what was happening and chased them away.

Amid the arrests and attacks, the Haitians were scared. Rumors flew that the Dominican government was rounding them up to take them back to Haiti, just as it had done the year before. But later in the week, Sister Boyer's nephew was released, along with the others arrested. The little merchants say that one of the men, a soldier, was released only after his friends paid 10,000 pesos to the drug authorities.

Fanciful landscapes, cascading waterfalls, peasant women carrying baskets on their heads, colorful shacks, wispy trees covered with bright fruits—these images fill the walls of many of the rooms where the Haitian painters live. In their dim studios, Little Haiti's artists paint pictures to sell to the tourists who meander through the market down the street or up and down the Malecón seaside boulevard, just a ten minutes' walk away. Haitian artists have composed these pictures, which are stenciled on canvases and colored in—hundreds of copies of the same images. The work is not so different from the pictures that immigrants in Hispaniola have painted in their heads: pictures of a better life, a life they can create only if they leave home.

The pictures are often not what they seem. On the Malecón Boulevard, across from the Caribbean Sea, hundreds of paintings are lined up along the streets. At night, a sleepy watchman guards them. During the day, the hot sun beats down on the paintings except when the four o'clock thundershowers soak them. Little by little, they fade, as do the pictures in the minds of the residents of Little Haiti, of New York and Miami.

Once, they imagined themselves kings and queens in a land of promise and opportunity. But soon, they find these strange new worlds offer harsh welcomes, and they are no longer kings or queens but instead treated by their hostile hosts as barely human, barely people.

In the afternoons, Haitians pull out chairs to chat and drink beer in the street in front of Clarisse's beauty salon at the entrance to the painters' hotel. People can always tell you how to find Clarisse. She wears her hair under a mesh cap, but everyone around her has beautiful hair: red, brown, black, or gray curls, braided in with their own locks or a wig. In her beauty salon, painted pink, Clarisse can transform anyone, even the transvestite who comes regularly. She has just learned to paint pictures; soon, she hopes, her brush will transform canvas as miraculously as her fingers do hair.

Every room of this building is a studio. Sometimes, three people at once will paint, one at an easel, another touching up a picture on the floor, the third working on a canvas propped up against the head of the bed. Underneath the mattress are other paintings, removed from their wooden frames and laid flat in piles so they will take up less room. Above her salon, Clarisse climbs three stories up the winding iron staircase to the tiny studio where Haitians paint pictures to sell in the market. On the roof of the painters' hotel, the fresh air is a relief after the climb past the odor of urine on the third floor. From here, you can look over to where the statue of Fray Montesinos towers over the seafront Malecón. The Mexican government had the statue built here to honor the friar's eloquent defense of the Indians of the New World.

Today, little Francia (named for that old colonial power for which the slaves sweated out the wealth of an empire) is a princess, her hair in long Clarisse curls. Francia is four years old. Her mother is dead, killed in a demonstration in Port-au-Prince. Her father came to Santo Domingo to paint. Today, Francia hides behind a painting, then runs and ducks behind another. She makes another mad dash behind her father's easel and knocks over the jug of paintbrush cleaner. He sits calmly at his easel and keeps painting fantasy landscapes. Her little sister runs around covered with paint from her father's palette. Maybe it's not just for the clients that he chooses these dreamy scenes. You couldn't blame him for wanting to walk right into one of them, right through the mountains.

The Karate Man's grunts echo down Delmonte y Tejada Street as he lets air out with each blow: "Whup! Whup!" Above his black pants and red sash, the muscles of his bare chest and arms glisten as he feints with an imaginary enemy. The Karate Man does not seem to notice the bustle on the street. The merchants and shoe-shine boys step around him, just as they avoid ankle-high mounds of market refuse—rotting mango peels, bits of plastic bags, sardine cans, and old chicken parts buzzing with flies—piled between the gaping holes in the road and sidewalk.

"*Moun fou!*" Crazy man! The people who live here warn visitors who must pass by the Karate Man when they go to Little Haiti. Everyone seems to have a different version of who he really is. One story has it that he was once a brilliant professor of languages in Haiti before he moved to Santo Domingo. Beyond Haitian Kreyol and French, he has mastered Spanish, English, Japanese, Chinese, and Russian. At least, that's how the story goes. "He even speaks African!" say the Haitian merchants who live in the hotel above the flower shop in front of the patch of street where he practices martial arts. The Karate Man, they say, came here to follow the woman he loved. He and the woman married and lived in a comfortable small house as he taught part-time in the university. But something went horribly wrong; nobody knows how it happened, but five years ago, the Karate Man's wife left him. After that, he went crazy. To fill the loss of the woman who was his whole life, the Karate Man passed his days losing himself in the martial-arts maneuvers he learned in his studies of the exotic cultures of the Far East. That is why he is always there, in the streets of Little Haiti, say the Dominicans and Haitians who live here and watch him every day.

Like many things here in the center of Santo Domingo, the Karate Man is not what he is imagined to be. When he is lucid, the Karate Man will tell you in Kreyol that he has never been a professor of languages. His travels take place only in his mind, or in the imaginations of the people who share the streets of Little Haiti with him. He barely even speaks Spanish, though he has lived for years in the Dominican Republic.

Today, he has changed his appearance. Above his black pants, he is dressed in a turquoise polo shirt and over it a black long-sleeved cotton shirt. The red sash around his waist is gone. He is no longer the dramatic martial-arts master but instead a fervent missionary. His name is Yvon. He says he has a wife and children, who live in a house on a hill on the edge of Santo Domingo. He doesn't remember exactly how long he has been here in Little Haiti, but it has been a long, long time. He says he used to sell clothes, whatever he could. But now, it is hard to figure out what he does. It is not clear if he even knows. "Times have been hard lately. So I'm not selling things right now," Yvon says under the hot sun. "I just write, write to New York so things will get better."

In this world of merchants and refugees, he is a hero of sorts, even to those who warn that he is *moun fou*. Instead of a lost soul in the streets, a man with nothing, the Karate Man lives in the eyes of his neighbors as something more, someone who achieved great things but lost them through a massive personal tragedy. In Little Haiti, people are not always so fortunate as to be built up to something more than they are, like the Karate Man; more often, they find themselves victims of myths created to make them less than themselves, less than human. Yet they keep on, trying to find the key to make their lives better.

"If you are going to New York, can you take a letter for me? A letter to Brooklyn, New York," the Karate Man asks one day. "I don't have the address. Do you think it will get there if I just send it to Brooklyn?"

Life on the Batey

A mí me llaman el Negrito del Batey, y para mí el trabajo es enemigo.

They call me the little black man on the batey, *and work is my enemy.*

—"El Negrito del Batey"
A Trujillo-era merengue by Medardo Guzmán,
popularized by Alberto Beltrán

Under the visor of his blue baseball cap, Julien Emanuel's right eyelid is permanently shut. All that remains where his eye should be is a small hollow. He lost the eye seven years ago, when an errant spear of sugarcane hurtled into his face from one of the creaking train cars carrying harvested stalks to be processed. After the accident, Julien spent a month in the hospital, and then couldn't work for another three months. He still can't imagine how he managed to live through the time after his accident.

Julien's thirty-five years have worn into his face as if they were sixty. On his back, he wears a red shirt, to go along with his blue cap. Together, they make up the colors of his country's flag. Fourteen years earlier, in the lovely town of Jacmel in southern Haiti, Julien listened carefully to the words of the Dominican men who came there one week: to work in the cane fields of the Dominican Republic—the land to the east Haitians called Dominikani—they promised pay of twenty-five dollars a day, real U.S. money, not Haitian gourdes or Dominican pesos. After hearing what the men had to offer, Julien joined a large group of workers who piled into a truck headed for the vast cane plantations in the southeastern Dominican Republic, at La Romana, on the coast. The workers stood up in the back of the truck, where cattle would ride, during the whole dusty day's journey to the Dominican fields of the Central Romana corporation.

When they arrived, the Haitians went to work cutting cane under the hot Caribbean sun. Their thin shoes hardly stood up to the deep piles of cane stalks under their feet. Dust from the fields filled their lungs and worked its way into the cuts the sharp cane spears etched into their arms, legs, and chests. Their lunch was the same as breakfast: nothing but the sweet juice they chewed from stalks of sugarcane. At night, the cutters returned to their *bateyes*, the islands of cement-block barracks far out in the *cañaverales*, waves of cane that go on for miles and miles outside of La Romana. If the Haitians were lucky, dinner was a bit of rice, maybe with a tin of sardines, eaten by starlight, since there was no electricity.

When the plantation managers decided to move their workers somewhere else, the workers had no choice. After several years of cutting cane at La Romana with the others, Julien learned he was to be transferred along with a group of workers to the sugar plantation at Consuelo, about an hour northwest. That was bad news, because La Romana had a reputation for treating workers better than anywhere else. Julien's two children and their mother stayed behind in La Romana, where she could find work in the market.

At Consuelo, the barracks of the *batey* where Julien lives have no doors. Inside, the damp air rusts the stark iron beds and molders the few thin, ragged pallets that serve as mattresses. An empty light socket dangles from a dead wire in the ceiling of the main hallway.

Ruefully, he remembers the promise of dollars that brought him here from Jacmel in the first place. "There are no dollars," Julien says with a laugh too frank even to be ironic. The pay is so low that there are barely even Dominican pesos. It was at Consuelo that he lost his eye. He lived only by going into deeper debt to the plantation store. The store already had taken most of his pesos when payday came. For months after the accident, a whole paycheck wasn't enough to cover what he owed.

Scores of thousands of Haitians like Julien Emanuel have made the trek to the Dominican Republic from Haiti to cut sugarcane. Years ago, most of these migrant workers—or *braceros*, from the Spanish word *brazo* (arm)—came by contract between the Dominican and Haitian governments. Only a few came informally, *an ba fil*, under the wire, as they called it in Kreyol. In those days, hardly any of them had much of what could be called rights, but the *an ba fil* workers lived even more tenuously, not sure where they would work or whether they would be hauled off in the middle of the night. There has been no formal contract between the Dominican and Haitian governments since 1986, so many workers arrive on their own and hope for an individual contract. Between sixteen thousand and twenty thousand Haitians arrive each October and November, when the harvest begins in the south. Officially, they stay only through May or June, when cane cutting ends in the northern Dominican Republic.

How many Haitians are in Dominikani is not certain. It depends on whom you ask. The Dominican politicians say there are a million—many, many more than the 300,000 to 500,000 Haitians that more judicious scholars have estimated. The more Haitians there seem to be, the more righteous a senatorial or mayoral candidate sounds when he pledges to protect Dominicans from the black hordes. For campaign purposes, it doesn't really matter whether the number, or the ostensible threat posed by the immigrants, is accurate.

Using charts and academic jargon, studies explain the same things that Julien Emanuel will tell you. The Dominican historian Frank Moya Pons and his team of researchers, in a thick study called *El batey*, estimated that a workday cutting cane averages 11.48 hours and brings a man or boy to the fields approximately 6.4 days a week, averaging 74.47 hours at thirty-one cents an hour, or twenty-three U.S. dollars a week. Barely a third of the Haitian workers can read; they are only half as likely as Dominicans to be literate, and slightly less likely than the average Haitian. The typical *bracero* has attended only a year and a half of school. One in five cane cutters is hurt seriously each year. Even the Dominican government recognizes that 85 percent of all workplace injuries in the country happen in the cane fields. The studies do not count the eyes or limbs damaged by the cane, the gallons of children's tears, the miles of cuts in black skin, the nights without dinner.

During the harvest, workers are not allowed to leave the plantations. The police, working with the state cane corporation and with the righteous conviction that they are protecting their communities from filth and disease, keep a sharp eye out for the Haitians and make them return if they rebel and go out on the streets of neighboring towns.

In July, *el tiempo muerto*, the dead season, begins. Work pauses for a few months, and the cane cutters are left to fend for themselves harvesting either coffee or rice. Over the years, many of the Haitians have stayed on the cane fields after the harvests are over: some of them have been able to start little garden plots or cobble together jobs here and there, right in the cane barracks, to sustain themselves over the months when there is no work. They stay through season after season. Many of the *braceros'* children become cane cutters too, beginning when they are barely taller than a machete. The *braceros* who have been here longer are the old hands, the *viejos*. Often the Dominican guards give the *viejos* authority over the newcomers, who are called *kongos*, a derisive term that refers to their African roots.

Under the harsh noon sun, the feathery green leaves and brilliant red-orange flowers of a flamboyant tree cast little shadow over a small group of cane cutters gathered for a break. Sego Germain scratches his stomach through his white T-shirt, which has been cut to make long, knotted hanging fringes. Like most of the others here, he has no passport, because the soldiers tore up his papers when he first arrived years ago.

Because of turgid Dominican bureaucracy, difficult transportation, and ignorance of the importance of documents, most cane cutters do not register births with the authorities. As a result, Sego's children will most likely not have passports either. They will be nationless, paperless. They will not be recognized in the world outside the *batey*. In the eyes of the authorities, these people do not exist or, more precisely, are not people at all. To the Haitian soldiers, Sego Germain is no Haitian. Nor is he a Dominican. In short, his life is not of much concern to either of the countries that share the island of Hispaniola.

"Here, I often work until seven o'clock in the evening. Then, even if I am home and have just gone to bed, they can come call me and say, 'Do this.' And that is after I have started work at seven in the morning," says Sego Germain in a rapid mix of Kreyol and Spanish. A red plastic comb juts out of his hair. "I can't exactly say life is not good, but . . ." He pauses. "We need people in the *bateyes* to help us, but there aren't any. When the children are sick, there is nobody to take them to the hospital. There's no school for them." He hesitates again, then switches to Spanish from Kreyol. *"Los grandes chupan a los chiquitos."* The big ones are sucking the little ones dry.

His shirt is open to his navel. You can see the diet of rice, plantains, and potatoes doesn't go far to cut the hunger from a day of *koupe kann.* Sego Germain's wages leave little room for much more to eat, for him, his wife, Lotilia, their five-year-old boy, and their eight- and nine-year-old daughters. He is paid every two weeks with a slip of paper that he can cash in at the corporation store on the *batey.* His wages are calculated according to how much cane his work team has cut. Each ton is worth just 30 pesos—about $2.40. Even so, a ton is not always paid as a whole ton of cane.

Why? The *pesadores,* Dominicans who weigh the cane to determine how much the Haitians will be paid, often cheat the workers. If a team has cut seventeen tons, the *pesador* will vouch for, say, thirteen tons but turn over the full seventeen to the *ingenio* and pocket the difference. In another trick used to cut wages paid to the Haitians, cane is often left to dry in the sun before it is weighed. As much as a third of the weight evaporates, and so does a third of the *bracero's* pay. But the workers can do little to protest. In Florida, the average cane cutter harvests eight tons a day. In the Dominican Republic, he cuts only a ton or a ton and a half. It's hard to tell how much of that difference comes from the weakness of the workers, from the lies of the *pesadores,* or from the sun's sucking the liquid from the stalks.

"Papa Doc" Duvalier still ruled Haiti when Jacques Pierre first came to Dominikani, when he was eighteen years old, from the hamlet of Ouanaminthe, on the northern tip of the Dominican-Haitian border. "It was hard to get enough to eat even then. Worse, when I came here, they were killing people in Haiti," he recalls.

Even before Papa Doc became President of Haiti on October 22, 1957, martial law had settled on the country. A military junta took over after his election to make sure that terrorist attacks would not prevent him from taking office. Despite Duvalier's meek appearance, the doctor ruled unsparingly, using states of siege and assuming emergency powers to quiet constant unrest. He established a personal security force named after Tonton Macoute, Uncle Strawsack, the bogeyman who steals children from the Haitian countryside and stuffs them into his straw sack.

The name Duvalier became synonymous with terror. The first people to leave Haiti under his dictatorship were called the "Boeing People," middle-class professionals and intellectuals who could afford airplane tickets and qualify for U.S. visas. The poorest Haitians, like Jacques Pierre, left Haiti under contracts by which the Haitian government sold workers to the Dominicans.

Now fifty years old, Jacques is still cutting cane. He has never looked for work outside the cane fields and doesn't plan to do so. "Other work, like construction? I don't know how to do that kind of work."

Like Jacques, few of the *braceros* still think Dominikani can offer them a life better than the one they left, but they do not want to return to Haiti. Resigned, Julien Emanuel softly puts himself down, describing himself as one who, like his colleagues, has no choice but to remain at the mercy of the indifferent owners of the cane fields: "*Nou pa gin tet pou aide nou.*" We don't have the head to help ourselves.

Jacques Pierre speaks up: "*Nou pa gin tet ansanm.*" We haven't put our heads together. The other *braceros* nod in agreement. "*Fok nou mete tout tet ansanm.*" We need to put all our heads together, says Jacques. "If we would do that, we would maybe be able to solve some of our problems. But the minute we try to organize, they send the leaders to prison. They don't want us to put our heads together."

A woman walks down the sidewalk, flipping her feet out at each step. It appears that she broke her hip once and that it never healed right. Each leg goes up at the hip, swings out from the knee, and ends with a quick snap of the foot. It is a laborious process. When she finally arrives, she squats at the foot of the flamboyant tree and watches the men. But her stare seems to go beyond them, into nothingness. It could reach all the way back in history.

Columbus wrote glowingly back to his Spanish sponsors that Hispaniola's lush soil would yield riches as dazzling as the mineral wealth that could be mined from the hills. In his vision, the sugar fields of Hispaniola might eventually rival those of Andalusia and Sicily. Sugar was introduced to the island in 1505. In 1516, Columbus's men completed its first sugar-mill (*trapiche*), a crude affair powered by horses, oxen, or men turning a giant wheel. Slaves began arriving on Hispaniola in 1518. In 1546 the historian Gonzalo Fernández de Oviedo recorded that four *trapiches* and twenty water-powered *ingenios* were operating on Hispaniola.

By the seventeenth century, Spanish explorers had abandoned Santo Domingo in search of gold in Mexico and South America, while the French had established sugar plantations to the west. By the late eighteenth century, Saint-Domingue boasted 723 *ingenios* and half a million slaves. In Spanish Santo Domingo, to the east, the sugar industry shrank to nine *ingenios* and eleven *trapiches* worked by six hundred slaves. By the time of the French Revolution, sugar exports were the mainstay of the economy of Saint-Domingue. But after the war for Haiti's independence (1791–1803), all that was left behind was charred fields. The war had also cut off channels of trade to Europe, and Haiti's sugar industry never fully recovered.

For most of the nineteenth century, Hispaniola's sugar fields lay all but fallow as fights for power on the island sucked manpower and resources into conflicts instead of cultivation. The Haitians failed to revive agriculture during their 1822–44 occupation of Santo Domingo. Nor did the Dominicans' uneasy reannexation to Spain in 1861 bring the sugar fields to life in Santo Domingo. Sugar came back only after Spain left for good, in 1865.

In 1868 Cubans fleeing the civil war that had erupted on their island, fifty miles northwest of Hispaniola, brought to Santo Domingo new technology—most important, steam power. Meanwhile, civil war in the United States and the Franco-German wars had devastated American and European cane- and beet-sugar industries; entrepreneurs looking for new sources of the sweet stuff found it in the Dominican Republic. Flush with new money and technology, Santo Domingo's sugar industry entered a golden age, launching a perpetual-motion machine that would swing the Dominican Republic from boom to bust and back, knocking around the humble men who cut the cane.

The new Dominican sugar barons rolled in: the Hardys, the Hattons, and the Smiths; the Basses with their Central Romana and Consuelo mills; the Zanettis and the Vicinis. By 1875 money was flooding into the south of the Dominican Republic as foreigners snapped up land and Dominican peasants sought work in the sugar mills. Wages during harvest time were far higher than what the peasants could eke out tilling the earth. Even so, the new plantations could not find enough workers to cut the cane and feed the mills. The Dominican plantations began importing workers from the English-speaking Caribbean (called *cocolos* for the way they cropped their hair so close as to be practically bald) to supplement the labor force. Times were very good.

As Santo Domingo prospered, the economy on the western end of Hispaniola was imploding. Haiti drifted from one dictatorship to another, and Haitians, despairing, took hope from word of the reviving Dominican sugar trade. By the last decade of the nineteenth century, a handful of Haitians had already begun to cut cane on the other side of Hispaniola, in a trickle that would later become a torrent.

Economic booms invariably attract charlatans looking to make easy money. The Dominican dictator Ulíses Heureaux (Lilís), who became President in 1886, was in the right place at the right time to lure money from foreigners overeager to profit from Dominican sugar. Lilís was clever and greedy enough to line his pockets generously with foreign money. He drew loan after loan from foreign bankers and corporations, who provided the funds in return for lucrative concessions and, of course, a hand in the customs receipts for sugar and other exports. Just as much money from the leaky loans slipped into the pockets of Heureaux and his associates as found its way into productive investment.

With so much money falling by the wayside, it was impossible for the Dominican government to earn enough to pay back all it had borrowed. The debt spiraled out of control; by the turn of the century, it was close to $34 million, while only $2 million a year was coming in through customs. Just to service the debt, Heureaux had to line up new loans. He secretly sold off borderlands to Haiti for 1 million pesos, only 400,000 pesos of which made its way into the Dominican Treasury. The rest disappeared, and it is not hard to guess where it went.

By the time angry Dominicans assassinated Heureaux in July 1899, ending his fourteen years of dictatorship, Dominican finances were a disaster. The country was tilting toward civil war. And, as we have seen, the new political parties named themselves after fighting cocks, the long-tail-feathered *coludos* and the tail-featherless *bolos*.

With foreign creditors clamoring for their money, warships from Italy, Belgium, and Germany appeared off the coast of Santo Domingo in 1901 and 1903 to try to force the Dominicans to pay up. U.S. President Theodore Roosevelt looked on disapprovingly. The ships intruded on the U.S. sphere of influence and threatened the security of Roosevelt's pet project, the Panama Canal. American creditors had to be paid back, too, and the Europeans had to be placated. Roosevelt's solution in early 1905 was for the United States to guarantee the Dominican debt and to take over its customs procedures and 55 percent of the revenues, which would be used to pay customs salaries and repay creditors; 45 percent would be retained by the Dominican government.

With state coffers empty and Dominicans demanding jobs, the new Administration under President Ramón Cáceres knew that encouraging foreign companies was the only means by which it could bring the country back to prosperity. Cáceres was ready to exploit investors' short memories and consequent willingness to throw good money after bad wherever it looked as if a profit might be had. In April 1906, Cáceres lifted all taxes from sugar production and export, then turned his head when foreign companies acquired all the best sugar lands in the country, along the southeastern coast, often conniving to buy the property at far less than its real value. His sugar gamble was to pull apart the social fabric of Hispaniola, shifting masses of people around the island and creating pockets of near slavery that survived until the end of the century. Though he succeeded at bringing in foreign money, he angered so many Dominican businessmen (not to mention workers unhappy about the new rum taxes) that he lost control. In November 1911, a group of conspirators ambushed Cáceres on his Sunday-afternoon drive on the highway west of Santo Domingo, to Haina. In the ensuing gun battle, Cáceres died. Foreign investors and creditors, many of them still waiting to be paid back from the Lilís years, watched nervously as the Dominican Republic descended into civil war.

Across the island, meanwhile, Haitian politics similarly disintegrated. A mob in 1915 attacked the Presidential palace in Port-au-Prince and pulled the corpse of the unfortunate President Guillaume Vilbrun Sam to pieces. U.S. Marines took over Port-au-Prince and began a nineteen-year occupation of Haiti. They landed on Dominican shores a year later to keep disgruntled Dominicans from similar violent unrest against elderly President Juan Isidro Jimenes.

As the Marines kept a lid on Haiti and the Dominican Republic, the

Great War was raging in Europe, where sugar-beet farms were destroyed, and sugar once again became scarce worldwide. With their boys running things on Hispaniola, American corporations moved full force to the island. Between 1893 and 1934, when the Americans left Hispaniola, sugar land under cultivation expanded from just over 200,000 *tareas* (a Dominican land measure equal to one-sixteenth of a hectare) to nearly 3 million. Now the pattern of boom and bust was about to repeat itself.

By the early 1920s, when world sugar prices reached a new high of twenty-two cents per pound, the U.S. companies running most of the Dominican sugarcane industry were in a frenzy to boost production. To keep their mills running, the plantation owners experimented with hiring workers from Puerto Rico and more *cocolos* from the English-speaking Caribbean; but these reinforcements were not enough. For the man-hours they needed, the sugar growers looked to Haiti for desperate men who would accept lower wages than the Dominicans would. In 1920 there had been 28,258 Haitians in the Dominican Republic; by 1935, a year after the Americans left Haiti and eleven years after they had left the Dominican Republic, the number had nearly doubled, to 52,657 legal residents. The corporations had relied so heavily on cheap foreign labor that Dominicans no longer considered cutting cane themselves. That was "Haitian work," unfit for native sons.

The flow of foreign workers peaked just when the U.S. stock market crashed in 1929, beginning the Great Depression. Sugar prices plummeted. Dominican exports to the United States tumbled by two-thirds. Prices fell to under two cents per pound, less than a tenth of what they had been just seven years earlier. Two years later, the sweet stuff sold for under a penny a pound and stayed that way for ten years. That tens of thousands of migrant workers had come to the Dominican Republic for work and wages now seemed a cruel irony. How could the Dominican Republic support all these foreigners, producing crops worth nothing, when its own people did not have jobs?

When sugar prices fell, Rafael Trujillo had already risen to the Presidency from his humble early career as a cane-field guard. As the Great Depression began, Trujillo was well aware that the Presidents before him had fallen from power because they could not deliver prosperity, and he had no intention of letting the same thing happen to him. His plan was to deflect attention from falling sugar prices by focusing on the many workers who had come to the country to support the sugar machine. If Dominicans directed their anger at foreigners, he would become a hero for fighting to keep the intruders out.

In January 1932, with the sugar harvest in full swing, Trujillo issued migration law number 279. The decree imposed a tax on all foreigners of $6 for each entry and $6 per year of residence—except for anyone unfortunate enough to be of Asian or black-African descent, who had to pay annual fees of up to $300. The U.S. companies that depended on immigrant labor reacted with alarm. How could workers earning sixty cents a day pay this new tax? The ones who would foot the bill, obviously, were the multinational sugar corporations.

Three days after the migration law was passed, the administrator of the Central Romana sugar corporation paid a visit to Trujillo, an incident that the Dominican historian Bernardo Vega recounts. Reminded of the Americans' past generosity to him (and, most likely, pleased that he, a once-humble sugarcane guard, was now in a position to grant or deny favors to the United States), the dictator was persuaded to cut a deal: the *braceros* would be exempted, a loophole that virtually guaranteed that the majority of sugarcane cutters would remain Haitian.

Times were even worse in Cuba, where sugar became a symbol of all that was wrong with the times: at its height, the industry there had produced five million tons a year (supplying half the sugar demand of the entire United States), employed one out of five workers, and made up 90 percent of exports. When sugar's price collapsed to a tenth of its previous level, so did the country's fortunes. Even though the majority of the plantations in Cuba and Hispaniola were owned by U.S. companies, Washington's loyalties were to the producers back home; in 1930 stopgap protectionist barriers were created, and then the 1934 U.S. Sugar Act set up an elaborate system of quotas and domestic price supports that severely limited sugar imports and would continue to dictate the fortunes of the Caribbean sugar economies for decades.

The dramatic drop in the volume as well as the price of Cuba's sugar exports coincided with political turmoil; a general strike and the withdrawal of U.S. support had forced President Gerardo Machado y Morales to resign in August 1933 and ushered in what would become the long rule of Fulgencio Batista. During a period of intense political intrigue, the government late that year moved to appease the masses of workers clamoring for jobs: it said it would employ no more foreign workers and barred Haitian boats carrying workers from docking; early the next year, it began expelling the tens of thousands of Haitians who had been lured to Cuba to cut cane during the previous decade. Fifty-four miles of ocean separated Cuba and Haiti, so it was nearly impossible for the expelled workers, once back in their Haitian homeland, to return to their old jobs in Cuba. They moved instead to the Dominican Republic, there being no watery barrier to keep them out.

As the new influx of Haitians arrived, Trujillo was doing scapegoating of his own. In 1933, he passed a law "Dominicanizing" the cane harvest, requiring that 70 percent of workers in the cane fields be Dominican. Again, the multinationals won exceptions, but Haitians working outside the sugar industry paid the price for the lenient treatment of the *braceros*. In July 1934, as the U.S. occupation of Haiti was about to end, the Dominicans deported eight thousand Haitians, in the first of many expulsions. A month later, the Dominican Congress passed yet another migration law, followed by a law promoting Dominican colonization of the border area. But the Haitians kept coming, until Trujillo decided to solve the problem permanently in October 1937, just as the cane harvest was about to begin.

How fitting that the massacre called *El Corte* stopped at the borders of the plantations where the real harvest took place, and the Haitian *braceros* on the property of the great multinational corporations were spared. Their blood did not mix with that of the more than twenty-five thousand Haitians that spilled into the waters of the Massacre River along the border.

Because the harvest had not yet begun that year, there were, in fact, very few workers in the fields. The Haitians stopped coming, leaving the plantation managers scrambling to find workers to cut the cane when the harvest began in November. Trujillo had his revenge on the corporations that had thwarted his efforts to keep Haitians out. In the end they were forced to import *cocolos* from the English-speaking islands, paying 30 percent more in wages. The *cocolos* were just as black as the Haitians, but when the Dominicans sent them home, they could not return to Dominican soil so easily.

Like the cane-growing season itself, sugar prices move in cycles. So did the whims of Trujillo. As the world economy recovered and sugar prices began climbing, Trujillo saw the Haitians in a new light. By 1948 the price of sugar had more than doubled from its Depression low, edging above four cents per pound. That year, Trujillo bought his first sugar property, the Catarey mill and fields near Bonao, an hour north of Santo Domingo. By 1952 he boasted (erroneously) that his new possession, the Rio Haina mill, near his hometown of San Cristóbal, was the world's largest.

Using threats, creative accounting, and selective strict enforcement of laws to buy land at close to nothing, Trujillo snapped up one plantation after another and drove out Dominican and foreign owners alike. In one memorable example, recounted by the historian Robert Crassweller, Trujillo extorted the Laguna Blanca fields to supply Rio Haina by ordering the assassination of their recalcitrant owner. Informed of his unfortunate predicament, the man agreed to sell Trujillo his land for a pittance, and the dictator graciously withdrew his murder command.

Once again, Haitians were not only welcome but in demand. In 1952, Trujillo and Haiti's President, Paul Magloire, agreed on a plan to ensure a steady supply of cane cutters: Dominican sugar mills would simply buy the workers straight from the Haitian government. The first year of the contract, the Dominicans "bought" 16,500 Haitians. Future harvests filled Trujillo's accounts with sugar dollars and the Haitian government's with profits from its sale of human beings. By the late 1970s the Dominican government was paying Haiti as much as $3 million a year for the *braceros*.

By 1957, however, President Magloire was gone and François Duvalier was installed in the National Palace in Port-au-Prince. This strange little doctor, who had made his name fighting the disease yaws in the countryside, would soon rival Trujillo for excesses of monomaniacal rule. Though the two dictators on opposite ends of the island eyed each other with distrust, they shared an interest in making money, so they renewed the contract for Haitian workers. Duvalier's firm grip over Haiti guaranteed that workers would be available and pliant; his spy network extended to the Dominican cane fields, where Haitian monitors (ostensibly sent to defend the workers' rights) ensured that the Haitians were not causing problems or plotting against Duvalier. The Dominican dictator thanked his Haitian counterpart in cash.

In the dusk on May 30, 1961, Trujillo's rule ended when gunmen ambushed his car on the highway west of Santo Domingo.

In 1966 the new U.S.-backed government headed by Joaquín Balaguer nationalized Trujillo's sugar holdings and established a new state agency to supervise the operations. With Trujillo gone, the Dominican Republic stood to profit handsomely from this new sugar arrangement. Still using the quota system it had set up in 1934, the United States decided each year how much sugar it would import, then allotted portions of its purchase among the world's sugar producers. Trujillo had hoped to win a portion of Cuba's share of the U.S. market when the quota of the world's largest sugar producer fell casualty in July 1960 to an American embargo as part of efforts to unseat Fidel Castro. But as one U.S. congressman pointed out during debate on the matter, it made no sense to take away the share of a left-wing dictatorship only to give it to a right-wing regime like Trujillo's. So Congress only reluctantly added 29,893 tons to the Dominicans' normal allotment of 81,457 tons—but slapped on an "anti-dictator" duty of two cents per pound. By 1966, however, the Dominican Republic had received the official international stamp of democracy and so was able to export lower-cost sugar to a vast new market. In *Sugar and Modern Slavery*, Roger Plant cites as having been close to $23 million the annual cut in duties on Dominican exports when the United States finally rescinded the special tax.

On November 14, 1966, the Dominican Republic signed a new contract with Duvalier for the annual supply of broad backs, strong arms, sweat, and blood. Trujillo was gone, but his inhuman labor system remained. As the years went by, the Duvaliers and the Dominicans came up with new and creative ways of siphoning money even from the pittance the workers were paid. Article 11 of the *bracero* contracts authorized the State Sugar Council to withhold, on behalf of the Haitian government, part of the workers' wages (as much as 5 percent), which in theory would be returned to them when they finished the harvest and returned to Haiti. In reality, the *braceros* never saw the money. The funds went directly into the Duvalier family pockets. Eventually, the automatic discount was changed to a flat payment, the "head tax," which the Dominican government paid the Haitian government for each worker.

Even when global sugar prices dropped, there were plenty of ways to make money off the workers. Entrusted with monitoring the trafficking of Haitian workers, the armed forces of both countries also enriched themselves: in Haiti, soldiers hiring workers took bribes, forcing those who did not pay to wait for hours, sometimes days; in the Dominican Republic, soldiers carried out *redadas*, or forced roundups, near the end of the harvest at one field, then sold the workers to other cane fields.

After Papa Doc Duvalier died in 1971 and his overweight son Jean-Claude, "Baby Doc," became President for Life, not much changed. In June 1974 a Trujillo collaborator and rich landowner, Felix W. Bernardino, sprayed with gunfire a group of Haitians resting in their rooms. These workers, part of a shipment of one hundred *braceros* whose contracts at Central Romana were up, had boarded a truck, thinking they were returning to Haiti. Instead, they were abducted to Bernardino's ranch. The men had refused to work and demanded to be taken to Haiti, the Dominican press reported. For their "crime," the Haitians were shot. That incident, and many others like it, happened when sugar prices were high. When the world sugar market dropped, Haitian workers could count on even worse treatment.

In 1974 and 1975 a temporary double stroke of good fortune hit the Dominican Republic and helped propel rapid economic expansion, to Balaguer's benefit. In 1974 world sugar prices nearly tripled, to an average of 29.6 cents per pound (and at one point in the year, nearly 60 cents). This meant that for only the third time since 1948 (when the United States added price floors to its byzantine sugar-import regime) the world price was above that which U.S. producers received. In 1975, making a wrong bet that world-market prices would stay high enough to keep U.S. farmers happy, the United States allowed the 1934 system of quotas and price supports to expire: in other words, it let foreign producers compete on equal terms with domestic producers for its huge sugar market. The subsequent worldwide rush to boost production soon created a glut and drove prices down. By December 1976 sugar producers were earning just 7.5 cents a pound. The next year, Congress approved new price supports to ensure that U.S. producers received no less than 13.5 cents per pound. To prevent cheaper sugar from undercutting U.S. producers, it raised import duties in a preamble to more drastic measures soon to follow.

Baby Doc was greedy but not as crafty as his father, and he lacked Papa Doc's sense of timing. He apparently didn't understand that sugar profits were down when he tried to wring more money out of the *bracero* contract in late 1977 by increasing the "head tax" for each worker from sixty-five dollars to seventy dollars. The Dominicans balked and threatened to have their own soldiers cut the cane if necessary. Duvalier backed down.

Just outside the town of La Romana, not far from where the cane cutter Julien Emanuel lost his eye, tourists swarm through a replicated seventeenth-century Italian artists' village, Altos de Chavón. Lining its charming cobbled pathways, there are four restaurants, a large coral amphitheater where international music stars come to perform, a design school, a writers' workshop, art shops, boutiques, and jewelry stores selling necklaces and earrings made from Spanish doubloons retrieved from shipwrecks off the coast of Hispaniola. The site is a perfect complement to Casa de Campo, a resort that began as an executive retreat for Gulf & Western (G&W) and is now playground to the rich and famous, including the likes of Henry Kissinger, Gloria Estefan, and the Dominican dress designer Oscar de la Renta. You can golf, play chukkers of polo, lounge on the beach, take a trail ride, pamper yourself at the spa, enjoy the good life.

The origin of the resort is as troubling as its contrast with the fields of workers around it. In the late 1970s, Charles Bluhdorn, chairman of G&W, the U.S. multinational that owned the vast cane plantations of Central Romana, struck a deal with Dominican officials, a deal that has been analyzed by the journalist Roger Plant. The plan was to speculate on world commodities futures markets using Dominican government, as well as Central Romana, sugar. Bluhdorn, making the right bets, walked away with $65 million in profits. Under the verbal agreement, the Dominicans were to receive more than half of that money. But G&W used smoke and mirrors to hide some of the gains, then balked at handing over the funds. When the Dominican government threatened to sue, G&W agreed in 1979 to contribute funds to "important infrastructure projects." Altos de Chavón, the artists' colony at its retreat, was the project the corporation chose to finance. Apparently, it defined broadly the concept of important infrastructure.

While wealthy North Americans and Dominicans cavorted in designer resorts, the workers who sweated to harvest the sugar were forgotten. In early August 1977 at the Rio Haina sugar mill, thousands of Haitians who had completed their work were ready to go home. Instead, they were forced to wait seventeen days during a bout of bad weather, which officials used as an excuse to delay repatriating them. Finally, the workers rebelled; they tried to storm the Rio Haina sugar mill offices before army officers violently put down their uprising. Haitian officials who were supposed to be helping the *braceros* barred them from speaking to reporters about the situation.

In 1979 the world began to take notice of the plight of the Dominican cane cutters. The Anti-Slavery Society of London picked up the case, on which it prepared a damning report that it presented to the United Nations High Commissioner for Human Rights in Geneva in August. The proceedings irritated the Dominican government, but the guilty parties did not bear the brunt of the scandal; the workers at the bottom of the system did. In June 1980, as the end of the harvest approached, the government took out newspaper ads warning that any employers hiring illegal workers would be prosecuted to the full extent of the law. Never mind that the migration statute invoked had not been dusted off for use in nearly twenty years or that the Dominican government itself was the country's largest employer of Haitians. That year and at the end of harvests in the years to come, Dominican soldiers rounded up all the Haitians they could find and deported them.

The Dominican government responded to a 1983 International Labor Organization inquiry into the status of the cane cutters with a disingenuous but accurate argument: "One of the worst forms of slavery today is practiced by the developed countries when they keep down the prices of basic products by subsidizing and dumping products competing with those that are vital for the countries of the Third World."

In 1981, President Ronald Reagan signed into law the highly protectionist Agriculture and Food Act. It spelled disaster in the Dominican Republic, for it established a sugar-price floor at 16.75 cents a pound, to increase to 18 cents by 1985. With this attractive price for sugar virtually guaranteed, U.S. farmers immediately began making plans to increase their yields. Of course, the more sugar they grew and processed, the further prices fell, the harder it was for the government to maintain the price support, and the harder it was for countries like the Dominican Republic to get reasonable prices for their crops. World sugar market prices plunged from 29 cents per pound in late 1980 to just over 4 cents in mid-1985, when the worst blow fell.

With the U.S. budget deficit ballooning from Reagan's tax cuts, Congress voted to prevent Uncle Sam from using tax moneys to hold the sugar price up. Under that constraint, there were only two ways to support sugar: quotas and tariffs. Neither was good for the Dominican Republic (nor, for that matter, for Panama, Guatemala, Barbados, Honduras, Peru, Nicaragua, or the Philippines). The United States limited the foreign sugar allowed into its market by using quotas that allowed each country to sell it a specified amount, which would be changed each year according to U.S. needs; it slapped tariffs on amounts above those limits. Since the United States buys one-quarter to one-third of the world's total sugar production, the law sent world sugar prices into a downward spiral.

Cane sugar was still expensive for U.S. food manufacturers, who began switching to cheaper domestic substitutes: beet sugar, high-fructose corn syrup, crystalline fructose, dextrose, and honey. At the same time, the health craze caught on, replacing sugar with saccharine, then aspartame. By 1985, U.S. food manufacturers were using processed sweeteners more than sugar. By 1988 cane-sugar use had fallen to sixty-two pounds per person per year, down 40 percent over twenty years. And as the U.S. sweetener industry grew, imported sugar dipped from 25 percent of the sugar Americans consumed in the 1970s to just 6 percent by 1981. Things were so bad for the Dominican sugar plantations that even G&W gave up. In 1984, after Bluhdorn's death, the multinational sold its Dominican holdings to the Fanjuls, a Cuban sugarcane family exiled in Florida.

The economy of the Dominican Republic, which continued to rely heavily on sugar, was heading for disaster. Because it still had the advantage of a cheap, docile source of labor, however, the government postponed the hard decision of ending its dependence on an industry that had kept it swinging from boom to bust and back again and again. It made little sense to invest in a dying industry; it was more efficient to direct economic resources to growing enterprises that could provide a higher income in the future. Yet more than half of the country's capital investment was in sugar; the crop provided half of Dominican jobs and one-quarter of the country's exports. By 1983 the Dominican Republic was having trouble paying its foreign bills and had to turn to the International Monetary Fund for more than $450 million in help, in exchange for which it devalued the peso. By 1985 the government had raised gasoline prices by 33 percent and food prices by as much as 60 percent. Food riots followed in which more than one hundred people died. The country had not even hit bottom.

Sugar mills started closing, and the Haitians who had worked in them spilled out into the rest of the country. Some sought work in other cane fields, and the more ambitious of them went into other agricultural industries: rice, coffee, cacao. Some moved out of the fields into light assembly work in the industrial free-trade zones, service jobs in the hotels, construction, anything at all. With good reason, Dominicans feared that these Haitians would push down wages in this other work as they had in agriculture and take Dominican jobs. At the same time, Dominicans were emigrating in greater numbers to the United States.

In the fields outside Hato Mayor, near the Ozama sugar mill in the Dominican Republic, a Dominican handyman named Florentino Jesus melts down car batteries to retrieve the lead. He throws oil onto a cauldron of smoldering lumps of lead. On the floor lies a row of completed bricks he will sell to factories. His wild hair flops down over his Charles Bronson–like features. "Before, people used to throw out batteries," he says. "Now they don't. They want to get whatever they can for them."

On the side of the dirt road not far from his laboratory, a yellow mini station wagon is stopped next to a water pipe and spigot. A Dominican girl is stomping up a sidewalk complaining that she has to help the man kneeling at the faucet fill bottles of water to bring to the cane cutters. "I don't care if your work does help a Haitian," he yells at her in disgust. "Dominican. Haitian. Shit, chickens probably have bluer blood than we do."

Up the road, Liberades Pérez awakens from an afternoon nap in her crazy-quilt-painted aluminum hut. "Oh, how my head hurts," she laments, patting the blue-and-green scarf above her freckled forehead and hazel eyes. Chatting with strangers as she stands on her tiny porch overlooking seas of cane, she points a mile away to a row of large, long pastel-colored apartment buildings standing incongruously against the sky. Those are the government housing complexes that President Balaguer built for the squatters he forced out of shacks they had erected on land where he wanted to build the Columbus Lighthouse. The complexes are eerie in this context—among the cane fields nearly an hour from the capital, out of their urban element—and stranger to the Dominicans of the *campo* than even the Haitian cane cutters are.

"Sabe lo que es, un animal?" You know what an animal is? Liberades mutters, rolling her eyes. "I'll tell you. That's it." The lighthouse people keep to themselves, and nobody can figure out what exactly they do in their concrete government apartments or why they insisted, before, on living in their crowded tin shacks in Santo Domingo. "They are all crazy, stupid," says Liberades. But she gets on fine with the Haitians who live down the hill and steps confidently down the path on the way to visit Cesar Saint Charles.

He came to the Dominican Republic from Ti Tanyin, in Haiti, fourteen years before, under the government of Antonio Guzmán. The story they told him was the same as always: If you go to Santo Domingo, you can earn fifteen dollars a day. The Dominicans didn't even have to tell him, because all the Haitians knew. His whole family except one son has left Haiti, too, but they've all gone to New York. He won't go because it's too cold and expensive: "All you do is spend money." Besides, he saved enough in the cane fields to build a little house. He had to pay 500 pesos to a Dominican lawyer a few months ago when the police took him to prison for living in a house he didn't have a title to (who did out in the cane fields?). But he solved the problem and went back to his work fixing shoes, picking potatoes, and gardening. He also paints. Cesar does a slow dance to show how he paints a room: he reaches up, around, and stretches on one bare foot, then another, pointing to imaginary corners, covering them completely with paint in his imagination. "Life here isn't particularly good," he says. "But when you compare it . . . well."

Isolated in the *bateyes*, the *braceros* see no future beyond the waving stalks of sugarcane. They hardly exist on paper. Their children have no country. They are lucky if they get medical treatment. They have no hope. Dominicans will not do the work they do, and most Dominicans hardly blink at the subhuman treatment meted out to the immigrants. The cane cutters are animals, says Dominican common wisdom. They are good for labor and no more, worth consideration only to make sure they do not leave the *bateyes* and spread their dirty diseases, their inferior culture, their black, black skin. What concern is it that the Haitians do not receive proper medical care? They chose to come to Dominikani. What matter if Dominicans brought them here? They agreed to come.

To speak with cane workers is to learn how incredible it is that these powerless men, forced to work for almost nothing and prevented from leaving the *batey*, could be a threat to Dominicans, as the government argues. The voiceless Haitians cannot even defend themselves. Human-rights advocates say they are modern-day slaves. And in many ways the *braceros'* situation is like that of the original slaves who harvested sugar-cane centuries ago. The Spanish colonizers justified working the Taino of Hispaniola to death in their barren gold mines with their belief that the Indians were not human. When the Taino died out, the black slaves brought from Africa harvested coffee, tobacco, and sugar for Europe, and they, too, could be mistreated because their owners believed they were not human.

It has been nearly two hundred years since Haiti abolished slavery and the white planters fled Saint-Domingue, but this denial of the work-ers' humanity persists. In a way, today's situation is even more tragic: Haitians who are in the Dominican Republic to cut cane have come on their own. They may be deceived about the opportunities in Dominikani, but they are not dragged to the cane fields in irons.

The *braceros* are caught in the logic of a time long ago, of the days of slave merchants and colonial plantations. This modern form of slavery is harder to define and more difficult to end because the driving forces behind it are intertwined. International human-rights groups blame the Dominicans, but the Dominicans are not alone. The United States, which has contributed to the problem, has been silent on the issue. It, too, is constrained by the past. Though U.S. interests left the island in the 1940s and 1950s, when Trujillo seized much of the best sugar land by force, later U.S. sugar policies did serious damage to Dominican sugar. And the Dominican government criticizes Haiti for failing to provide for its people and protests that its own resources are too scarce to do more. Why should Haitians get better treatment when so many Dominicans themselves have no work? It notes that the Dominican Republic was doomed by U.S. sugar policy, which set up massive plantations, then cut back the market for Dominican sugar. It has blamed everyone but itself.

Few Dominicans argue that the Haitian cane cutters' lives are good. But rather than eliciting compassion, the truth of Haitian misery often becomes a circular argument: the *braceros* live miserable lives because they are pathetic, because they can't help it. In this twisted logic, the Haitians' sad circumstances are of their own making. What matter that the Dominican government made the mistake of depending too heavily on the caprice of sugar prices? What difference does it make that without the *braceros* the Dominican sugar mills would grind to a halt? International human-rights groups are embarrassing the Dominican Republic. There are too many Haitians in the country. Haitians are guilty; Haitians deserve their fate.

Bitter Sugar

Never again will our brothers and sisters give blood to make
bitter sugar.

—Jean-Bertrand Aristide

In the shining white National Palace in Port-au-Prince, the Duvalier family lived high off the payments they received for Haitian cane cutters sweating under the hot sun in Dominikani. The profits from selling human labor, horrible as they were, could be called the most honest of the Duvaliers' schemes for making money. At least the corrupt Haitian government was delivering something of value in return for the money it received.

When François Duvalier died in April 1971, his nineteen-year-old son, Jean-Claude, became President for Life. Papa Doc's mysterious, austere ways disappeared, replaced by Baby Doc's lax, free-spending lifestyle. In 1980, Baby Doc married a rich mulatto divorcée, Michèle Bennett, in a wedding that cost $3 million. The First Couple's lifestyle was lavish: $50,000 monthly flower bills, Michèle's frequent shopping trips, all financed by graft on an impressive new scale. Money flowed out of the government and into Duvalier bank accounts at the speed that blood had run under Papa Doc. The Central Bank, for example, paid a $100,000 "salary" to Michèle each month. An International Monetary Fund monitoring team estimated that in December 1980 alone $20 million leaked out of state accounts into Baby Doc's hands.

It was rare that the Duvalier family business left behind anything except gaping holes in government finances. One project, the Bon Repos Hospital, was different. It stood out not because there was no theft but because it had buildings that the Duvaliers could not spirit out of the country like dollars. As ambitious as she was greedy, Michèle Duvalier badly wanted to polish her public relations, especially with the foreign press. Seeking a cause to portray her as a woman of good deeds, she dreamed of building a hospital with an operating wing of international caliber and repute. Cooler heads convinced her that a charity maternity, children's, and teaching hospital was a more realistic goal, and one that would better project the image of a pious, warmhearted First Lady.

As so often happens on Hispaniola, the finished project did not resemble its glowing promise. The $4 million spent to build Bon Repos by no means created a sparkling, competent facility. Who knows how much money creative accounting siphoned away from the building fund? Once the facility began operating, graft continued in an even more insidious way. In a particularly disgusting account in *Haiti: An Insider's History of the Rise and Fall of the Duvaliers*, the historian Elizabeth Abbott tells us how physicians abused the hospital as well, performing unnecessary surgeries—such as cesarean sections or hysterectomies, at a cost of twenty or thirty dollars—to pad their salaries. "The water used to bathe patients was so germ-ridden, it caused serious infections," she writes. "And when patients appeared to be dying, the staff rushed them to the General Hospital so they would not be criticized for having so many deaths on their hands."

If halfhearted attempts at charitable works could not lend an image of sanctity to the Duvalier regime, the First Couple hoped the approval of the Pope could. In March 1983, preparing for Pope John Paul II's trip to Haiti, Baby Doc and Michèle decked out the country. They spent $4 million to redecorate the François Duvalier International Airport to welcome him. They hoped the visit would present a bright and shining image of Haiti, with throngs of smiling Haitians turning out to see the pontiff.

Instead of thanking the Duvaliers for their generosity, however, John Paul II delivered them a severe message: "There must be a better distribution of goods, a fairer organization of society, with more popular participation, a more disinterested conception of service on the part of those who direct society," he warned, speaking in Haitian Kreyol to an audience delighted that he had learned enough words in their language to address them directly. "I appeal to all those who enjoy power, riches, culture, to understand their urgent responsibility towards all their brothers and sisters." The throngs of Haitians who turned out to see Pope John Paul II cheered on hearing his command: "*Fok sa chanje.*" Things must change here.

Change was coming in Haiti. On Hispaniola, sugar is a force so strong that it even drives political change. But like the crop, once the old stalks have been cleared out and burned, new political leaders and the men around them grow back to create a landscape that closely resembles the one that came before.

The Pope's forceful words must have come as a shock to the Haitian clerical hierarchy, which openly supported the Duvalier regime, especially because the dictator had helped its highest officials. When François Duvalier became President in 1957, Haiti's many light-skinned foreign-born clergy were a threat to his black-oriented, nativist politics of *négritude* (which stressed the values of African culture) and of the Vodou syncretic religion. For a decade his *tontons macoutes* threatened, bullied, even killed clergy; Duvalier was excommunicated. Nonetheless, in 1966 a Vatican concordat granted him the power he wanted to shape Haiti's Church: the right to appoint a new Haitian-born local Church hierarchy. For most of the next thirty years, many of those priests were largely complacent in the face of the Duvalier regime. But by the mid-1980s, that was changing.

Only a year before the Pope spoke in Haiti, a young priest had been sent out of the country because of his calls for change in the nature and tone of Haitian government. "Can we continue to find normal this situation of violence imposed on the poor?" Jean-Bertrand Aristide had demanded.

Aristide was born on July 15, 1953, in the southwestern town of Port-Salut. His father died not long after his birth, and his mother supported him and his sister, Anne-Marie, from her small business selling clothes and doing odd jobs. She arranged schooling in Port-au-Prince for the children, who returned each summer to their grandfather's home and taught their playmates to read and write. Aristide's grandfather was a peasant who had acquired some land and taught the boy to help those less fortunate. In 1966 the thirteen-year-old Aristide completed grade school and was on his way to the seminary to study languages and work with the poor, following the teachings of the Salesian St. John Bosco. Aristide excelled at the seminary, both in the classroom and out. He was captain of the soccer team and became leader of the Roosters scout patrol.

The year Aristide entered the seminary, Joaquín Balaguer was elected President of the Dominican Republic. In 1974, at the end of Balaguer's second elected term, Aristide turned twenty-one, finished his seminary training, and went to study at the Salesian novitiate in the Dominican Republic. He then returned to study philosophy and psychology at Haiti's state university; in 1979 he received a three-year scholarship to study in Israel, Greece, and Egypt.

Against the wishes of his superiors, who urged another year of study, Aristide returned to Haiti in June 1982 to put his years of scholarship to work. His dissident preaching at St. Joseph Parish soon prompted Interior Minister Roger Lafontant to protest to his superiors in the Salesian order, who, complying with the official dissatisfaction, stripped the young priest of his assignment and sent him to Montreal for "pastoral reorientation." During nearly three years in Canada, Aristide completed a master's degree in biblical theology and course work toward a doctoral degree in psychology, two courses of study he linked under the theme of neurosis in the Old Testament.

When Father Aristide returned to Haiti in January 1985, the Pope's words were still echoing: Things must change here! Haitians no longer feared saying that they wanted no more of a government that had forced tens of thousands of their neighbors, cousins, sons, and brothers to brave hostile waters and possible death in rickety boats in hopes of reaching Miami. They wanted an end to Jean-Claude and Michèle's cronies' looting of what remained of their poor country, an end to the shopping expeditions in Paris while peasants starved or departed for Dominican cane fields. How much longer would Haitians prefer selling themselves into the hands of a pitiless foreign government to remaining in their own homeland?

Aristide was now assigned to a parish in Les Cayes, on the southern peninsula several hours south and west of Port-au-Prince. He spent a day each week journeying back and forth to Port-au-Prince to teach a seminary Bible class. Ignoring the possibility that he might again be reprimanded, he resumed the fiery protests he had begun in 1982. The young priest's followers recorded his sermons and passed audiotapes around the country. *"Va-t-en Satan"*—Satan begone!—Aristide commanded Duvalier in January 1986.

The flesh of Haiti was wasting away. The country's vultures saw that soon there would be nothing left to gnaw. Alerted to the open looting of government accounts, multinational organizations were threatening to cut off economic aid. After fifteen years of Baby Doc, there was little left of Haiti to pillage. What else might the country have expected from a spoiled boy who became President at the age of nineteen? At least Duvalier *père* had once been a physician who had done something useful, but his son had never had much of a vocation beyond fast cars and fun. Soft-bellied Baby Doc did not have the strength to keep Haiti together.

Even the army was disgusted. For a system based on corruption to work, it must not appear that the opportunities for enrichment are being made available disproportionately. Jean-Claude Duvalier had failed to understand that and had given too much rein to his wife's father and brothers. Not only had they not left enough of the spoils for the armed forces, but also their drug trafficking in the United States brought trouble. Shut out of the sweetest deals, Haiti's military officers began to plot the end for Baby Doc. All they needed was an excuse that would make their takeover plausible. Aristide and the cane cutters would give them what they needed.

As the Duvaliers' hold on Haiti weakened, so did Haiti's arrangements with the Dominican Republic for contracting *braceros* to harvest sugar. As protests grew louder in Port-au-Prince, compliant workers grew scarce. For decades, Haitians had been hearing about the Dominican harvest from the official accounts given in radio broadcasts. Haitians believed they could provide well for their families by joining the truckloads of workers who went to Dominikani each winter. But in the last days of Baby Doc, more realistic accounts slipped through. As the 1985–86 harvest was about to begin, the story spread of what had happened the year before to workers returning from the Dominican Republic, their pockets filled with the meager wages they had somehow managed to save over the year. Officials responsible for changing Dominican pesos into

Haitian gourdes had robbed them at the border. To be sure the workers had not hidden money, the officials even stripped the Haitians of their thin clothes coated with the greasy black grime of the cane fields.

Meanwhile, the Dominican government was tired of foreign meddling and irritating human-rights groups. It was no longer sure it wanted the trouble that the Haitian workers brought with them. More important, by late 1985 the Dominican State Sugar Council (CEA) was running out of money to pay for them. And the country could not export as much of its crop at favorable prices after the United States drastically slashed its sugar quota. The United States imported 302,016 short tons of Dominican sugar in the 1985–86 harvest but in September announced that the next year's quota would drop by 44 percent.

Just as the harvest was about to begin in November, the Dominican government stated that it would not bring in more *braceros*. Instead, the state sugar company would recruit Haitians already in the country and try to attract Dominicans to do the work—a plan doomed from the start. The CEA had no money to pay for new recruits to work under barely human conditions, and even less to improve the *bateyes*. Even the government's heavy-handed recruiting, often at gunpoint, didn't fill the need. Independent cane growers, *colonos*, protested. With government sugar mills using most of the available manpower, there were not enough *braceros* to keep the *colonos'* mills open.

By 1986 the government had no choice. The cane was already taller than a man, ready to be harvested or rot. It had to pay for Haitian workers or lose the cane. On January 18, Haitian Ambassador Hervé Denis and two Dominican officials flew from Santo Domingo to Port-au-Prince on an urgent mission. The three of them delivered Duvalier two suitcases, each bearing $1 million in cash: payment for nineteen thousand Haitian cane cutters.

The Dominicans never received the human cargo they had purchased. On January 28 thousands of Haitian peasants lined up at the recruiting center at the Leogane market, where Dominicans came every year to hire workers. A mob of demonstrators massed around the potential recruits and stoned the soldiers who were to have signed the peasants up. The Haitian army sent out backup forces, but the violence escalated. Twenty-six people died in two days of riots. When the government tried to move the registration center to the south, at Jacmel, the townspeople protested, making that plan impossible to carry out.

It became clear that the sugarcane trade had been siphoning off the strong young men who might have risen up against the regime had they stayed in Haiti. By leaving for Dominikani, the *braceros* had unwittingly helped to keep Haiti from blowing up. Now the *braceros* themselves were at the center of protests. The same practice that had financed the Duvaliers, the pressure valve that had bought them time, would bring them down. The *bracero* protests gave the army the credible excuse it needed to push out Baby Doc. At first, it seemed like poetic justice.

On February 7 a black Mercedes whisked Jean-Claude and Michèle Bennett Duvalier to the airport in Port-au-Prince, where a U.S. military plane waited. The First Couple carried into exile the $2 million in cash the Dominicans had given them not even a month earlier. A month later, when the Duvaliers had settled in the South of France, the street in front of the Dominican consulate in Port-au-Prince filled with throngs of protesters. Led by Aristide, they carried a coffin to bury symbolically the hated practice of selling Haitians to the Dominicans to cut cane.

On February 23 the Episcopal Conferences of the Dominican Republic and Haiti jointly issued a protest against the treatment of sugarcane workers. Haitian exiles in Canada and human-rights groups in the United States and Europe all joined in. The protests failed, however, to propose a solution. The meager sustenance the Dominican cane fields provided was better than what workers could expect in Haiti: nothing at all. Even knowing how badly the Dominicans would treat them, many Haitians saw no alternative but the Dominican cane fields. Misery in Dominikani was better than starvation in Haiti.

The Haitians tried their luck crossing the border on their own, without even the façade of protection in the official contract. Under the old formal arrangement, at least they had had a sure way of getting work. Standing in line at a migrant-cane-cutter center was one thing. Agreeing to accompany an unknown recruiter to whatever job he offered was another. Offers abounded for light farmwork, construction, anything that sounded better than cutting cane. They were all fictitious.

As the year went on, the Dominicans, desperate for workers to cut the grown cane before it rotted, created a new system of individual contracts for the *braceros*. Still, there was no one to explain to the workers, many of whom were illiterate, what their few rights were nor anyone to translate from Spanish into Kreyol. Besides, as it turned out, the slips of paper, ostensibly "contracts," carried no legal weight at all but were merely identification cards, and then not even properly that, since the officials who filled them in inked in errors as often as not. Depending on how sloppy the bureaucrats were, the name on a worker's card could be somebody else's or nobody's. Most often, a *bracero* could not read well enough to tell the difference.

Even the new contracts didn't make up for the nineteen thousand missing workers. Strapped for manpower, the Dominican government had its soldiers patrol the streets looking for Haitians, round them up, and take them to the *bateyes*. Sometimes police would rush into one field where the harvest was drawing to a close, herd the hapless cane cutters into a truck, and sell them to another plantation.

As Haitian politics descended into chaos, the economy of the Dominican Republic became worse and worse. In seven years the Dominican harvest had shrunk by a fifth. From just over a million metric tons in 1980, the harvest dipped to 815,500 metric tons in 1987, the year the government closed the mills at Catarey, Amistad, and Esperanza. Rumor was that the New York real-estate mogul Donald Trump would build a five-hundred-room hotel on the north coast, on the old Montellano land, near the resorts of Puerto Plata. But like most rumors, this one never came true. Dominican workers, themselves desperate for jobs, worried that Haitians would stream from the cane fields into the cities. When the mills closed, many Haitians found work harvesting coffee and rice, but others headed for the cities. Dominicans began seeing more and more Haitians in heavy-construction jobs; these soon joined cane cutting as dirty "Haitian work." Despite the old paradox that Haitians were doing work Dominicans refused to do, the immigrants were nonetheless blamed for Dominicans' lack of jobs. The more Haitians appeared in Dominican cities, the more pressure grew to keep them on the fields and to make sure they remained docile.

But sometimes it was impossible to ignore the Haitians' plight. In February 1989 a Mack truck carrying Haitians to a cane field careened along a cliff-side Dominican highway. The truck's violent swerves and lurches threw its passengers up against one another and against the rough sides of the truck. Their discomfort didn't matter much to the Dominican driver, who was drunk on rum he had coerced the Haitians to buy for him: he had promised that if they gave him drinking money he would take them to a field where they would be treated well. How much better conditions did they expect? Did they imagine running water, mattresses on the iron bed frames, perhaps a little medical clinic? Instead, the inebriated Dominican drove the truck over the edge of the cliff, killing the forty-six Haitians riding in the back.

The accident shocked the country, but a few months later it was all but forgotten when the police again started rounding up Haitians to meet a surprise boost in the Dominican sugar quota to the United States. In September 1989 the Americans cut off Panama's sugar quota and distributed the Panamanian share around; the new calculation nearly doubled the Dominican allotment from 185,328 to 333,035 tons. If the Dominicans couldn't meet the increased quota, they would lose windfall hard currency.

As the State Sugar Council sent everything it could produce to the United States, sugar disappeared from Dominican grocery shelves. Supposedly the government was importing inexpensive supplies from the world market to fill Dominican sugar bowls, but very little made its way to Dominican households. At the height of their own cane harvest, Dominicans could not find sugar to sweeten their dark, strong coffee.

After the fall of Baby Doc, Haitians wanted to inter forever the symbols of death and suffering from the Duvalier years. On April 24 demonstrators, led by Jean-Bertrand Aristide, gathered outside his church to cast away the past. On their shoulders they carried mock coffins, many representing the *bracero* system, to take to a symbolic funeral at Fort Dimanche, the dark prison where Duvalier's henchmen had tortured their victims. As word of the mock funeral spread through Port-au-Prince, soldiers from Fort Dimanche appeared, arrested protesters, and brought them to the prison. Late that night, Aristide drove to Fort Dimanche and convinced the guards to let them go.

"Haiti is a prison," Aristide wrote later, recounting the events. "In that prison, there are rules you must abide by or suffer the pain of death. One rule is: Never ask for more than what the prison warden considers your share. Never ask for more than a cupful of rice and a drink of dirty water each day, or each week. Another rule is: Remain in your cell. Though it is crowded and stinking and full of human refuse, remain there, and do not complain. That is your lot. Another rule is: Do not organize. Do not speak to your fellow prisoners about your plight. Every time you get two cups of rice, another prisoner will go hungry. Every time another prisoner gets two drinks of dirty water, you will go thirsty. Hate your fellow man."

Two days later, on April 26, demonstrators worshipped in a Mass of Mourning at the Church of Sacré Cœur, then marched to Fort Dimanche—where, exactly twenty-three years earlier, François Duvalier had ordered a mass execution of political prisoners in retaliation for an attempted kidnapping of his children. The Duvaliers were gone now, but repression was not. As the demonstrators broadcast the mock funeral over the Church-owned radio station, Radio Soleil, truckloads of soldiers bore down on them, ejected canisters of tear gas into the crowd, then opened machine-gun fire. Throughout this shocking sequence of events, Aristide announced over the airwaves what was happening.

Loyal to the regime and intent on preserving the status quo, Haiti's Church leaders were displeased. Within a few weeks, the Salesian order warned Aristide to stop taking part in politics; when he did not, it transferred him out of Port-au-Prince. His angry parishioners went on a hunger strike until the order allowed him to return. He was building a new history of Haiti—telling the stories of the forgotten cane cutters, the murdered prisoners, the victims. One man, even backed by the soundless voices of the unheard, could not hope to stand up against the Haitian system. This new mythic history, though, had within it the power for change. In the meantime, the situation in Haiti remained the same, with its patterns of intimidation and theft. But as there was less and less to steal, the repression intensified.

The first Sunday in August 1987, shortly after he was reinstated at his church, St. Jean Bosco, Aristide said Mass, then headed to Port-Sonde for a memorial service for hundreds of peasants who had been murdered by soldiers at Jean-Rabel the month before. As Aristide stood up to speak, three white-clad men wearing hats waved their revolvers wildly and fired into the crowd. Aristide recalled later: "One of them pointed his gun directly at me, standing there . . . I was standing there because at that moment I was unable to run and leave everybody. I could not take to my heels like a bad pastor, and leave my sheep behind to face the guns . . . I felt calm, and I stood there, and I saw the gun pointed at me and I saw the smoke coming from the gun and I heard the noise of the bullets. He missed me, and began again, and again I saw the smoke and heard the noise, and he missed me again." Finally, a woman pulled Aristide down under a pile of people. Somehow they all escaped, through a harrowing night and past treacherous roadblocks. Aristide lost a shoe, his car was crushed, but he was safe. The priest now had a reputation for having divine protection, and the military junta ruling Haiti was losing power.

Under intense international pressure, the armed forces were preparing to hold elections, planned for November 29. The eve of the elections, gunshots filled the night air, and on the morning of the balloting, hooded *tontons macoutes* descended on the Argentine-Bellegarde school, a voting place, and killed twenty-four voters. Terrified Haitians stayed home, and the elections were canceled. The junta followed that sad charade with a mock election in which a sociology professor named Leslie Manigat was "elected" President by barely more than 5 percent of the populace.

The armed forces had imagined that Manigat would be a weak puppet. Thinking himself a real President nonetheless, Manigat in June 1988 tried to assert his power over them. He fired General Henri Namphy as head of the armed forces, put him under house arrest, and replaced him with the notorious drug trafficker Colonel Jean-Claude Paul. But the army was loyal to Namphy and in three days made it clear to Manigat who really ran the country. It gave Namphy his job back and toppled the puppet president, sending him across the border out of the country. Poison found its way into Colonel Paul's pumpkin soup, and he suffered a fatal heart attack. In Santo Domingo, on his way to exile in New York and France, Manigat denounced Namphy as mentally ill. He was only the first of a long line of deposed Haitian leaders to make their way through the Dominican Republic. Soon there were so many that the rooms they occupied in the Dominican Concorde Hotel became known as the Haitian Presidential suite.

Namphy and his gang were as corrupt as the Duvaliers had been and showed no more propensity to let Haitians choose their own leaders than their predecessors had. For all their dissatisfaction about the faucet of foreign aid having been shut off at the end of the Duvalier regime, the military governments that followed could not keep aid money flowing either. They resorted to random attacks and terror to create the illusion that they had real control of Haiti, but for all their guns and power to intimidate the soldiers were powerless.

Aristide kept on attacking the regime. The soldiers decided to silence him on September 11, 1988. At St. Jean Bosco, Aristide was preparing to consecrate the Sacraments when a band of armed men dressed in black and red burst in amid a barrage of stones and bullets. Parishioners whisked Aristide into his house adjoining the church. The thugs cut down parishioners trying to flee, then torched the church with people and corpses still inside. They searched Aristide's house hours later, then inexplicably let him go.

The next day, a Salesian superior flew in from Santo Domingo to speak sternly with Aristide. Three months later, the order expelled him; he was now a priest with no parish. Because he preached class struggle, Aristide was no longer qualified to speak the Word of Christ in public, they said in a four-page document removing him from his priestly duties.

On September 17, General Namphy, like Manigat only months before, found himself on the way to the Haitian Presidential suite at the Dominican Concorde Hotel. The general who sent him packing, Prosper Avril, lasted for a little more than a year before he, too, was on shaky ground. In March 1990, Avril handed the Presidency to Ertha Pascal Trouillot, president of the Supreme Court. She began the process that would lead to Haiti's first free elections ever. In October 1990 the leader of the *tontons macoutes*, Roger Lafontant, announced that he would run for the Presidency, but the leading candidate was Marc Bazin, Duvalier's Finance Minister and a former World Bank official. With the backing of the United States and tacit approval of the Dominicans, Bazin seemed a shoo-in.

Then came the surprise. A new party, the National Front for Change and Democracy (FNCD), named Father Jean-Bertrand Aristide as its candidate. Aristide was ready to step out of the Duvaliers' long shadow into the light. He entered the ring of politics under the symbol of "the cock, the bird that sings and rouses." His slogan was *"Kòk la chante, fok sa chanje,"* The cock sings, we must change things—an echo of the words of Pope John Paul II. The image was ambiguous: though it suggested dawn, promising a new future, it also evoked the violence of the cockfight. Aristide was the *kòk kalite*, a top-notch fighting rooster, king of all fighting cocks.

Election day came on December 16, bringing with it brigades of international election observers. Haitians lined up early in the morning to cast their votes. When the ballots were counted, Aristide had won 67 percent of the votes. Marc Bazin, the second-place candidate and the favorite of the Dominicans, earned only 14 percent. The *kòk kalite* would be President.

For the first time since the days of Papa Doc Duvalier, Haiti had a leader whose personal mythology threatened that of the Dominicans' Balaguer. Aristide had already escaped death several times in public, making Haitians wonder if he were immortal. The young President-elect seemed to be under the protection of the Vodou spirits. But in Santo Domingo, Balaguer's power had been waning. When the May 16, 1990, Dominican elections approached and he prepared to fight desperately to be elected President a fifth time, popular frustration ran high. There had never before been so many *apagones*, blackouts. A popular merengue tune complained about mosquitoes biting when the power failed and the electric fans turned off. Dominicans joked that the government didn't do anything about the blackouts because the President couldn't see that the lights went out, which literally was true: when a *New York Times Magazine* reporter was interviewing the President shortly before the elections, the lights went out in the Presidential palace and Balaguer didn't even blink. Traffic continually jammed around stoplights that went dark every time there was a blackout. In the past the government had always brought blackouts under control for at least the few months before an election, but this time it couldn't even manage a week of consistent power. Prices were doubling each year. Housewives complained that they could barely afford their *pan de agua*, the soft, small "water bread" rolls that are a Dominican staple. Chickens were slaughtered and left to rot because businesses couldn't get dollars to buy imported feed. *"Ojalá que llueva café,"* Juan Luis Guerra's hit merengue, pleaded: "So the people on their little farms do not suffer so much, O Lord, let it rain coffee in the countryside." He sang of the peasants' dreams of filling the mountainsides and their dinner tables with strawberries, sweet potatoes, wheat, and rice. While Dominicans went hungry, the government kept spending enormous sums on the Columbus Lighthouse. Lines of Dominicans wanting to leave their country formed at the U.S. consulate before dawn. By the time the doors of the ugly white building opened, the hopefuls stretched almost out of sight. Businesses popped up around the line: a cafeteria and a passport shop across the street, a swarm of kiosk vendors and taxicabs hovering around the corner of Máximo Gómez and Cesar Nicolás Penson.

Balaguer and his old rival Juan Bosch were both in their early eighties, with thin white hair. For months polls showed Bosch in the lead. Trailing in third place was José Francisco Peña Gómez, the black leader of the Dominican Revolutionary Party who had won the nomination over Jacobo Majluta, who had served forty-three days as President after Antonio Guzmán killed himself in 1982. The disgruntled Majluta, running as the candidate of his own Independent Revolutionary Party, trailed a very distant fourth.

Bosch's Dominican Liberation Party (PLD) presented a politically and economically moderate platform that appealed enough to the nation's business interests not to cast it out of favor with the United States, which had invaded Santo Domingo in 1965 to keep him and his allegedly pro-Communist leftist ideology from returning to the Presidency. But now, a week before the elections, Bosch inexplicably announced that if elected he would disestablish Roman Catholicism as the national religion. This dramatic statement, in a vastly Catholic country, stirred the same old fears that an older generation of Dominicans had always had about Bosch. His 1963 Presidency, after all, had ended after only seven months and had led to civil war and an American invasion. Was he so unpredictable as once again to bring chaos to the country? People wondered about his mental state. They shrugged off the many rumors of Alzheimer's disease as concoctions of Balaguer's Reformistas; the story of the Cuban doctor who allegedly had treated him turned out to be a ruse. But what about his speech at Puerto Plata, in the north, which had begun with his addressing "my beloved people of La Romana," in the southeast?

When Bosch then announced that if elected he would stop all government construction projects—not just the Columbus Lighthouse boondoggle but even the housing projects that brought hundreds of jobs each—Dominican truckers jammed the streets in protest. Quickly, Bosch's lead in the polls slipped to a slim, slim margin, surely not enough to overcome Balaguer's bag of tricks for winning elections. "Balaguer?" chuckled a Dominican sociologist. "He's won every time, but he's never really *won!*"

The morning after the election, the front pages of Dominican newspapers were filled with photos of rallies of Dominicans clad in purple and yellow: the colors of Bosch's PLD. Early returns showed that, as Bosch had promised, it would be *"el año de la victoria morada,"* the year of the purple victory. By noon, however, official electoral council bulletins showed Balaguer in the lead. As darkness fell, it was clear that Balaguer had stolen another election.

Dominicans locked their doors that night and stayed inside. Word was out that Bosch was calling for blood on the streets to reclaim what was his. The next morning, all was calm. Bosch's party, realizing that his erratic behavior of recent weeks made it unlikely the country would rally behind him, had ignored his call for violence. The third-place candidate, Peña Gómez, working with former U.S. President Jimmy Carter, helped to mediate the situation. It was weeks before a recount of the votes was completed, but the fighting red rooster of Joaquín Balaguer was victorious with just over a third of the votes, and Bosch and Peña were not far behind him.

Balaguer was very weak. In Haiti, Aristide was just beginning to fight. Hispaniola had rarely supported two strongmen at once: each *caudillo's* power depended on his ability to preserve an aura that reminded his people that he was the only Great Leader on the island.

Rafael Trujillo stayed in power for only the first two years of Papa Doc Duvalier's rule. When Duvalier was first elected, the long-established Dominican dictator did his best to make sure he did not become a threat: he broadcast Kreyol-language anti-Duvalier propaganda into Haiti, harbored dissident Haitian exiles, and dispatched his feared security chief, Johnny Abbés García, to Port-au-Prince to stir up trouble. He backed off only after Duvalier threatened to welcome Dominican exiles in Port-au-Prince. Their uneasy truce could not have lasted long, and if Trujillo's own people had not assassinated him, he and Papa Doc would surely have escalated tensions to a breaking point.

After his father's death, Jean-Claude Duvalier was the ideal Haitian counterpart to a Dominican strongman like Balaguer. Once Baby Doc was gone, none of the military governments that followed him lasted long enough to merit the blink of an eye. But with Aristide's election, Balaguer faced a real threat. Aristide was at the beginning of his political career and Balaguer at the end. The young priest was impetuous, erratic, and his political power came from his public rejection of the Duvalier regime before him. Balaguer was calculating and patient, traits he learned from his mentor and predecessor, traits Trujillo had shown in his rise from sugar-field guard to President. When Trujillo fell out of favor with the United States, some of Balaguer's old school companions had called him from exile in New York, urging him to leave the government and help them form an opposition party. "No," Balaguer had told them, "I'll stay here and pick the mangoes from the low branches." In opposing the past, Aristide was attacking the basis of Balaguer's entire political career.

Their differences were all the more provocative because the two men had much in common. Both were solitary, enigmatic. Aristide, mysterious, impulsive, let Haiti and the world wonder whether he was prophetic or power-mad. Balaguer shuffled his cabinet, issued cryptic pronouncements, kept Dominicans guessing as to who he really was. Aristide and Balaguer, the priest and the bachelor, remained aloof, mirror images of each other. It was little wonder that each had chosen the fighting rooster as his political symbol. And it was inevitable that they would face off.

Sugar was the obvious issue, the cane fields the obvious arena where Aristide would choose to fight. When he came into office, his country had empty coffers and people with high expectations. He needed symbolic moves that would produce quick psychological results while he waited for international aid to return to Haiti and boost its economy. The cane cutters had already proved their political strength: their plight had helped bring down Baby Doc. But what benefit had they received from his departure? The tragedy of the cane cutters was as dramatic as before, if not more so.

In the spring of 1991, wasting little time after his February inauguration, Aristide denounced the treatment of Haitians in the cane fields as no better than the slavery of colonial times. Every few years a chorus of international groups had launched staccato attacks on the Dominican Republic on this issue; they gave Aristide ample weapons.

Since 1988, the Quebecois Committee for the Recognition of the

Rights of Haitian Workers had waged a campaign urging tourists to boycott Dominican resorts—which was brilliantly well-timed, since the Dominican government was pouring money and cement into new hotels, resting much of its economic policy on attracting sun-hungry visitors, many of them Canadian. In March 1990 the UN Human Rights Committee had chastised the Dominican Republic for its glacial progress in submitting a requested report on the cane fields. Americas Watch, the National Coalition for Haitian Refugees, and Caribbean Rights all demanded that the United States withdraw its more than $200 million in preferential trade benefits until the Dominican Republic dramatically improved its treatment of Haitian workers. U.S. trade representative Carla Hills came to investigate whether the country was indeed violating worker rights, in which case it would be ineligible for Generalized System of Preferences and Caribbean Basin Initiative trade benefits that allowed Dominican imports into the United States duty-free.

The Dominican Republic also stood to lose trade preferences and aid benefits from the European Community's Lomé Convention, an agreement to which it had been admitted only because it had applied jointly with Haiti. Combined, the populations and economies of Lomé's thirteen tiny Caribbean member states barely equaled those of the Dominican Republic, so the Dominicans represented an economic threat, but members could not justify refusing admission to Haiti, the poorest nation in the Americas. The Dominicans rode in on Haiti's tattered coattails but apparently hadn't given a thought to the continued rapprochement that they would need if they were to keep the benefits.

International pressure had intensified. In a September editorial headlined "Slaves of Dominicans," *The Miami Herald* had argued in favor of boycotting Dominican agriculture. When the International Labor Organization wanted to send a delegation to the Dominican Republic to investigate the cane fields, the Dominican government had flatly refused. Balaguer had called the allegations untrue, "foul and offensive," and a contradiction of Dominicans' "hospitality" to Haitians. On October 15, as the 1990 harvest was about to begin, he issued a decree providing individual contracts for the workers, giving them legal status as temporary residents or fixed-term day laborers. He promised to improve health, education, and basic living conditions on the *bateyes*. "The human rights of the *braceros* must be respected in the Dominican Republic," he declared. His words rang hollow. Decree 417/90 was nothing but cosmetic, a cynical response.

Four months later, in February, Haitian Ambassador Albert Chassagne bluntly told *El Siglo* that he was still waiting to see action, not just words. The U.S. State Department's 1990 "Country Reports on Human Rights Practices" called the decree "essentially a reiteration of labor code provisions which in the past have rarely been enforced in practice."

Yet, strangely, it didn't seem to matter. Balaguer had made a clever move in erecting a paper decoy. For the United States the decree was enough. In April 1991 the U.S. trade representative reported that the Dominican Republic was taking steps to improve worker rights recognized under international law. What were those steps? Balaguer had created a blue-ribbon commission to reform the labor code (completed and neatly published a year later) and issued the October decree that in theory allowed Haitian immigrants to legalize their status. (This would work fine for new migrants, but what about the workers who had lived in the *bateyes* for decades? Or the children born there of parents without papers?) The U.S. Commerce Department turned down the Americas Watch petition. The Dominican Republic kept its trade benefits.

The United States' role in the whole Dominican-Haitian confrontation was a charade. It threatened Dominicans with economic sanctions in an industry it had, in effect, created; the Dominican cane fields were dying in part because powerful U.S. agricultural interests had won protectionist policies that shut out foreign sugar; and now the Commerce Department was accepting a farcical declaration as proof that things were getting better. Which was the greatest irony?

The human-rights groups did not give up. In May the New York City–based Lawyers Committee for Human Rights issued a report on Haitian children cutting cane in Dominican fields. In a 1991 interview given at Batey Palamarejo, on the Rio Haina cane plantation, two fourteen-year-old boys described to the Lawyers Committee representative how Dominican recruiters had convinced them to come to the Dominican Republic by promising that all they would have to do was gather eggs from henhouses and other light farmwork. A reporter and a cameraman from ABC's *Primetime Live* confronted a Dominican State Sugar Council official about the miserable treatment of an old, sick *bracero* they had interviewed: the bureaucrat pursed her lips, sighed, and in florid, formal Spanish replied that she lamented it greatly but nothing could be done.

The truth was the sugarcane issue could not have emerged at a better time for Balaguer, who needed something to take his people's minds away from their other economic troubles. No one in the Dominican Republic had forgotten the food riots of 1984 and 1985, and the economic crisis of 1990–91 demanded austerity measures very similar to the ones that had brought those riots on.

Things were spinning out of control. The country had run out of dollars. Even the business community, which normally supported Balaguer, was restive. Dozens of vehicles were lined up at each gas station waiting in vain for fuel that never arrived. Poultry farms had to let chickens starve because they could not get dollars to import feed. Medicines disappeared from pharmacy shelves. Even toothpaste was hard to find. The government was arresting hotel owners who failed to convert their dollars to pesos with the Central Bank.

In the Dominican political calculus, letting things go to the brink of chaos was the only logical thing for Balaguer to do. Taking the measures needed to bring dollars back in would have been political suicide before the election. Halting his massive public-works projects would have left many Dominicans jobless. Slowing government spending would have slammed the economy to a stop. Balaguer allowed just enough uncertainty that his campaign slogan—*Un Camino sin Peligro*, A Path without Danger—resonated. What would happen if he were not there to run the country?

By holding food prices and the peso steady, Balaguer had kept the people on his side as long as he needed them. When the business community chafed under the currency crisis and criticized the government, Balaguer called a prominent insurance man who was also a vocal advocate of business-community interests to the National Palace and proposed that he become the director of a new investigation he was commissioning into fraud in the insurance industry. The businessman immediately picked up on the veiled threat that he would be investigated and agreed to become part of the Administration, from which point, of course, he could no longer protest against the government.

Shortly after his new term began Balaguer removed subsidies on flour, sugar, cooking oil, and other basic foods. He boosted gasoline prices and began negotiations for funding from the international financial community. Businesses were relieved, but poor Dominicans were out in the streets protesting.

The Haitian cane cutters provided just the issue Balaguer needed to distract Dominicans. Cleverly, the octogenarian President turned the international scandal over the cane workers to his advantage. Just as Trujillo had done after the 1937 massacre, Balaguer more than fifty years later was rallying his people to the defense of their country, painting his government as their savior.

Balaguer's position had always been that, since the days of Toussaint Louverture and Boyer, Haitians had made no secret of their dream of uniting the island under Haitian rule. This time, he claimed, the Haitians were trying to fuse the island quietly, by sending hundreds of thousands of poor peasants across the border into the Dominican Republic. It was Balaguer's destiny to defend the Dominican reputation against accusations of practicing slavery. The *bracero* problem was not the Dominicans' fault, nor was it his. It was the Haitians' fault.

On June 14, President Balaguer issued a new decree ordering that all Haitian immigrants over sixty or under sixteen years old be expelled. If the human-rights groups did not like the way Haitians were treated in the Dominican Republic, they could all go home. The Dominicans had been hospitable enough. Why continue to accept the Haitians if scandal was all one got from it? Pragmatism and ideology went hand in hand. The harvest was over, the workers were not needed until November, and the Dominicans could be rid of the Haitians and the human-rights groups. Haiti's impertinent Aristide could have back the workers about whose fates he had been so concerned. No more Haitians in Dominican cane fields? That suited Balaguer fine. Let Aristide find them jobs in Haiti.

The "repatriations," Balaguer said, were "merely friendly interventions in order to look for certain arrangements." The soldiers rushed to follow his orders. They not only combed the cane fields for Haitians but patrolled the cities and roadsides for anyone they thought looked Haitian. Refugee organizations estimate that fourteen thousand Haitians were expelled; another forty thousand fled in fear.

Dominican and Haitian priests who publicized the cane workers' plight received death threats. Soldiers prowled every neighborhood where Haitians were known to live, arresting people in Santo Domingo's Little Haiti and on the streets of beach and sugar towns like Boca Chica and San Pedro de Macorís, east of Santo Domingo. Haitians whose families had lived in the Dominican Republic for generations were torn from their children and spouses. Deported to Haiti, they had no family or friends in the country that was, yet was not, their own.

Dominican intellectuals watched the frenzy with dismay. "If it certainly created a euphoria among the anti-Haitian forces, it did nothing to confront technically the problem," commented the Dominican sociologist Rubén Silié. "Balaguer allowed to awaken anew among 'the good Dominicans' the idea that just as under Trujillo, they were protected by Balaguer against the new Haitian attempts at domination."

The Dominican authorities did not just deport cane cutters. Soldiers marched down Delmonte y Tejada Street, where they knocked on doors one by one, checking the documents of anyone who lived there. They helped the Haitians without visas to gather their things and carry them downstairs to a waiting bus, which took the Haitians to San Cristóbal, half an hour west of Santo Domingo. There the Haitians stayed for a week before many were released or escaped.

It took only a few weeks for them to return to the hotels, where their merchandise was waiting. The owners had the keys to their rooms ready.

"Hah! Within a month, they were back here!" Doña Julia laughs, retelling the story a year later. "I was glad to have them back. The Haitians you can trust. Almost all of the people who live here have been with me four or five years."

The second time the soldiers came, a month later, Doña Julia was ready. When she saw them coming down the street, she led the Haitians up to the attic, where they waited safely until the police left.

Doña Julia hardly rents to Dominicans anymore. In a country where family and community ties are strong, a Dominican who must rely for lodging on a cheap hotel for Haitian merchants is automatically suspect: a drug dealer or worse. "The Haitians are more simple people, good people," she explains. "I give them credit if they can't pay rent, because I know that it's just because business is bad. When they are doing better, they'll pay me, I know. And even if it's a thousand pesos they owe me, I know they will pay. But the Dominicans you can't trust like that."

Fifteen hundred miles away, Haiti's President was about to speak up, too late, for the rights of repatriated Haitians. On September 27, 1991, Aristide strode slowly to the front of the chamber of the General Assembly of the United Nations. A bevy of aides ushered the little priest to the podium and helped him climb up. Aware that his words would ring out across the world, Aristide paused, surveying the long wooden tables where the diplomats sat, looked up at the high banks of balconies above, and took in the gray-green color of the place.

He began to speak softly, in clear, lyrical French, pronouncing the necessary, proper salutations. The opening of his address to Haiti's "dear Latin American friends" was both poetic and political. "We share the same experience of struggle, struggle against the enslavement of men by men, struggle for the dawn of peace and full liberation of the Latin American continent and of the entire world," Aristide began in a quiet voice.

But quickly, in the dramatic style that earned him the attention and devotion of Haitians, he switched to a more lively tone, punctuated with exclamations: "Liberty won! Pride regained! Dignity restored!" Aristide soon took up Spanish, the first of nine other languages he would use.

The words in Spanish were stronger than the French ones of his hopeful beginning, and he aimed them precisely at Haiti's neighbor to the east:

> We must denounce, before the eyes of all humankind, the flagrant violation of the rights of Haitians living in the Dominican Republic. Though we recognize the sovereignty of the Dominican Republic, we must protest forcefully against this violation of human rights. Haiti and the Dominican Republic are two wings of the same bird, two nations that share the beautiful island of Hispaniola. Hearing the voice of all the victims whose rights are trampled, engaged in respecting human rights despite the social problems and financial difficulties created by this forceful repatriation, we must respect both wings of the bird . . . Never again, not ever again, will our Haitian sisters and brothers be

sold in order to transform their blood to make bitter sugar. Blood made into bitter sugar is not acceptable; the unacceptable will never be accepted.

Slowly, deliberately, his voice rising, he repeated his words: *Never again, not ever again, will our Haitian sisters and brothers be sold in order to transform their blood to make bitter sugar.* The audience in the balcony cheered wildly. Aristide ended his speech with an anthem-like exhortation to the United Nations to defend human rights and to Latin American nations to defend unity. His chant slipped in and out of Kreyol, a jubilant rallying cry. The balconies cried out along with him the mantra of his Lavalas movement: *"Youn sel nou feb, ansanm nou fo, ansanm ansanm nou se lavalas."* Alone we are weak, together we are strong, together, together, we are Lavalas, the cleansing flood sweeping away everything in its path. Giant red-and-blue flags unfurled from the front balconies as the audience and diplomats gave Aristide a standing ovation in the normally staid General Assembly.

That night, New York's Haitian immigrants, giddy at the sight of the President they believed held out hope that they could return to their country, turned out by the thousands to hear Aristide speak at the massive Episcopal Cathedral of St. John the Divine. Haitians who had been in New York for years were talking about going home, even about setting up vacation time-shares for tourists. The cathedral overflowed, leaving hundreds of Haitians standing along Amsterdam Avenue in a torrential rainstorm. Holding up umbrellas colored Haitian red and blue, they danced and sang: *"Nou se lavalas!"* We are Lavalas, the flood, the cleansing downpour!

In the end, none of Aristide's beautiful General Assembly speech mattered. The plight of the sugarcane cutters was to bring Aristide down as well. The Dominicans had not liked him even before this embarrassment. But by the time he finished at the United Nations, their determination to see him gone was cemented. If the Haitian army wanted to rid itself of the President who had pledged to end corruption, it was assured of Dominican support. A high Dominican government official visiting the United Nations commented dryly to a Dominican reporter, "He won't be around long." Four days after Aristide's jubilant address at the United Nations, his words came true.

In New York, the Haitians who danced in the rain could hardly believe it when the sonorous voice of New York Consul Wilson Désir announced on his Kreyol-language radio program that Aristide had been overthrown shortly after his return to Port-au-Prince. Throughout the agonizing day of September 30, Aristide was held prisoner in the National Palace as the French, American, and Venezuelan ambassadors negotiated for his life. Finally, a midnight flight out of Port-au-Prince sent him into exile, first in Caracas, eventually in Washington. Unlike other former Haitian Presidents, Aristide did not make a stop at the Haitian Presidential suite of Santo Domingo's Dominican Concorde Hotel.

A month after the coup, as the sun eased its way up into the sky, tensions were high at Bon Repos Hospital, Michèle Duvalier's old pet project, which had been temporarily renamed Centre d'Accueil des Rapatriés Haitiens (Welcome Center for Repatriated Haitians). The hospital, once a lasting monument to the shame of the kleptocratic Duvalier family, was now a symbol of the sugarcane slave trade too. The Haitians expelled from the Dominican Republic waited there, lost, their lives in Dominikani gone, their families split up, their possessions seized, and the future of their country uncertain.

Jobs were disappearing by the day. The United States had imposed an embargo on Haiti and asked the international community to join in to try to convince General Raoul Cédras and Police Chief Michel François to step down and allow Aristide to return. Soon oil deliveries would stop altogether, and the economy would rumble to a near halt. There is no way the workers expelled from Santo Domingo could make a new start in Haiti, a country many had never known or knew so long ago that it was only a mythical land in their childhood memories.

A *bracero* named Gaston lifted his feet, one at a time, to show the ragged green-and-white flip-flops he was wearing when soldiers burst into Batey Santa Rosada, where he lived, and arrested all the cane cutters. "They didn't even give me time to change into shoes," he said. "They almost didn't let me put my shirt on," he added, fingering its maroon cloth. The soldiers tore up his documents, including the newly issued residence card created the previous October, and rushed him to a bus that carried him across the border.

He looked at least fifteen years older than his forty-six, most of which were spent in the Dominican Republic. In Haiti, he knew no one. It had been thirty-two years since he left his country. In all that time in the Dominican cane fields, his Kreyol had slipped away. Spanish now came more easily to his tongue.

The Dominicans did not really care whether or not the dark-skinned men, women, and children they deported were cane cutters, or within the age range President Balaguer's decree had specified. The numbers that Bon Repos officials gave, only a month after the coup, are disturbing, though not surprising. As many as 14 percent of the adults who passed through the Welcome Center were born in the Dominican Republic, not Haiti. Of the children expelled, nearly half were born in Dominikani. Of the "repatriated ones" at Bon Repos, 41 percent had been expelled without their children.

Joseph, a twenty-five-year-old Haitian studying data processing at the Autonomous University of Santo Domingo (UASD, pronounced WuAHSS), was working his route collecting public bus fares in September in downtown Santo Domingo when the Dominican police arrested him at the busy commercial corner of Duarte Street and 27th of February Avenue. His dark skin had given him away. His passport and visa were at home, giving him no immediate proof of his legal status. He was sent back to Haiti and was still waiting at Bon Repos in early November.

Many more Haitians had escaped before the soldiers came. By the end of August, a month before the coup, the Haitian government had already estimated that as many as forty thousand Haitians fled the Dominican Republic. By October, the Lawyers Committee for Human Rights put the number at sixty thousand or more. More than seventeen thousand men, women, and children had passed through the Bon Repos Welcome Center, not counting the workers who fled through the mountains along the border rather than wait for Dominican soldiers to get them. The center had room for only six thousand residents at once, so by the end of October more than ten thousand had been sent out into the streets to fend for themselves.

This particular November morning, something had to give. Trapped inside the crumbling white walls of Bon Repos, desolate over the loss of everything he had managed to save in Dominikani, one man released the pressure building inside. "Why do we allow this to go on?" he yelled at the other men waiting in the yard for nothing in particular. "We should demand to be given better treatment. They should find us jobs!"

At first the others just listened, familiar with this peculiarly Caribbean trait: like a torrential but brief afternoon thunderstorm, a man from time to time declaims loudly on some topic, releasing his anger in a dramatic display of rhetoric, gesticulation, and grimace; if you let the aggrieved person carry on, his anger, like the afternoon cloudburst, will expend itself.

Something about this particular morning, however, induced another resident to intervene. "Look, man, we're all just as unhappy as you. Nobody has any more right than the other to special treatment. Where are they going to get these jobs from?"

The first man's rage tore loose and set itself upon the man who disagreed. Before anyone knew what was happening, a machete appeared. By the time the group pulled the two apart, the first man's stomach was an ugly gash, spilling blood. The commotion attracted the attention of the authorities, and a white van pulled up to take away the injured man. Others, their shirts bloodied, watched from the shade along the wall of a small office building. Would each of them one day soon reach an explosion point and lash out at their equally unfortunate neighbors?

The Cockfight

*Con rapidez asombrosa, le fue metiendo las agujas, sin darle un
segundo de respiro, neutralizando así el manejo de las patas a su
contrincante. El pico era el arma más poderoso de Juanito. Cuando
agarraba era muy difícil desprendérsele, salve que el adversario
dejara en tributo una gran cantidad de sangre.*

*With stunning speed, he struck with his spurs, without a moment's
respite, thus neutralizing his opponent's control of his feet. His beak
was Juanito's most potent weapon. When he clamped on, it was
extremely difficult for his adversary to escape his grasp without
leaving as a tribute a large pool of blood.*

—*Viriato Sención*
Los que falsificaron la firma de Dios
(They Forged the Signature of God)

Three kinds of men go to the cockfight: breeders,
players, and gamblers.

The breeders, the true cockers, get involved in every aspect of the lives of their roosters. They decide which hen
will be matched with which cock, what mix of feed the birds
will get, at what age a young rooster is ready to fight. Breeders supervise every aspect of the *traba*, the home of the roosters, as if it were their own home and the roosters their
children. At the fights a real breeder puts himself in the ring
with his bird. For him the cockfight is not a game.

Players appreciate well-trained birds and know more
than a bit about the history of the sport. Though they do
not let emotions carry them away, they enjoy the passion of
the fight, the heat of battle. A player may keep a *traba* of
his own, but it is not his main occupation. He passes by
often to check on the roosters and the men who are paid to
take care of them, but the *traba* does not consume his life

as it does a breeder's. Because he is in the game for money and the prestige that goes with it, the player may do something a true breeder would never do: he will bet against himself if he sees his own cock losing. He has no more attachment to his bird than an investor has to a stock he sold short or bought options against to protect himself from losses if the market, or the fight, does not go his way. The player does, however, participate in a brotherhood: he knows the other players and their birds.

Gamblers thrive on chance and the thrill of cash. For them, the cockfight inspires no more emotional attachment to the birds than a turn at roulette would inspire for the spinning wheel and marbles. Gamblers change the odds quickly if they see their pick is behind. The best can play at almost any ring; they rely on minuscule clues from the owners and birds that show whether to stick with the odds or hedge the bets. Or the gambler is blessed by chance.

In politics as in the cockfight, there are those who put themselves in the ring. The political leaders of Hispaniola are like the true cockers, whose selves are in the ring. Others, lining the ring, have much at stake in each combat, but they do not put themselves on the line. On Hispaniola, the Roman Catholic Church, the armed forces, and the business elite are such players. So, too, are the two governments; usually, the President of one country can rely on his counterpart to bet against him. Finally, the spectators gamble. At times, the United States is a player. Often, it is more like a gambling spectator, casting its fickle support to whichever side best serves its own interests.

Politicians claim to invoke the will of the people, though in reality what they do is send the population into battle for them. The citizens of Haiti and the Dominican Republic suffer when political fights break out far above them, for conflict at the top usually means there is less of everything. As the people on the bottom scramble to survive, they begin fights of their own until order returns above them.

Twenty-five years before Jean-Bertrand Aristide won and lost power in Haiti, a young President traced a hauntingly similar path in the Dominican Republic. Like Aristide, Juan Bosch was a leftist reformer who had lived abroad (exiled under the Trujillo dictatorship). Bosch, like Aristide, was his country's first democratically elected President, winning with an overwhelming majority of votes (62 percent in Bosch's case,

67 percent in Aristide's). At Bosch's swearing in on February 27, 1963, U.S. Vice President Lyndon Johnson embraced him.

Like Aristide years later, however, Bosch could not convince the United States that he would be open to its way of doing business, which was a key condition for staying in power; as President Franklin D. Roosevelt reportedly said of Trujillo, "He may be an S.O.B., but at least he's our S.O.B." Trujillo, knowing that the Americans would do anything to keep the Communist bloc from gaining influence in the Caribbean, convinced them that however distasteful he might be, the alternative would be worse; it would be Communist.

Bosch quickly lost the support of the United States because of his populist economics and because of rumors that he was sympathetic to Fidel Castro and to Communism. He never had the blessing of the armed forces or the Church. Even before his election, powerful Dominican archbishops had opposed him because of what they considered his Marxist leanings. He had not courted them, and then he angered them further by introducing legislation legalizing divorce. Months into his Presidency, a Church statement accusing him of being a Communist helped to seal his fate.

To make matters worse, Bosch's Dominican Revolutionary Party suffered from serious internal strife. His cabinet and advisers failed to inspire confidence. A controversial land-reform proposal raised fears that his intended social democratic policies leaned further to the left than was comfortable for the business elite or for the Americans. (The land involved was former Trujillo property, nationalized after the dictator's death, which Bosch intended to hand over to small farmers.) The business community, whose sentiments for him were only lukewarm in the first place, tended to go along with the other players in Dominican politics, and François Duvalier, watching from across the island, resolved immediately to prevent Bosch from becoming an adversary as formidable as Trujillo had been.

Clashes began soon with Duvalier. The first serious crisis happened quickly, in April 1963, after a sniper shot the chauffeur and bodyguards of Duvalier's children on their way to school and Lieutenant François Benoit, a young marksman whom Duvalier believed guilty of the attack, sought refuge in the Dominican embassy in Port-au-Prince. Duvalier's enraged thugs searched the embassy, then stormed the Dominican ambassador's residence, where they arrested twenty-two refugee Haitians, including Benoit, then took them to Fort Dimanche and executed them along with hundreds of other Haitians. Infuriated that Duvalier had violated Dominican territory, Bosch called him a madman and threatened to invade Haiti. Duvalier retaliated by inviting Trujillo loyalists to come to Haiti to plot against Bosch. Bosch ordered troops to the border and warships to the seas around Haiti. With the two nations on the verge of war, the Organization of American States (OAS) had to intervene to convince Bosch to back down.

Escalating a dispute that many believed he should have regarded as a tempest in a teapot was a blunder on Bosch's part. But even more damaging was his failure to convince his own armed forces that he supported them. The journalist Bernard Diederich has written that right-wing officers believed Bosch was trying to weaken the armed forces by diverting their attention to Haiti. They did not want to be used to help make Bosch appear to be a decisive leader. The clash with Duvalier, they believed, was simply a ploy to distract Dominicans from Bosch's domestic failings.

In mid-May, just as the embassy crisis was dying down, another crisis began to develop. Word leaked in Santo Domingo that Haitian exiles were training in a camp at Dajabón with the approval of the army but without Bosch's knowledge. When Bosch learned of the camp, he angrily denounced officers for conducting strategic activities without his approval and ordered its dissolution. He was quickly using up what little goodwill he ever had from the armed forces. And in July, ignoring Bosch's opposition, the Dominican army began training Haitian exiles in a new camp just outside Santo Domingo. Bosch again ordered it to break up the camp; again, the camp disbanded but soon restarted. Through late August and early September, the exiles launched three failed invasions of Haiti from near the Massacre River. After the first attacks in August, the Haitian government went to the OAS to denounce the Dominican Republic for interfering in its internal affairs. During the third attempt, in September, Haitian border soldiers returned fire from their border holdout across the Massacre River from Dajabón. The river is narrow enough for Haitian bullets to have hit the Dominican customshouse and a nearby school along the river. Now it was Bosch's turn to complain to the OAS about Haitian aggression. But days later, on September 25, accusing him of "dangerous improvisation of international incidents . . . endangering the prestige of the Republic," the army sent the foundering President into exile. Bosch had lasted seven months as the Dominican Republic's first democratically elected President. Twenty-eight years later, in Haiti, Aristide made it for only a few days more.

With Bosch gone, an interim government linked to the business community and supported by the United States, the Church, and the armed forces took over. Run by a car dealer, Donald Reid Cabral, it quelled street disturbances by sending out the police to arrest worker and student activists. Calls were immediately made for a return to democracy. From exile, Bosch temporarily allied himself with Balaguer, who was biding his time in New York. Both urged a return to a constitutional regime: Bosch because he wanted his Presidency back, Balaguer because he wanted to run in elections he suspected he could win easily.

Knowing Reid Cabral had little popular support, pro-Bosch rebels toppled his regime on April 24, and civil war broke out the next day. Three days later, President Johnson ordered in the U.S. Marines to "restore order" and to prevent Bosch's return. After four months of fighting the OAS brokered a compromise under which Santo Domingo's two parallel regimes—the pro-Bosch one, and the one led by the armed forces with U.S. support—would hand over power to a transitional government charged with organizing new elections.

Bosch ended his alliance with Balaguer, whose Reformist Party still relied on the support of Trujillo's cronies. The two men returned to Santo Domingo to run for President. Intimidation by army officers loyal to Trujillo kept Bosch largely confined to his house during the campaign, and Balaguer, backed by the United States and promising stability, was elected President on June 1.

Why did the U.S. government care enough to send troops to a country that its citizens thought of, if they thought of it at all, as a two-bit banana republic? It invaded not because the Dominican Republic was intrinsically important but because Washington considered it yet another Cold War arena. Just five years earlier, Cuba had fallen to Fidel Castro, giving the Communist powers a Caribbean stronghold. As 1965 progressed, U.S. soldiers were heading to Vietnam, and many people in government were obsessed with stopping the Red Menace. All across Latin America, preventing Communism became an accepted excuse for helping to topple democratic leaders.

Jean-Bertrand Aristide never joined the brotherhood of players, the men of power in business, the army, and the Church, though he accepted the grudging support they gave him early on. Because he had a strong popular mandate in elections that the United States had encouraged, the latter had little choice but to support publicly the man who had defeated a U.S.-favored candidate and spoke derisively of "the cold country to the north." An elected President, even Aristide, had to be better than the directionless military juntas he replaced. Haitian businessmen naturally liked the idea of foreign money returning, though they were not sure Aristide's leftist leanings would help the economy. The wealthy white and mulatto families that make up Haiti's high-bourgeois class, and that own most of Haiti's few resources, viewed him as a dangerous maverick who wanted to take forcibly what was theirs and give it to Haiti's poor. Even before he took office, it was clear his Presidency would be fragile.

Early on, long before he entered politics, the impetuous Aristide had clashed with his conservative superiors in the Church, since he chose the path of liberation theologians, the *ti kominote legliz*, the little church community, and declared himself an ally of *pep-la*, the Haitian people, who had never counted much in Haitian politics. "In what we call theology of liberation, we look at what is going on and we ask ourselves, What would Jesus do? What would Jesus say confronted with this situation: people are hungry, people have no jobs, I don't agree with this situation, I'm going to change it. And he would do something. All of us trying to do something for the poor are doing what Jesus did," Aristide told the American journalist Mark Danner.

The upper hierarchy of the Church, however, had been allied with the Duvaliers. Archbishop François Ligondé preached a New Year's homily in 1991 accusing Aristide of Bolshevist and authoritarian tendencies and beseeching the Virgin Mary to come to the succor of the Haitian people. Then, on January 6, a month before Aristide's inauguration, Interior Minister Roger Lafontant seized the Presidential palace and declared the December election void. (Lafontant had been struck from the ballot because the constitution drawn up in 1988 banned Duvalier associates from running for office for a decade.) But his coup was short-lived: called by the ancient lowing of *lanbi*, conch horns, just like those that had echoed during the Haitian Revolution, people poured into the streets of Port-au-Prince to support Aristide. The rest of the army refused to support Lafontant. Jailed, the would-be President had to give up. Still remembering Bishop Ligondé's diatribe against Aristide, the people in the street decided that surely the Church was linked to Lafontant's coup attempt. Seeking revenge, they attacked the home of the papal nuncio. The Dominican Church, already no fan of Aristide, sent a plane to rescue the prelate; in a skirmish in Delmas, on the outskirts of Port-au-Prince, more than twenty coup supporters died, among them a number of Dominicans.

Taking his Presidential vows on February 7, Aristide proclaimed a "marriage," as he put it, between the army and the Haitian people, in an allusion to the army's timely refusal to support the Lafontant coup. He then sacked seven high officers in the army and named as its new head a young mulatto officer, Raoul Cédras, who had guaranteed the security of the elections.

But Aristide soon used up his goodwill with the new military leaders, for he was governing as if Haiti were his own parish. He failed to assure the army and the nation's well-to-do that he considered himself responsible to them as well as to the two-thirds of the Haitian people who had elected him, and he alienated Haiti's minute middle class when he purged the civil service in an otherwise admirable effort to reduce corruption and free up government spending for worthier causes.

In July, when it was time for Roger Lafontant's trial, Aristide's fragile government was barely holding together. As Haitian judges deliberated, mobs of Aristide supporters surrounded the court, demanding that Lafontant be sentenced to life in prison, though fifteen years was the longest sentence allowable under Haitian law. If the judges did not impose a life sentence, the protesters threatened, they would attack the judges with the weapon of popular justice: a gasoline-soaked tire placed around a victim's neck and set on fire. (Haitians called this the "Père LeBrun," after a local tire merchant.) The judges gave in and sentenced Lafontant to life imprisonment at hard labor.

Less than a month later, Haitians again took to the streets around Parliament to prevent a vote of confidence being taken against Prime

Minister René Préval, a longtime friend of Aristide's who was, however, better suited to his career as a baker than to governing. The terrified legislators, remembering the grisly fates of the *tontons macoutes* whom the mobs had captured after Baby Doc fled, gave in to the crowds and let Préval stay. On both occasions the army and Haiti's elite waited for Aristide to call for calm, but his word never came. Most of them had never liked the idea of Aristide in the first place, and now they watched the mobs with grim resolve that he be brought down.

Back in Santo Domingo, Dominicans saw an unusually large number of luxury jeeps bearing Haitian plates passing up and down the John F. Kennedy Highway, and they knew something was going on. Duvalierist exiles who had been living in the Dominican Republic turned up in Haiti. Reports of Dominican helicopters crossing the border added to the general suspicion that Balaguer had probably offered help to Aristide's opponents. Busloads of expelled *braceros* arriving in Port-au-Prince in August and September were, Dominicans and Haitians speculated, part of Balaguer's plan to destabilize Aristide's government.

The coup against Aristide came on September 30, twenty-eight years after Juan Bosch fell in Santo Domingo. There was no more Soviet Union. Everywhere else in Latin America, except for Cuba, where Castro was still in power, citizens elected their leaders or at least gave the appearance of doing so. Free markets and democracy were the buzzwords. In Haiti, however, the political scene, like the economic one, was grim. A million Haitians lived in the United States, and many more were trying to come. The U.S. interest in the Caribbean was now no longer military security vis-à-vis Communist expansion but demographic: it wanted to keep images of starving black boat people off its television screens. The players and the arena had changed dramatically since 1965 and the Marine landing in Hispaniola, but not all the players recognized it right away. It took three years and a change in political administrations before the U.S. government decided that Aristide's fate should be different from Bosch's. During that time the Dominican government did all it could to prevent the young President from returning to Haiti.

In New York City, shocked Haitians gathered to protest the coup against Aristide. Sixty thousand strong, they filled Brooklyn's Flatbush Avenue, then marched across the Brooklyn Bridge toward City Hall, shaking the structure with the force of their footsteps. Many carried signs—DOWN WITH BUSH! DOWN WITH THE CIA! NO ARISTIDE, NO PEACE. DEMOCRACY, NOT DEATH! As they marched into Manhattan, they fanned out around City Hall, then into the streets of the financial district. Amazed bankers stood helplessly on street corners watching the crowd pour past the Merrill Lynch bull and around the staid stone banks. The Haitians sang the famous rebel song "Guantanamera" but with new Kreyol words: *"Kraze lame-a, woh-oh-oh, kraze lame-a!"* Destroy the army, oh-oh-oh, destroy the army!

The Haitians didn't believe U.S. President George Bush meant it when, immediately after the coup, he denounced the military government headed by General Raoul Cédras and Police Chief Michel François. They wanted to see more done to bring back their President, and they pledged not to be silent until that happened: they wanted an embargo imposed against the coup government, at the very least, and some of them even spoke of an invasion to depose Cédras and François. If the Haitian New Yorkers could not return to Haiti, they could bring Haiti to the United States. Until now, diaspora Haitians had been divided among themselves, segregated into groups based on their hometown, their class, their color, or the number of years they had lived in the United States. But over the months following the coup, they united and kept up the pressure. For many of them, Aristide represented a dream of returning to Haiti; without him, they felt, they would never go back. By the busloads, New York and Miami Haitians descended on Washington to protest the plight of their President. In Brooklyn, they picketed the businesses and homes of exiled *tontons macoutes.* At the United Nations, they met each evening for candlelight vigils and sang *"Ke-m pa soté"* (My heart doesn't leap, I'm not afraid), a song by the pop group Boukman Eksperyans that became an Aristide campaign rally. They picketed *The New York Times* over its reporting, which they saw as overly sympathetic to the coup supporters.

Aristide had already given a name to the more than one million Haitians abroad, many of them in New York and Miami: the Tenth Department—as if they were a new province added on to Haiti's nine existing administrative departments. The Tenth Department was learning to participate in American politics. In the spring of 1990, after the United States had banned Haitian blood donations, thirty thousand Haitians had marched across the Brooklyn Bridge to protest the insinuation that they all carried the AIDS virus. And now, after the coup, the Tenth Department took its cause to the Congressional Black Caucus, to New York Mayor David Dinkins, to Jesse Jackson, to the filmmaker Jonathan Demme. The legendary dancer Katherine Dunham, who has a home and dance school in Haiti, went on a hunger strike. The Haitian leaders met with labor leaders in New York to publicize their plight. Dominican union activists, many of whom moved to the United States because they or their families opposed Balaguer, were among their strongest supporters.

The struggle for Haiti moved to the streets of New York and Miami and down the halls of the State Department and Pentagon, no longer confined to Haiti or even to Hispaniola. Refugees streaming out of Haiti since the coup made an even stronger impression than the voices of the Haitians already in the United States. They set out in crowded wooden boats, leaving their homeland to cross the often stormy waters between Haiti and Florida, and became a familiar image. Before them, refugees from the Jean-Claude Duvalier regime had taken to the seas in leaky boats in hopes of making it to Miami. During 1981 nearly thirteen hundred Haitians arrived on Florida's shores each month.

At first the boats were old, but then refugees embarked on brand-new vessels. Boat makers had much to do, because there were not enough boats already in Haiti to carry away all the people desperate to escape the bullets. Nearly every night, television news showed an image of another tiny vessel being accosted by the U.S. Coast Guard, some of the boats capsizing as their occupants were hauled up to the American ships. More disturbing still were images the viewers never saw: of boats that sank when no camera was around to record the deaths of the refugees huddled on board.

Shadows reached long from the graves in the Port-au-Prince cemetery as All Saints' Day turned to night. Soft light filtered through the humid air, touching the intricate wrought-iron fences, which cast delicate crisscrossing patterns on the pale pink, yellow, and turquoise tombstones. The last straggles of mourners, little girls in frilly dresses following parents dressed in their somber best, shuffled out of the cemetery after paying their respects to their ancestors on this annual holiday.

"Mwen mal!" I am suffering! A man's shout echoed among the graves

near the entrance, next to the pile of chalky dirt and stones that was once the tomb of François Duvalier, before the crowds who drove his son Jean-Claude out of the country ripped the monument to pieces. His long arms waving in the air cast shadows that stretched beyond the cemetery, making the yelling man seem even taller than he was. "We have no President! How can we be all right?" His voice rose feverishly. "We have no food. The army is killing people." He swung his head and arms around and pointed behind him, up the hill that swells to a mountain. "There are many fresh graves up there."

On All Saints' night, for the first time since the coup, the military government lifted curfew so Haitians could honor the dead in the most important Vodou ceremony of the year, the festivals for Papa Guede, *lwa* of the dead. The candles lit and rum poured paid tribute to the hundreds of Haitians killed in the coup, as well as to all the ancestors who had come before them, especially those back in *Nan Ginen*: in Africa, where all Haitian spirits would return.

Prohibited by colonial French plantation owners from African worship, the slaves in Hispaniola disguised their ancestral spirits as Roman Catholic saints. Catholic holidays are holy in Vodou as well; the feast days of Catholic patron saints are the same as those of the corresponding *lwa*. Haitian Vodouists are devout Catholics. Their *lwa*, like the saints, all serve one God, known to Haitians as Bondyè (from *Bon Dieu*, in French). But Bondyè is so grand and busy that most life problems are delegated to the *lwa* who serve him.

In the parallel world of Vodou, each spirit-saint represents aspects of character on which humanity must rely to survive. St. Jacques, riding a white horse with a flag held over his head, is Ogou, the war spirit who gives strength and persistence. The Madonna, or Erzulie, represents motherhood, beauty, love, and sex. St. Peter, who opens the doors to the afterlife in heaven; St. Lazarus, who emerged from the tomb; and St. Anthony, patron of the needy and lost, all embody aspects of Papa Legba, the gatekeeper, guardian of crossroads and cemeteries. St. Patrick, who drove the snakes out of Ireland, is Danbala, the great serpent who is the spirit of life.

Corresponding to St. Joseph, the rooster spirit Papa Loko is master of ceremonies, reprimanding devotees if they are neglectful in their preparations. Papa Loko is invoked with Papa Legba at the start of each ceremony. He makes sure devotees pay attention to details and perform the ceremonies properly. As guardian of the temple and patron of the priesthood, Papa Loko has an obvious corollary in Aristide, the Catholic priest. Aristide once even acknowledged that he sewed into his vestments a *veve*, or sacred Vodou line drawing, representing Papa Loko. Now that Aristide is gone from Haiti, the symbol of the rooster spirit has added importance. But not all roosters are Loko. Other roosters are offered to the pantheon of *lwa*: black roosters to the death spirit, Papa Legba; white roosters to the female spirit, Erzulie; red roosters to the war spirit, Ogou. Loko is a yellow rooster, his color being that of the sun. The rooster is all at once a symbol, a spirit, and a source of nourishment for both humans and *lwa*.

On All Saints' and All Souls' Days, the high feasts of Papa Guede, all the *lwa* are honored. In the worldview of Vodou, the departed ones are always present, despite their physical absence. This makes sense in a culture of people whose ancestors were forceably taken from their homeland, and whose contemporaries are making their own exodus by choice—to New York, Miami, Boston, Montreal, Paris, anywhere but the misery of Haiti. What the departed leave behind is part of daily life. Papa Guede, lord of the dead, who mediates between life and afterlife, is the Haitians' final appeal against death, part of the powerful family of spirits who preside over the cosmic crossroads. But Papa Guede also can guide Haitians forward. After the coup, Haitians turned to him.

Just outside Port-au-Prince, at Leogane, lightning crackled in the dark sky above the high spiked sisal fences leading from the road to the *hounfort* where the ceremony was being held. Inside, paper flags draped from the ceiling, and the sacred drummers began to play. One of the first spirits to answer their invocation was Ogou, with his red military hat and vestments, gold epaulets, cigarette hanging precariously from between his teeth, rum bottle gripped tight. Tears rolled down his cheeks as red-robed *hounsi*—his assistants—whirled around him and he sank, sapped for a moment, into a wooden chair. He was soon up again, careening around the *hounfort* with the chair held on his backside. Ogou, the *lwa* of fire and battle, had responded to the people's call. But whose side he was on was not clear.

At the posh Hotel Montana in Pétionville, high above Port-au-Prince, expensively dressed members of the Haitian high bourgeoisie—

boujwazi, as Haitians call them—argued among themselves. They did not disagree on the main issue—that the OAS delegation to arrive the next day should not be allowed into the country—but were competing to be the most indignant. They were determined that Aristide not be allowed back, ever. It didn't matter that the OAS, followed by the United States, had imposed economic sanctions on Haiti (including a trade embargo excepting only basic food and medicine and commercial flights) to try to force its antidemocratic government to give up power, that the impending cutoff of fuel from abroad created lines stretching far down the streets leading to the gas stations that still had any to sell, that fuel prices had risen above ten dollars a gallon. Whatever the *boujwazi* had to do to keep Aristide out, they would.

Two days later, a crowd of rock-throwing, jeering Haitians (many of whom openly told reporters they were paid to be there) met the international delegation at the airport. When the OAS group left a few days later, they were visibly shaken and already wavering about Aristide. Haiti's *boujwazi* settled back in, confident that they would prevail over the international community's momentary commitment to the deposed President.

The Dominican government, across the island, shared that sentiment. In the cool piney hills above Port-au-Prince, Dominican Ambassador José del Carmen Acosta sat in his breezy office and lifted his eyebrows at the thought of the coup being undone. "I think the medicine might be worse than the illness," he said. His government certainly had no intention of helping Aristide return, especially now that he was accusing it of conspiring against him. Acosta complained that the embargo would hurt the Dominican Republic as well as Haiti. "We, too, are a poor country," he sighed. "We do not have the resources to feed all of the tens of thousands of refugees who would come across the border. And we don't have a Berlin Wall to keep them out." How much the times had changed that it was so easy to forget that the Wall had kept people in, not out.

The most visible refugees were not the ones who fled over the mountains to Dominikani but the boat people trying to reach Miami. Kreyol already had a word for these refugees: *botpippel*. Haitian Kreyol is an immensely adaptable, ironic, imaginative, and practical language, and this was not the first time it incorporated American influences. During the Alliance for Progress years in the 1960s, for example, Haitians called used clothes sent from the United States *kennedy* and diesel-operated home power generators *delcos*. From the 1950s to the early 1990s more than a million Haitians left their country, but not all by boat. First, there were the Boeing people, as they were called: middle-class professionals and intellectuals who had the means to get out even before Papa Doc Duvalier came into power in 1957. In the early 1970s the urban poor formed another wave of refugees. But *botpippel* became a word in 1980, when so many Haitians fled to Florida that the Immigration and Naturalization Service set up a detention center there to house them temporarily and, when that was insufficient, shipped them to another camp, Fort Allen, in Puerto Rico. To put an end to the streams of desperate black people Floridians did not want to see, the United States coaxed Jean-Claude Duvalier to agree to allow U.S. Coast Guard ships to patrol the waters around Haiti to prevent illegal immigrants from heading to the United States. Over the next decade the Coast Guard seized twenty-three thousand Haitians. Only eight people—*eight*, few enough to be counted on two hands—were allowed into America.

The new refugees, after Aristide's fall, made these earlier waves look like ripples on a pond. Nearly forty thousand Haitians would try to reach the United States in 1992, nearly doubling in just one year the refugee flow of the entire decade before. But these new boat people, the Bush Administration argued, did not deserve asylum because they were fleeing the economic—not political—situation in their country. The argument, of course, undermined the Bush Administration's supposed condemnation of the coup leaders: the military government could hardly be objectional and repressive if these were not political refugees (indeed, State Department criticism of the Haitian regime's human-rights abuses stopped in late October 1991, after the U.S. government suspended trade with Haiti and ordered home all nonessential U.S. employees; by this time the State Department had also begun to question Aristide's own human-rights record). And the economic situation the refugees were fleeing was the result of the international embargo imposed at U.S. insistence to change the political circumstances. Even more insulting was the way the treatment of Haitians contrasted with the policy for Cubans, who were welcomed as legitimate political refugees from Castro's dictatorship even though many of them openly admitted that they were fleeing poverty, not politics.

The Bush Administration, worried about Florida votes heading into an election year, urged Caribbean nations to accept Haitian refugees that the Coast Guard vessels were plucking from the sea: the world's most powerful country was saying it could not afford to absorb the refugees but nonetheless expected poor Caribbean nations to do so. When it became clear that the token offers from other countries would not be enough to absorb the flow, the U.S. government began to repatriate the refugees by force.

On November 19 a boat carrying two hundred Haitians capsized near Cuba. That same day, the U.S. district court in Florida, agreeing with Miami's Haitian Refugee Center that the Administration's policy violated international law, issued a temporary restraining order against the repatriations. The Coast Guard complied by ordering its vessels to deposit their human cargo at a tent camp at the U.S. base in Guantánamo Bay, Cuba, fenced around with barbed wire. By January 1992 more than ten thousand Haitian boat people were living at Guantánamo as the courts tossed around the question of what to do with them.

In May 1992, U.S. Ambassador Robert Pastorino proposed to Dominican officials that they allow a refugee processing center, with capacity for fifteen thousand Haitians, near the Dominican-Haitian border, where the refugees could have a chance to apply for asylum in the United States. The Dominicans refused flat out, arguing that they had "too many Haitians already." More to the point, they did not want to be accused of abusing the Haitians in the camp. But even without a processing center, Haitian refugees poured into Santo Domingo. The owners of the Dominican cane fields, emptied just months before, now would have no trouble finding workers when the harvest began in November.

Meanwhile, the U.S. government, the UN, and the OAS threatened and cajoled Haiti's military regime to give up. They tried tightening the terms of the embargo in an effort to flush out Haiti's de facto government, but it is difficult to close off a country completely, even an island. Haitian military officers cooperating with friendly nations and mercenary traders had ways of getting around the bans on trade. In Pétionville, the markets were full of Belgian charcuterie, French butter, all sorts of European delicacies. Gasoline found its way into Haiti to fuel the army's and the *boujwazi*'s giant Land Rovers, Mitsubishi Monteros, and Mercedes-Benzes.

In Santo Domingo, President Balaguer denounced each addition to the rules of the embargo. With crocodile tears he pleaded that the ban on trade with Haiti was also hurting the poor Dominican Republic. Meanwhile, the Dominican army sat back and got rich smuggling goods into Haiti. Giant oil trucks, freshly painted to read WATER, rumbled west to give the Haitian army the fuel it needed. At night they returned empty, bouncing and rattling without the weight of their cargo to keep their wheels and axles quiet on the road. Dominican business delegations rushed to Port-au-Prince to set up import-export operations to circumvent the embargo. In the satellite-dish-spotted suburbs up the mountain from Port-au-Prince, businessmen toasted the embargo.

Soldiers all but silenced Haiti's independent radio stations. They killed two radio journalists, "disappeared" another, and destroyed the equipment at many stations. Many reporters were in hiding. The ones still working no longer slept at home. Soon government-controlled radio was the only source of information, if you could call it that.

For a time, the main reliable news source was across the border: a radio station in the town of Tamayo, surrounded by cane fields in the southwestern Dominican Republic. Radio Enriquillo's 7 a.m. and 4 p.m. Kreyol programs carried news about the regime's repressions, the negotiations to end the political crisis, the violations of the international embargo. Rankling Haiti's military command most were Radio Enriquillo's interviews with President Aristide and his supporters. By now the post-coup government had settled in confidently enough to begin stretching its reach across the border. In early February, unknown attackers fired at Radio Enriquillo's antenna but missed. A few days later, men in civilian clothes broke into the station and began to take photos. Both times, neighbors chased the attackers off. Popular organizations, which relied on the broadcasts, formed night watch groups to protect the station.

The Dominican government and army were only too pleased to help when Haiti's de facto government requested that it control the radio station. On Valentine's Day, 1992, the Dominican government banned Radio Enriquillo's Kreyol-language newscasts, citing a 1966 law against foreign-language broadcasts. But the staff, many of them Dominico-Haitians who grew up in the cane fields nearby and could switch fluently between Spanish and Kreyol, carried on nonetheless. Father Pedro Ruquoy, the Belgian priest who ran the radio station, defied the order by singing the news, accompanied by a strumming guitar. Even to untrained ears, it was clear that the Belgian priest's calling was to work other than singing. "Well, he's not exactly an artist," the translator Ramón Batista said diplomatically. The human-rights group Americas Watch, which denounced the Dominican censorship, even noted in its board-meeting minutes that Ruquoy's voice left much to be desired.

In late May, Haitian strongman Raoul Cédras complained that the ban had not stopped the station from urging Haitians to resist his government. Dominican television reported that, indeed, the station was intended as a focal point for an invasion of Haiti by Aristide supporters. But, in fact, the station was running out of money. Worse, the controversy was causing problems for the Missionhurst international missionary congregation, which owned it. Ruquoy's superiors, though sympathetic to his efforts, had to think about the best interests of the mission.

In June, help arrived from Haiti when an exiled singer showed up at the station with a guitar and a sheaf of protest songs. Under the alias Mark, he sang the news to a ten-note melody repeated again and again: "After the announcement of Marc Bazin as the new Prime Minister for Life, the international community has rejected him. The OAS General Secretary has declared the nomination illegal . . ."

In July, the Dominican telecommunications commission ordered the Kreyol broadcasts suspended and threatened to close the station if Ruquoy did not comply. Archbishop Nicolás de Jesús López Rodríguez and President Balaguer justified this censorship on the basis that the radio's pro-Aristide broadcasts were an unwarranted interference in Haiti's internal affairs. Never mind that the Dominican Republic's leaders had no problem interfering with Haiti's internal affairs when Aristide was still President. If they saw the irony, they did not say so.

Louis-Jeune is tall, too tall. It is impossible for him not to stand out in a crowd. Perhaps in a token effort to blend in, he walks slouched over and shuffles through Santo Domingo's Little Haiti. Around his gaunt face he wears bright-blue radio headphones, taped together, with an antenna that sticks up like a space-age apparatus from *The Jetsons*. He is everywhere, popping up in the market, in church, in the merchants' hotels, and with the painters. He wants to write a book, he says. So he writes and writes, in a dark-green notebook with a dove on the cover. He lifts the book from his nightstand and opens it to show his notes in a curlicue script. His signature on the first page is a rococo confection of elaborate whorls and crosses.

Louis-Jeune was fourteen when his father died. When he was sixteen, his mother kicked him out of their house in Port-au-Prince because he refused to go along with her politics; she was a *filet lalo*, a female *tonton macoute*.

At twenty-eight years old, Louis-Jeune came to Santo Domingo as a political refugee after soldiers accused him of harboring arms to help bring back Aristide a year after the coup. Louis-Jeune says he is innocent, but later he pulls a glass bottle from under his dresser. He's ready to make a Molotov cocktail with it, he hints, and return to Haiti to fight for his President. On his arms and legs he shows the scars left by attacks in Haiti over the years. He lists the number of beatings he has suffered: in 1985 six hundred blows, in 1986 eight hundred, in 1989 one thousand, in 1990 twelve hundred . . . He offers his left forearm: "Here, this one I got in 1987. It was Franck Romain who did this to me." Louis-Jeune is talking figuratively about the former mayor of Port-au-Prince, a *macoute* who later took refuge in the Dominican Republic. As Louis-Jeune shows each of his scars, it doesn't matter that he is exaggerating the numbers—120 or 1,200.

The fan above Louis-Jeune's head shudders to a stop and the battered car radio on the nightstand is silent. It is another of Santo Domingo's incessant power cuts. "Blackout," Louis-Jeune says, pronouncing the word as Haitians do: blahck-ahh-woot. Without the fan the room is hot. Louis-Jeune pulls himself up and moves to catch the breeze outside.

Julian, the fluffy orange dog that belongs to the owner of the guest house, patters in and sniffs at a cup of sangria sitting on the floor. Two naked toddlers, sons of the Dominican owner, wobble in after the dog. It runs out the other door of the room and yips.

Life is expensive in Santo Domingo. Here, you can eat a meal for twenty pesos, roughly equivalent to sixteen gourdes, but in Haiti, you could get the same meal for seven or eight gourdes. "With sixteen gourdes, you can get fat!" Louis-Jeune says. The photograph on his passport shows a face much plumper than it is now. Since Louis-Jeune fled

Haiti, he has lost weight living frugally on savings and the little money he makes taping radio reports here. He pays forty pesos a day in rent for his little room overlooking the market. "This place is safe," he says. "The police can't come up here." On November 15, when two Dominican policemen threatened to arrest him even though he had a passport and visa, he was forced to pay them off with fifty pesos. "It's organized robbery," he says. He bends his tall, thin frame over the balcony rail. "Last Sunday alone, just sitting here on my balcony, I could see the police take in a thousand pesos," he says.

Fear is normal in Little Haiti. Many of those who live here have no papers showing that they are legal residents, and many of them aren't. But even those who do have the papers often won't show them for fear that they will lose them.

Across the street from Louis-Jeune's hotel, the Haitian little merchants go about their business quietly, fearing the soldiers will come after them, too. Gathering at lunchtime, surrounded only by other Haitians, they launch into intricate debates about their nation's politics. "The only man who is able to save Haiti is a prophet. But the disagreeable ones don't want that. They don't have any respect for Haiti. It's only with the help of Bondyè, the Good Lord, that the country will get out of the hands of the disagreeable ones."

Joseph is sad today, taking a break from selling clothes. He came here in 1988 to trade, because he could no longer feed his children working in a metal shop in Haiti. His wife, Lucienne, and their four children still live in Jacmel. Lucienne sells food while they wait for Joseph's visits, more and more infrequent when business is bad, as it is now because of the embargo.

"If they have any conscience, they can see how many people are dying every day.

"In Haiti, I won't tell just any old Pierre or Jacques what I'm thinking," he says. "There, any of them could be bought, their words twisted and used against you. I stay still, immobile. Because I never know. I don't want to get myself in any trouble. If I am in Haiti, if I see a person die in the street, I can't say a single word, because I am a Haitian.

"But if Aristide were to return one morning, that afternoon the fear would be gone. But until then . . . as we say, if your head is cut off, you don't worry about where your hat has gone."

Joseph pauses only briefly before launching into his opinions on the United States. "The Americans say they have democracy in their house. I don't believe it. Wherever there is democracy, everyone has the right to choose what they want. The Americans don't permit that. The world's policemen, that's how the Americans see themselves." He pulls a pair of pink panties from the pile of yellow, blue, and pink underwear in his hand. "If they like pink, it's pink for everybody."

"It's the Americans who caused this hurricane that came to Haiti, all these things that have happened in Haiti. The Americans aren't waiting for Bondyè to bring the end of the world. They are doing it themselves in Haiti.

"But nothing is eternal. Even George Bush is going to die. He's playing God on the earth. But he's not all-powerful. He's very powerful, but he's not all-powerful."

The words are running out now, tripping over each other, faster and faster. "We come here to work to save our children. What else can you do when you see them crying in front of you, because they are so hungry?" Suddenly he is quiet. "When the end of the world comes, it will begin in Haiti."

Joseph walks away, then turns back. "It has begun in Haiti."

November 4, 1992. Haitians were ecstatic when Bill Clinton defeated George Bush. Throughout the U.S. election campaign, Clinton had strongly condemned the Republican refugee policy as cruel and inhumane. Taking at face value Clinton's promise to change things, Haitians reassured themselves that his election was a sign that the U.S. government at last would give them asylum. After months of not going to sea because they knew they wouldn't make it past the Coast Guard, they had new hope. Haitian boat makers set to work again.

Scoffing at the world's inability to topple it, the junta in January ran sham elections that packed the Haitian Parliament with new, anti-Aristide legislators; the exiled President's supporters boycotted the election. Clinton took office on January 20, but he almost immediately reneged on his promise to end the forced-repatriation policy he had denounced as cruel.

On February 16 eight hundred Haitians drowned as the refugee ship *Neptune* sank on its way to Miami. Pressure was rising for Clinton to do something. In June, the United States froze the U.S. bank accounts of coup supporters who appeared on lists compiled by Aristide loyalists. It also announced that in addition to the existing embargo it would block any ship that attempted to deliver oil or arms to Haiti. At last, Haiti's military leaders appeared to be backed against a wall. Cédras finally agreed to negotiate with Aristide in a session that yielded an agreement under which Aristide would name a new Prime Minister, then return to Haiti himself by October 30.

The new Prime Minister, Robert Malval, took his place in Parliament at the end of August, but the military regime tightened the screws. It murdered two prominent supporters of Aristide: the businessman Antoine Izméry and the Justice Minister Guy Malary. UN peacekeepers refused to set foot on Haitian soil because it was so unsafe. On October 10, as the U.S.S. *Harlan County* tried to dock at Port-au-Prince, a mob of protesters supported by the military junta and its political arm, FRAPH, filled the docks and attacked U.S. embassy officials who had come to greet the ship. The *Harlan County* left Port-au-Prince harbor along with any hopes that the July agreement would become reality.

Balaguer and the Dominican army sat smug in their confidence that Aristide would not come back to Haiti. As long as the crisis continued, they were protected from his attacks, assured of a compliant supply of cane cutters, and making money from the embargo. And they knew that the United States did not want to try to control both ends of the island at once. While the Americans were preoccupied with Haiti, Balaguer virtually had free rein in his own country.

As the Haitian crisis approached its last long, hot summer, Santo Domingo's campaign for the May 1994 elections was about to begin. The government had printed brand-new voting cards, embossed with a gold ballot box printed over an identifying photograph; fingerprints and a magnetic strip were on the back. To prevent multiple voting, there were spaces for the ballot-box supervisors to punch the card when it was used to vote. This election, the government claimed, would be cleaner than any before.

Haiti's crisis provided the perfect campaign backdrop for Balaguer's nationalists. Whispers continued that José Francisco Peña Gómez, the leading opposition candidate after Bosch's humiliating 1990 defeat, was

Haitian. Stories circulated that there was an international plot to force Haiti and the Dominican Republic to become one country, the implication being that Peña, "the Haitian," backed such a scheme. Since Peña supported Aristide, other rumors had it, he would welcome a rush of Haitian refugees into Santo Domingo.

The insinuations notwithstanding, Peña Gómez and his Dominican Revolutionary Party (PRD) stayed ahead of Balaguer and the Reformistas in the polls, but just barely. As the elections approached, he was leading by only four points.

When election day arrived on May 16, everyone already knew what would happen; even so, the brashness and ingenuity of the fraud still shocked Dominicans. When voters in Peña strongholds showed up at the polls at dawn, many of them found that the polling stations were not yet open. They stood and waited for hours. Others, their valid voting cards in hand, discovered their names mysteriously had disappeared from the lists at their assigned polling stations. The affected voters were, not coincidentally, largely Peña supporters, as inspections later confirmed. By evening the protests were loud enough that the Central Electoral Board agreed to allow the polls to stay open an extra three hours, but the announcement did not come until 6:20, after most polling stations were already closed.

The first returns showed Peña in the lead in Santo Domingo, and with more than a third of the population there, the winner in the capital usually takes the whole country. But by the next morning Peña's majority (echoing Juan Bosch's experience four years earlier) had fallen; the Central Electoral Board reported Balaguer ahead by just 1 percent of the votes.

It was the most sophisticated fraud Balaguer had ever pulled off. Peña claimed that 200,000 PRD members had been kept from voting, far more than Balaguer's plurality of less than 30,000 votes. By the time the votes were counted and recounted three months later, Balaguer's lead had slimmed down to 22,281 votes, 0.74 percent of the total. International election observers reported that as many as 45,000 Dominicans were kept from voting, a vast majority of them supporting Peña. The names of 60 percent of those not allowed to vote had been mysteriously replaced with fictitious names, and the observers noted dryly that such an alteration was unlikely to have been caused by a computer error.

An international scandal over those stolen elections proved the perfect chance for the United States and the OAS to urge Balaguer that his government close the leaks on the border with Haiti. The day after the elections, U.S. Ambassador Pastorino met with Balaguer. The two refused to say they discussed the election, but they did say that they discussed the border accord. Two weeks later, the Dominican and American governments announced that they had reached an agreement under which Dominican soldiers would police the border to slow the flow of contraband into Haiti (putting the fox to guard the chickens, perhaps, since the Dominican army had been a key player in much of the smuggling; but the plan was an effective show nonetheless). Balaguer, it appeared, had bought himself some time. The Americans were in a bind, he knew: they needed his support on Haiti. Though he would have to put up with their preaching about democracy, they would have to use a soft hand with him if they wanted their way in Haiti. (Trujillo used the same logic to carry out his coup; in 1930, when pressure was growing for the U.S. Marines to leave Haiti, Haitian President Louis Borno announced he would not run for reelection, so the Haitian crisis demanded the full attention of the Americans, who grudgingly let Trujillo stay.)

The stakes rose in both Santo Domingo and Haiti as the days passed, then turned into weeks. Refugees kept trying to leave Haiti. More important, midterm elections were approaching in the United States, and it was already clear that the Democrats would take a drubbing. President Clinton's Administration was mired in scandal as the Republicans trumpeted his failure to lead the country. His foreign policy, most notably in Haiti, had been as haphazard as many of his domestic initiatives. It was an embarrassment that the pack of thugs in Port-au-Prince for three years had thwarted U.S. efforts to get them to give power back to a democratically elected President. Worse, after months of relative silence, maintained so as not to endanger U.S. support for his return to Haiti, Aristide himself had finally spoken out against Clinton's policy of immediate repatriation of refugees intercepted on the high seas; he now denounced the U.S. Coast Guard interdictions as "a floating Berlin Wall." It was time for a clear strike to remove the coup government and, with Aristide's return, end the refugee problem.

The price of gasoline was still falling in Haiti, despite the supposed better policing of the border. But the American government came up with other ways to pressure the Haitian army. In July commercial airlines stopped flying to Haiti, and on July 31 the UN Security Council authorized the United States to lead an invasion of Haiti to remove the military leaders of the antidemocratic junta.

On August 1 the Dominican Republic and United States announced that they had signed another accord: this one would station eighty-one international observers on the Dominican border, and the United States would provide $13 million worth of military equipment. On August 3 the Central Electoral Board declared Joaquín Balaguer the winner of the May 16 election. The United States, issuing a statement of "disappointment," urged Dominican authorities to move to hold new elections. As the U.S. government prepared to send its troops to Haiti, it would tolerate Balaguer for some time longer because it needed his cooperation, but it could not justify an invasion if it condoned this election fraud.

The following week, Balaguer agreed to shorten his term to eighteen months and to hold new elections for his successor in the interim, and this compromise was stamped with the approval of the OAS. It was the best Peña Gómez could hope for, but even that limited success would be diluted: the week before the inauguration, Bosch's Dominican Liberation Party (PLD) allied with Balaguer's Reformistas to betray him; Bosch had despised Peña Gómez ever since he usurped leadership of the PRD two decades earlier. Balaguer's term was lengthened to two full years. On the floor of the Dominican Congress, Reformista legislators, wrapped in giant Dominican flags, denounced international plots that they claimed would deny them sovereignty. The new American ambassador in Santo Domingo, Donna Hrinak, blasted the Reformistas for election fraud and for breaking the accord.

Speculation was rampant. Cynics accused the United States of criticizing Balaguer simply to have its way in Haiti but not intending actually to force the Dominican leader to hand over the Presidency to its true winner. "Sure, they cackle a lot, but they never lay any eggs," scoffed the economist Miguel Ceara Hatton. And despite a public spat with Vice President Jacinto Peynado, Ambassador Hrinak did, after all, attend Balaguer's inauguration on August 16. Not enthusiastic over her gesture, throngs of jeering Reformistas accosted her and assaulted her bodyguard.

In his seventh inaugural speech, Balaguer played on the Dominicans' suspicion of the outside world. He claimed that the pending refinancing of the Dominican Republic's foreign debt was evidence of an international plot to force the two nations of Hispaniola to be fused. His accusation drew indignant shouts and stamps. The crowd of people filling the auditorium with white suits and dresses smelling slightly of mothballs broke into yells demanding that Balaguer fill the entire Presidential term: "Balaguer! *Cuatro años!*" Balaguer! Four years! Just as he did during the campaign, Balaguer was inflaming passions against Haiti to strengthen his position. The attacks on Haiti were not about the neighboring nation but about Peña Gómez, the United States, and Balaguer's own reputation as defender of the Dominican people.

Balaguer's final jab was at those who criticized him for spending massive sums on monuments to himself, rather than on improving the lot of the poor. "Jesus himself justified poverty," Balaguer said, provoking more cheers. But behind his defiance had to be the recognition that the alliances supporting him had shifted. He had won two more years for himself, but he was old and blind. The United States, which had backed so many years of Balaguer government, was now no longer worried that Communism might take over its back yard. It was interested in keeping out immigrants. If making Haitians stay in Haiti meant returning the banished President, whom the Americans little liked, they would do that, even though it meant they must stop tolerating cooked elections in Santo Domingo. Ironically, as much as Balaguer continued to insist that Haiti and the Dominican Republic were separate, the events in Haiti mirrored his own country's past and shaped its future; without the crisis in Haiti, Balaguer could very well not have been making that inaugural speech.

In September 1994, with planes on their way to Haiti, former President Jimmy Carter convinced the military leaders in Port-au-Prince to step down and to allow U.S. troops to land peacefully in the harbor. The next morning, as the U.S. occupation began, Haitians jubilantly poured into the streets to welcome the Americans they called their liberators. On October 15 a U.S. Air Force plane touched ground at the Port-au-Prince airport. (Once called the François Duvalier International Airport, renamed Port-au-Prince International Airport when Duvalier's son fled the country, it was now the Guy Malary International Airport, in honor of the Justice Minister slain by Duvalierist thugs.) An entourage of high U.S. officials and international diplomats emerged; they were accompanying Jean-Bertrand Aristide, President of Haiti.

Aristide once wrote: "For us, there was no question of reconciliation without justice. A new regime could not be built without the *dechoukaj* (uprooting) of all the machinery of a corrupt regime that had imbedded itself down to the roots of society." As he returned to Haiti, ending three years of exile, he again spoke of reconciliation but without the accompanying talk of *dechoukaj*. He was promising a return to stability under the protection of the cold country to the north. It was the same pledge that Balaguer had made twenty-eight years earlier when he came back to the Dominican Republic and won the 1966 election as the candidate of the United States.

Four months after Aristide's return, American helicopters were swirling over Port-au-Prince as the city prepared for Carnival. The Americans had asked the celebrants to begin early, in the afternoon, so there would be less danger of violence after dark. But as the sun faded, the decorations were not yet all in place on the floats. It was considerably after dark when the parade began, the first real one in four years.

Rows of men danced down the street wearing giant papier-mâché rooster heads. Most of the crowd was too poor to have costumes, so they just danced in their street clothes, past the Presidential palace glowing white in the night. The Haitians pressed around the American troops posted at strategic points along the parade route. Haiti's best bands rode through the crowd as the drumbeats of celebration pulsed from giant speakers piled ten high on massive trucks, which spewed diesel into the crowd pressed against their fenders. The streets of Port-au-Prince, so silent at night except for gunshots for three years, throbbed all night long.

At ten the next morning music was still echoing up the foot of the mountain overlooking Port-au-Prince. In the city the music finally died down and gave way to the bustle of the day.

In the studio above the funeral home Edgar Jean-Louis runs, his assistants are finishing an intricate sequined banner, a *drapo* Vodou, honoring the spirits. Tall, with prominent round cheekbones and a sprinkle of gray in his hair, Edgar is a *houngan*, a Vodou priest. He surveys the work on this flag, which incorporates a giant red rooster, palm trees with silver trunks, a red number five representing Aristide (his number on the 1990 election ballot was five), fiery-orange trim. In the middle a photograph of Aristide covered in plastic is painstakingly sewn into place with delicate beadwork, just like the chromolithographs of the Roman Catholic saints Edgar uses for flags honoring the other *lwa*. Aristide's jacket and tie are covered in silver and gold sequins, making him look like a Haitian version of Elvis Presley.

While Aristide was exiled, the rooster began appearing in flags like this one. Aristide's *kòk lavalas* rooster, a political emblem that Haitians could be arrested for painting or carrying, was easily disguised as Papa Loko, the rooster spirit. Near the end of the military government, artists grew bold and began adding the words *kòk lavalas* to the flags. So strongly identified was the *kòk lavalas* with the flags that by the time Aristide came back from exile many of the flags were made for the *kòk lavalas* itself with no mention of Papa Loko. (And, some said, the red color of the rooster also evoked the war spirit, Ogou, and the ferocious female spirit, Erzulie Zè Rouj, who would fight for Aristide.)

Aristide's fusion with Papa Loko mimics the process by which Haiti's *lwa* emerged, the mix of images, spirits, and personalities reflecting the way Haitians see the world. Papa Loko, whose African ancestor was a wind and tree spirit, became a rooster in Haiti. Chromolithographs of St. Peter, who represents aspects of the gatekeeper Papa Legba, usually show a rooster in the background (the cock whose crows reminded St. Peter of his denial of Jesus). Since Loko is part of the Legba family of spirits who open the celestial gates to bring the *lwa* into the *hounfort*, the St. Peter rooster became Loko.

In Bel Air, not far from Edgar's studio, a *hounfort* honors Papa Loko. From the outside the temple doesn't look like much, just a large cement-and-corrugated-tin shed. Inside, gradually emerging from the dim light, the walls are covered with murals to the various *lwa*. Behind a wooden door at the corner of the *hounfort* lies Papa Loko's altar. At first Lolotte, the *mambo* at the temple, hesitates to open it, saying the key cannot be found, but she finally relents. Hanging on the wall is a spice rack, since Papa Loko is also the spirit of healing, herbs, and trees. The wind appears as a rustling in the leaves of trees. Papa Loko is the wind as well as a tree. In Africa, a Yoruba sacred tree spirit is named Iroko; he is the wind, son of Mawu and Lisa, the great parent spirits who are the sun and moon. In Haiti, the corruption of the name Iroko into Loko corresponds to the Spanish word for crazy, *loco*, a word many Haitians know. Papa Loko's rage when rituals are not performed properly has strengthened the connection with the "crazy" connotation. Loko is insistent about the way things are done. Loko, along with Legba, is a guardian of the gate. As mediator, director and master of ceremonies, guide to new initiates, and guardian of the temple, Loko is central to the ceremony. His simple altar has many bottles on it: drinks offered in his honor. Papa Loko likes foreign drinks, especially the most expensive ones: champagne, cognac, whiskey. Like any Haitian spirit, he also likes rum.

An *asson*—a gourd wrapped with beads and snake bones that is used as a rattle—lies by the bottles, and next to it lies a mirror, representing the duality of the spirit and real world. Papa Loko presides over the *asson*, which is used to call the *lwa*. It is the symbol of the Vodou priesthood. Each Vodou devotee enters the realm of the faithful under the protection of one particular dominant spirit, the *met tet* (from the French *maître* and *tête*), master of the head. The devotee honors the days sacred to that spirit, remembers which colors, food, and drinks it favors, and prays to it. Edgar and Lolotte are insistent that none of the Vodou faithful chooses the master of the head: "You don't choose the spirit; the spirit chooses you."

It does not seem strange that the rooster spirit has chosen the President of a country where the cock pervades life and politics. Vodou, like the cockfight, is a ritual in which spirits play out dramas for their human counterparts. It is a parallel world of expression to which the faithful can turn for order and understanding when the human world lacks sense. No wonder that it has come to incorporate politics too.

Outside the room containing Loko's altar, live roosters are tied with twine to cinder blocks on the floor that have been spaced so the roosters cannot attack one another. Near the roof, at the top of the center pole that supports the roof of the building—the *poto mitan*, which draws the spirits into ceremonial celebrations—is a painted gourd, a holy *asson*.

The quiet late-morning heat suffuses Papa Loko's temple. It is calm. But on a night of religious celebration, devotees will invoke the spirits; drumbeats and song will rise through the corrugated-tin roof and out through the alleys of Bel Air. Shaking the sacred *asson*, offering rum, food, and music, Lolotte and her acolytes will call the spirits, one by one. First Papa Legba, then Papa Loko, followed by myriad others, will descend the *poto mitan*. Like riders on horses, they will mount their devotees, and their personalities will overwhelm those of their mounts. Lolotte will take on the mannerisms of Erzulie, the flirtatious love spirit. When Erzulie leaves, Lolotte will perhaps begin to speak in the high nasal voice of Papa Guede, spirit of the dead and protector of the crossroads. The spirits will speak, connecting the present to the past and predicting the future, translating the stories of those who have died into lessons for the future.

The Old Man

*Mais, me direz-vous, si du côté des coqs les choses sont simples, elles
sont beaucoup plus compliquées du côté des hommes. Pas tellement.
L'essentiel est de comprendre la situation et de connaître les
personnages dont les coqs portent les noms.*

*But, you'll say, while things on the roosters' side are simple, they are
far more complicated where men are concerned. Not exactly so. The
essential thing is to understand the circumstances and to know the
personalities after whom the cocks are named.*

—*Aimé Césaire*
La Tragédie du roi Christophe

Overcome with emotion on a shining morning, a
schoolteacher wearing a cerulean dress thanked President
Balaguer for the money he had given her town for a new
school. The whole town had turned out for the President's
visit here in the northwest port of Manzanillo, near Haiti,
where a bright-red stand was set up for his appearance. The
teacher was invited up to meet the President and shake his
hand, which she did vigorously. Bobbing and gushing, she
started to rush back to her seat without realizing he was not
finished. Blind and unsteady on his feet, the leader stood
with his hand out until his aides, not so gently, nudged the
woman back to the dais. After he bid her goodbye, Balaguer
waved to the crowd with his black fedora, then replaced it
on his thin white hair before his trusted generals ushered
him out to prepare for the next stop on his whirlwind tour.

The President was exhausting the press corps following
him in a red minivan. How could such a frail man, almost
ninety years old, barely able to walk, blind, and hard of hearing, keep up this pace day after day? Was it sheer force of
will, the same drive that kept him at or near the center of

power for sixty years? The only emotion that can fuel such frenzy is anger, the fury of a desperate man grasping to prevent what he knows is the end.

It was a little more than a week before the May 16, 1996, Presidential election. Soon, for the first time in ten years, Balaguer would no longer be President of the Dominican Republic. For the first time in three decades, he was not on the ballot, though not by choice. Under his agreement after the stolen election of 1994, he was ending his term two years early and had agreed not to run. Yet this tour had all the marks of a Presidential reelection campaign, leaving Dominicans wondering if he really would step down. After all, when he gave his State of the Union address on Independence Day, February 27, he had said only that the speech would probably be his last as head of state. Probably? Dominicans speculated for weeks over the meaning of that word.

After seven terms as President, Balaguer refused to accept losing power over the forces of history and memory, as his predecessor, Trujillo, had done. All these years, he cultivated the image of a great father, the only person who could take care of Dominicans, his children. He wanted to be remembered as the builder of the nation, both physically and in character. He was out to cement his own legacy in his last days as President. But his rise to power had relied as much on stirring dissent and hatred as on building alliances, and his decline would follow the same path, leaving deep questions over where the Dominican Republic would end up. Could it replace his strongman tactics and nationalist rhetoric with more democratic ways? The last days of his campaign suggested that the answer was no.

Work was proceeding furiously on widening the treacherous highway from Santo Domingo to Santiago, the link from the capital and its market and ports to the agricultural heartland. Balaguer had built roads, dams, aqueducts, an aquarium, a ponderous stone lighthouse, and a giant tunnel through a cliff at the western edge of Santo Domingo, where street boys lived in caves. But he wanted to leave behind something more than stone and steel. This trip was about more than simply affixing his name to the public-works projects he had funded. It was about defining who would succeed Balaguer, who for thirty years had been virtually synonymous with the Dominican Republic, as the representative of the country. It was about making sure the myth of the Great Man did not die, about casting history's long shadow into the future; it was not necessarily about what was best for the country. Balaguer had always justified his actions with the idea that his destiny was to lead the country; by that logic, anything required to preserve his influence was what the Dominican Republic needed, too, no matter the consequences.

For most of the years Balaguer was President, he used his biweekly ribbon cuttings as press conferences to give public statements and grand pronouncements. This year, he had stepped up the pace of inaugurations to as many as six a day, but he was not saying a word. He presided, silent and still, his face blank, over the projects he was leaving behind. In March, exasperated with reporters' pressing him to reveal why he would not wholeheartedly support the Presidential candidate of his own party, Balaguer snapped: "I am blind, deaf, and dumb." End of story. Except for a seven-year-old girl he allowed to interview him for a children's television show about what he liked to eat, he had not spoken to journalists since the 1994 election.

The only people close to Balaguer were the generals, right-wing ideologues, and kleptocrats called the *anillo palaciego*, palace ring, an expression that plays on the word *ciego*, blind, suggesting a circle of men taking advantage of his blindness. But even the *anillo* members were not assured of their positions. A month earlier, Balaguer demoted his longtime trusted aide, General Pérez Bello, after their pilot brought his helicopter down north of Santo Domingo rather than trying to land in the capital in a torrential late-afternoon thunderstorm. In one version the detour was an attempt to force Balaguer to call off the vote. In another the blind old man was angry that Pérez Bello had not told him of the safety landing and snapped, "If you don't have the balls to pilot this thing, I'll do it myself."

These last few months, his public speeches insisted that there be no "foreign interference" in the Dominican Republic. He and his cronies deplored the presence of a delegation of international observers and blasted the fact that a new vote was being held at all. It went unspoken that Balaguer blamed the United States for having left him no option but to sign the 1994 accord in which he agreed to step down this year. The same nation that helped him to power in 1966 was now pushing him out.

Rumors swept the country. What was Balaguer trying to do? Would he agree to turn over the Presidency? Nobody knew. Nobody ever knew exactly what Balaguer intended; his mysterious behavior had spawned an entire profession of self-styled Balaguerologists, many of them disgruntled former aides. Their favorite adjective for him was "Machiavellian," pulled out whenever they had no good explanation for his intentions. Eyes glinting, the Balaguerologists would say, relishing each word: "The end justifies the means."

The last stop of the day was Navarrete, the town where, as a ten-year-old boy, Balaguer first met the U.S. Marines taking over his country. The crowd shielded their eyes from the sun and dust as a half-dozen helicopters appeared on the horizon, then buzzed toward the field where a bright-red platform and tent were waiting. A hush fell over the crowd as Balaguer's chopper, white with the faintest blue trim, settled onto the grass and bodyguards escorted the President to the special red-velvet chair waiting for him under the tent. A woman fainted from excitement and the heat. The Minister of Transportation read a florid speech about the new highway Balaguer had built and reminded those gathered: "Only Balaguer could do it!" When the official finished and a bevy of satin-clad women drowned Balaguer in flowers to thank him for a housing project, the President was nearly immobile.

With each stop to inaugurate yet another monument or public work bearing his name, Balaguer and his plans became even more of a mystery. His silence was almost a warning. *Without me*, his muteness suggested, *you are at the mercy of foreigners.* In the town of his early childhood, his silence seemed even louder, a sonic void created as memory imposed itself on the present. The strongest memory of all was that of the Americans, present at the end of his time as they had been at the beginning.

Joaquín Balaguer was just a boy when the U.S. Marines landed on the shores of the Dominican Republic. In 1916, a year after the United States had taken over Haiti, the Marines came ashore at Montecristi, on the north of Hispaniola at the tip of a V whose sides were the two neighboring nations. The American soldiers in their khaki uniforms tromped across the Dominican Republic from Montecristi southeast to Santiago de los Caballeros. They easily defeated Dominican resisters like Máximo Cabral, who gathered his men together at La Barranquita in the north but quickly fell to the invading forces.

One July afternoon, the Americans arrived in Navarrete, where the young Joaquín Balaguer and his friend Chimbolo had just returned from picking mangoes. As the boys neared the main street of the town, the echoes of the soldiers' boots rang out and halted the boys in their tracks. A line of soldiers, heavy weapons straight at their sides, stretched back farther than Joaquín and Chimbolo could see. The tall men were so strange with their sun-reddened skin and fair hair. When the front of the line drew even with the two, the leaders paused and stopped the boys, who were waiting to cross the street. Fascinated, the boys offered the soldiers some of the mangoes they had gathered. The soldiers thanked the boys and allowed them to scamper across the street on their way home.

When little Joaquín arrived at his house and told his parents what had happened, he was severely scolded. It was his second lesson in politics: outsiders could stir up powerful passions in his country. When he gave the mangoes to the Marines, he had already applied his first lesson: even a little boy can convince stronger men to step aside if he can offer them something they want.

As a boy, Balaguer, tutored by his seven sisters, studied literature. Grown into a bookish adolescent, he wrote poems and essays. His father told him to follow a pursuit more useful than burying himself in books. But the teenager was obsessed, devouring Greek classics and literature of the Spanish Renaissance. He read voraciously, following the exhortations of the Uruguayan writer José Enrique Rodó in the 1900 book-length essay *Ariel*, which had provoked much comment among intellectuals at the time. Reflecting on Shakespeare's *Tempest*, Rodó urged Latin American youth to strive to advance the greater cause of civilization by relying on Ariel's intellectual prowess instead of the half-human monster Caliban's sensuality and brute action; they should seek Old World culture as their guide instead of what Rodó considered the crass and vulgar underpinnings of the United States, which was expanding its military influence in Latin America at the time. The attainment of wisdom, in Rodó's vision, would allow an enlightened leader—in the mold of the exiled duke Prospero—to harness both intellect and force to serve his noble purposes. "The crowd, the anonymous masses, is nothing in and of itself. The mob will be an instrument of barbarity or civilization according to whether or not it lacks the coefficient of high moral direction," Rodó wrote, alluding to the French humanist playwright Ernest Renan's 1878 portrayal of Caliban as the embodiment of the basest qualities of the common people.

Rodó's casting of Ariel and his master, Prospero, as ideals to which Latin America's leaders should aspire influenced the region's intelligentsia at the time of Balaguer's adolescence. The Dominican scholar Pedro Henríquez Ureña, building on Rodó's writings, praised Prospero as "the magician-teacher who is also a man, the wise connoisseur of the world and its minutiae, strengthened by his solitude." But these ruminations on *The Tempest* downplayed Prospero's flaws: he allows himself to be driven by anger at the betrayal that deprived him of his dukedom and cast him out to sea; he depends as much on Caliban as he does on Ariel to tame the wild island where he is shipwrecked; he is a despotic master; and his magic is rough and dangerous. When Prospero gains a chance at revenge after twelve years on the island, the method he chooses is a violent storm. He achieves reconciliation only by employing questionable means. Had Shakespeare named the wild island setting for *The Tempest*, he could easily have called it Hispaniola and cast Prospero as the very embodiment of the island's mythical Great Man (and, by extension, Haitians as Caliban and the influence of Spanish culture as Ariel).

It was not until decades after Rodó's analysis that critics (notably, France's Jean Guéhenno, Argentina's Aníbal Ponce, Martinique's Aimé Césaire, Barbados's George Lamming, and Cuba's Roberto Fernández Retamar) developed an interpretation of the darker side of Prospero and began to portray Caliban as a victim representing the suffering masses of the region and Ariel as something of a mercenary. But by then, Balaguer had embraced Rodó's and Henríquez Ureña's philosophies, which would mold his entire political career. In his twenties, he taught philosophy in Santiago. His students recalled decades later that his passion was more for books than for the people whose young minds he was shaping. But Balaguer was turning words into power. He later distanced himself from his early poems, which he scoffed at as the idle musings of a teenager. Nonetheless, the words he wrote as a seventeen-year-old boy, the last year of the American occupation of his childhood and adolescence, mapped his obsessions:

YO—	I—
Soy de hierro. La fuerza toda en mí se resume	*I am made of iron. All force is gathered within me*
cual todas las maldades las resume Satán,	*just as all evil is gathered within Satan,*
por eso no me importa si no tiene perfume	*because of this it matters not to me if there is no perfume*
mi jardín que no escucha los quejidos de Pan . . .	*in my garden which does not hear the moans of Pan . . .*
Mis cantos son rugidos de furiosos leones;	*My songs are roared by furious lions;*
y quiero ser un fuerte trovador de alma macho	*and I want to be a strong troubador with a male soul*
y no un rimadorcillo forjador de ilusiones	*and not a silly rhyming forger of illusions*
que le tema a las burlas del hostil populacho.	*who fears the insults of a hostile populace.*
Tengo todo el orgullo de mi raza indomable:	*I hold all the pride of my indomitable race;*
por eso no ha flaqueado mi cuerpo miserable	*my miserable corpse has not weakened*
ante aquellos que quieren que yo acalle mi voz . . .	*before those who want me to quiet my voice . . .*
Soy de hierro. Y por eso con orgullo sostengo	*I am made of iron. And because of this I assert with pride*
que la fuerza y la audacia y el valor que yo tengo	*that the force and audacity and valor I possess*
no los he ido pidiendo en el nombre de Dios . . .	*I haven't gone begging for in the name of God . . .*

The "I" of the poem finds strength not in his frail body but in his mind. His weakness is not a handicap because his force comes from the power of the stories he tells and from the purity of his race. He is obsessed with the power of intellect. Solitary, resentful, he never marries.

Instead, he lives surrounded by books. Six decades later, Balaguer's words remain those of a man motivated by the desire to tame the world around him:

A veces una ola	*At times a wave*
por vientos tempestuosos	*battered by tempestuous*
combatida	*winds*
batiendo como una pez su	*thrashing its enormous tail*
enorme cola	*like a fish,*
se encrespa, ruge, se	*curls, roars, trembles,*
estremece, canta,	*sings,*
en cada acantilado se	*meeting each cliff it swells*
agiganta	*massively*
y hecha pedazos, pero no	*and, broken into pieces but*
vencida,	*not defeated,*
alza su blanca enseña	*raises its white standard*
y a todos nos enseña	*and teaches us all*
a triunfar de la mar	*to triumph over the angered*
embravecida.	*sea.*

◈ ◈ ◈

Small, simple, built of wood painted brilliant white, President Balaguer's adolescent home gleams amid a row of dingy bigger buildings on Máximo Gómez Avenue in downtown Santiago. The humble structure, one down from the corner, represents his middle-class upbringing and embellishes the mythology of a simple man dedicated to learning and to the people of his country: despite his elitist bent, Balaguer knew his strength lay in the devotion of the people. It is only a few blocks from the old headquarters of the Amantes de la Luz, the Lovers of Light Society, where, as a young law professor, Balaguer met with Santiago's intellectuals to discuss books and learning. The country's second city lies at the heart of the Cibao valley, which not only yields the country's best tobacco, pineapple, and mango but also is the biggest source of emigrants seeking work in the United States. (Other Dominicans mock the Cibaeño emigrants' broken mix of thick-tongued countryside dialect and English as "Ciba-English.")

While President, Balaguer rarely slept away from the capital, but things were different as the end of his term approached. By decree, he would move the seat of government to Santiago for a week at a time and stay overnight there. As the President traveled his country for the last time as head of state, he remained distant from his people. His aides left behind packages of food and money. Nobody commented on how weak Balaguer appeared; nobody complained about his silence. Buffered by bodyguards and functionaries, Balaguer was withdrawn; the man himself appeared lost in his obsessions, ignoring the show around him.

This particular day had been a long, hard campaign, halfway through a week of touring the interior. On the first stop, Cotuí, the President inaugurated a highway, then moved on to cut the ribbon for a school in Salcedo, where a stream of public officials pontificated, pouring lavish words of praise and gratitude on the President. Behind the barriers that kept the crowd back, rail-thin women pleaded with the press corps: "Give me a ticket for food. Please. We are hungry."

As the officials went on and on, the sky opened. A dark black cloud, which one moment had seemed small, swelled into a thunderhead that unleashed a torrent of rain on the crowd. Under a wooden structure set up to protect him from the weather, Balaguer sat just behind a steady drip. His bodyguards, generals in full regalia, pulled out an embroidered red shawl and placed it on a table next to him in case he should want it to keep dry. Balaguer was impervious to the fuss around him. By the time the locals were supposed to thank him personally, the rain had slowed.

Just as officials opened a side gate to let in women who wanted to present him flowers, Balaguer tried to stand but lost his balance and nearly fell. The guards rushed to steady him. Others headed off the women with flowers. The ceremony was over. The generals rushed him out to the helicopter. The next stop was canceled—"because of the rain," officials said. The President headed on instead to Moca, the fourth planned stop of the day.

At Moca, the bright-red "Balaguer-mobile," a bulletproof cage on top of a pickup truck, like John Paul II's "Pope-mobile," moved through streets still half filled with mud and green slime. Heavy rainfalls a week earlier had flooded parts of the town and left some residents homeless.

"Balaguer will build new homes for all the flood victims!" a loudspeaker blared. Cheers went up.

Maribel Gassó, an attractively plump young Vice Presidential candidate on Balaguer's Reformista Party ticket, walked alongside the Balaguer-mobile. A thirty-seven-year-old businesswoman and graduate of New York University Law School, she was fully conversant with U.S. culture. Still, she seemed at home when she paused to talk with the grandmothers of Moca and to dance the merengue with the younger Dominicans following the parade.

The Balaguer-mobile pulled off the road and into a large field, where it rolled to a stop next to his waiting helicopter. The crowd lurched forward. A row of bodyguards formed a human chain to keep them back, but only a few feet separated the mass of people from the rear end of the Balaguer-mobile. If something were to have startled the crowd, if they had pushed forward just a little harder, they would have crushed the old man right there. Inside the truck, Balaguer's aides were on the floor, unbuckling the straps that held his chair down. When it was released, they tipped it back slowly and gently lifted him, like an over-size baby, out the door. As he alighted on the steps, he wobbled for a moment and waved weakly. He appeared about to fall, but the security escort quickly steadied him and guided him the few steps over to the helicopter. As the door sealed shut behind him and the blades began to whir, other aides handed out envelopes stuffed with money. People dispersed under the wind of the helicopter as it carried him away, back to Santiago.

In the early evening, after Balaguer woke from his afternoon nap, guests gathered on the wooden porch of his childhood home hoping for a personal audience. Tan-clad bodyguards lined the steps to grant or deny access as they saw fit. From the looks of the crowd, the old President still had considerable power to grant large favors. Portly businessmen and political heavies, awaiting a turn, planted themselves along the railings. Overly perfumed and talcumed matrons, their corpulent figures draped in dramatic bright colors and blacks and encrusted in costume jewelry, waited for a chance to entreat the President on issues they considered vital in their social circles.

Slender teenage girls, looking as if they had just celebrated their *quinceañera*, hovered in high heels, miniskirts, and delicate blouses that sometimes did not even cover their midriffs. Their mothers fussed over them. A man who described himself as the President's doctor, tall, handsome, and freshly showered after the day's dusty campaign, circulated among the women, trying to charm them, though he stayed away from the girls. The jovial head of Presidential security strolled among the guests. Unlike the people in the small towns Balaguer had visited on this day, these Dominicans were well fed, secure, and confident that their requests would be honored. They were part of a privileged group that supported and benefited from his many Presidencies.

The porch afforded a view into the living room, painted the same searing white as the rest of Balaguer's house. Two large paintings over a pair of austere couches adorned the walls; otherwise, the room was simply furnished. On a hall table, a stuffed red rooster stared out the window with its glass eyes. The taxidermist had done a splendid job: dusty as it was, the bird seemed ready to fling itself off the table at any threat to its territory.

On the street the Dominican press corps waited in vain for some comment. They watched in envy two American reporters allowed up on the porch. When the foreigners left, disappointed, more than two hours later, the Dominicans accosted them, notebooks at the ready to take down any tidbits of information.

A block away, poor Cibaeños stood in a line snaking around three blocks and shivered in the night air. The line was really two lines, one for men, one for women. Soldiers separated them to keep men from pushing their way to the front. All were waiting for that evening's handout. The ones at the front had been there since 8 a.m., not willing to give up their places to escape either the noonday Caribbean sun or the early-dusk rain shower that washed off the day's sweat and dust and left them soaked and chilled. It was after ten by the time two soldiers rolled open the back door of the truck parked next to the barricade that kept the crowd from crossing the street to Balaguer's house.

Another pair of soldiers stepped to the front of the women's line to make sure everyone stayed in order. The first few women were allowed to pass, hurrying to the truck and opening their arms to receive the bulging red (of course, Balaguer's color) plastic bags of food. Waving the women along one by one, with just enough space between them to keep them from running up on each other, the soldiers moved the line efficiently; they had obviously practiced this routine many times. Disorder broke out only once, when a woman with her prepubescent son tried to push through and get two bags. As the women in the line pointed at the boy and protested, the soldiers pulled him aside and made sure the woman got only her due. The line began moving smoothly again.

Once they had grabbed their bags, the women ran back across the street to the median, where they tore the red plastic to inspect their haul: rice, beans, cooking oil, sundry nonperishable foods. A day of waiting for this, and they were satisfied. The women scattered across the street, emptied of cars, and headed home. One drunken old woman smoking a cigar with her white hair wild watched from in front of the President's house.

The men stood remarkably peacefully in line, where they waited until the soldiers finished giving all the women their packages. The last two nights, the food had run out before everyone received a parcel. But the men didn't mind. There was something else for the ones at the end of the line: envelopes holding hundred-peso bills, easier to blow on Presidente beer or Bermúdez rum than a bag full of rice and oil would be.

Balaguer won the hearts, or at least the pocketbooks, of the Dominican Republic's countryside peasants by building and passing out small favors, poor substitutes for what would have been a lasting contribution: education, training, and the tools that would have allowed them to provide for themselves. Instead, he fed his people's desire for myth.

In another election campaign, in 1974, Balaguer's helicopter had crashed when he was returning to the capital from a speech in the Cibao. Balaguer and the generals accompanying him survived. From the forest, where they had crashed, they made their way to a highway and back to Santo Domingo just in time for the President to reprimand the military brass who had presumed him dead and were preparing to announce the accident and take control of the country.

When Balaguer told Dominicans about the accident, he thanked the Virgin of Altagracia for saving him. But Dominicans in the know said that privately he thanked the Vodou charm he wore. Balaguer won the election that year, though thanks less to any miracles than to the boycott of the election by opposition parties.

When the 1978 election came around, he had been in office for twelve years—the time Dominicans now call, in hushed voices, *los doce años*. Though he lost the election and the American government gave him no choice but to step down, Balaguer went on building the myth of the great wise father, maintaining considerable political influence, even though he no longer occupied the National Palace. He had held office for three Presidential terms by taming the army and using it to silence the opposition. Now that he could no longer rely on guns, he turned to stronger tools: images and words. He passed most of his eighth decade preparing compilations of his speeches and writing books of history, poetry, and essays. His poems are filled, strangely for a man of the tropics, with images of ice. Balaguer was reshaping his personal mythology and waiting for his opponents to self-destruct. And he watched the Dominican Revolutionary Party (PRD) split into rival factions as President Guzmán handed out jobs and favors to family and friends.

When Guzmán failed to convince the PRD to nominate Vice President Jacobo Majluta to succeed him, he turned to Balaguer for help in attacking the party's nominee, Salvador Jorge Blanco. But Jorge Blanco defeated Balaguer in 1982 nonetheless, and the disgraced Guzmán killed himself. Balaguer waited longer, and the PRD divided further. Lacking Balaguer's charisma and authority, Jorge Blanco tried to win the army's loyalty corruptly, but his plan backfired as his enemies made the most of his errors.

Through all this, Balaguer reshaped his personal mythology. When he allied his Reformista Party with the Social Christians, a new Reformist Social Christian Party united his rooster and rising sun with the Social Christians' machete, a symbol of work and immortality. Even better than the rooster alone, this new symbol fit the image he had honed: a dedicated leader with powers to escape death.

In 1981, Balaguer lost his eyesight to glaucoma. His blindness remained an open secret for seven years, until he acknowledged it in a collection of poems, *La venda transparente* (The transparent blindfold), which was dutifully acclaimed when published in 1988:

Los ciegos recibimos	*We blind men, we receive*
Mensajes de otras zonas	*Messages from other mysterious*
misteriosas,	*zones,*
Vemos por intuición y	*We see by intuition and*
percibimos	*discern*
Con el tacto las formas más	*By touch the most indistinct*
borrosas.	*forms.*
La ambición de los hombres	*The ambition of men has*
siempre ha sido	*always been*
Congelar la corriente de la	*To freeze the currents of*
historia,	*history,*
Atar el tiempo ido	*To harness passed time*
En la hora triunfal de la	*In the triumphant hour of*
victoria,	*victory,*
Tornar al bien perdido	*To turn loss into gain*
Para hacerlo inmortal como la	*To become as immortal as*
gloria.	*glory.*

The old man had turned his weakness into a medium for public adulation. When the poem was published, Balaguer had been back in the Presidency for two years. Salvador Jorge Blanco and high military officers were being tried for embezzling as much as $60 million during the PRD period. Balaguer was building the Columbus Lighthouse as a monument to the past. He was trying to keep time from moving ahead, to keep the country in the days of the *caudillos*, who held the people so strongly that without them order was lost and the nation risked falling into the hands of foreigners. As long as the Dominican Republic was trapped in the past, Balaguer would give the people what they wanted: a strongman leader.

Not everyone agreed with this vision for the future of the Dominican Republic. Witty and charming, if sometimes abrasive, Narciso González was a university professor, lawyer, and journalist known for his satirical writings. He signed his articles under the pen name Narcisazo, a superlative of Narciso, to distinguish himself from Narciso Isa Conde, another activist in the Dominican Students' Federation. Days before the 1994 election, he scribbled off this list: "Ten Pieces of Evidence That Balaguer Is the Most Perverse Man Who Has Arisen in the Americas . . . Assassin, Gangster, Immoral, Delinquent, Perverter, Servile, Crook, Vermin, Miserable, Embezzler."

After the election on May 16, Narcisazo turned up the volume. On May 25 he urged top university officials to take a stand publicly denouncing Balaguer and the heads of the armed forces for a supposed twenty-five-million-peso payoff to keep him in power.

The last time anyone saw Narcisazo alive was on May 26, when he went to see the movie *Philadelphia* on Duarte Avenue. That evening, witnesses in front of the Ear, Nose, and Throat Center at the corner of 27th of February Avenue and Leopoldo Navarro saw a group of armed men in military garb force him into a blue Mitsubishi Montero, license plate 0-11172, belonging to the Central Bank.

Waiting for the 1996 election, Narcisazo's widow, Altagracia "Taty" Ramírez, sat on the campus of the Autonomous University of Santo Domingo. She was running the university station of the phone company, one of the three jobs she has to keep food on the table. Few students came in—one here, one there. Today she had with her a sheaf of documents related to the disappearance of her husband two years earlier. She had letters pleading with the police chief in Santo Domingo to answer questions and confront key evidence; an Organization of American States/Inter-American Commission on Human Rights study of the case; a timetable of the disappearance attributed to "intelligence contacts in the Armed Forces" provided by an unknown source; a biography of Narcisazo; and a copy of her husband's offending article. The pile held all the information she had been able to put together about her husband's last days.

His family declared him missing on May 27. The police called him "absent." His family received frantic phone calls: "He's on the third floor of the National Police offices." "Don't worry, he's alive." A friend said he saw someone who looked like Narcisazo in the guardhouse at the Department of Investigations and Forgeries. Reports emerged that he had been so severely tortured at the army headquarters that, when he was delivered to the National Police headquarters, the police refused to receive him because they feared he would die in their custody.

The mysterious timetable in her file pinpointed his death at June 7,

1994, at 11:30 p.m., when he was being taken from the secret police to the National Police headquarters. It took three days to find a place to hide the corpse, in a crypt in the cemetery of the far northwestern town of Montecristi. The day after Narcisazo was buried, the night watchman was found dead.

Often Balaguer simply neutralized his opponents with decrees, discredited them with a flip of his tongue. His speeches were his greatest weapon, spoken in a deep forceful voice that belied the frail body and blind eyes of the man pronouncing the words. But when his words were not enough to drown out those who opposed him, soldiers finished the job. The ones who received the worst of his wrath were those who used powerful words to attack him. They were the ones like Narcisazo, and like another dissident journalist nearly twenty years earlier.

In his 1988 autobiography, *Memorias de un cortesano de la "era de Trujillo"* (Memories of a courtesan of the era of Trujillo), Balaguer left blank a page that he pledged would be filled, twenty years after his own death, with the details of the disappearance of the journalist and activist Orlando Martínez, murdered March 17, 1975, after a series of his articles was published that were critical of Balaguer and the Crimson Gang of thugs. As an oddly personal touch in a book full of dry accounts of the President's meetings with various Latin American leaders, the note preceding the blank page was one of the few passages that seemed to shed light on the mind of the memoir's author. But what exactly did the promise regarding Martínez say about Balaguer? Did his mentioning the crime suggest a twinge of guilt? An ambivalence about using brute force in his service? Was it his way of seeking absolution? A plea of innocence? If it was any of these things, it did not prevent Balaguer's men from repeating the crime when they disappeared Narcisazo.

As the 1996 election approached, Balaguer enlisted the help of his aides to leave behind words that were strong enough to last. Ironically, the more that words surrounded him, the murkier his true intentions became. A large graying man wearing thick, 1950s-style glasses and a pressed linen *guayabera*, Ramón Lorenzo Perelló, the palace head of information, was the keeper, in a way, of the immortality of Balaguer's image. Lorenzo Perelló shuffled into a cool office of the Presidential palace carrying a heavy, glossy book, *Perfiles de Balaguer* (Profiles of Balaguer), which he edited in 1993. On the cover, a younger Joaquín Balaguer smiles, his eyes twinkling without glasses, his complexion flush and healthy, his hair still a dark gray. Lorenzo Perelló opened the book.

With his long fingers, he ticked off the authors of the many essays on the Agrarian, the Statesman, the Philologist, the Social Leader, the Intellectual and Critic, the Historian, the Storyteller, the Poet, the Sociologist, the Journalist. He intended the book to stand for a long time as Balaguer's official record. "These writers are objective. Look, they come from all around the political spectrum," said Lorenzo Perelló, going down the list of authors to prove his point.

This man also chose the three readers who fed Balaguer's voracious appetite for ideas and literature. He supervised them to make sure they gave the President an accurate reading of important documents. Often the President sat the readers down in front of him one by one, so he could listen to them separately. If one gave him false information, the others would reveal the treachery. Lorenzo Perelló epitomized loyalty and defended the information the leader received as well as the information that went out to the public.

Once Balaguer stepped down, however, there would be no coterie of devoted assistants with the power of the Presidency behind them. When Balaguer left office, he would no longer control the information that came out of the National Palace. For the first time ever, he needed a powerful person to protect his image, someone he could anoint his successor but who would not eclipse him.

The choice was easy among the three men competing to succeed Balaguer. The Reformista Party candidate, Jacinto Peynado, would become head of the party if he were elected President. Peynado had been presenting himself as Balaguer's heir ever since Balaguer chose him as Vice President in 1994. But a new party head, prepared to portray him as a has-been, was not what Balaguer wanted.

José Francisco Peña Gómez, Balaguer's old rival from 1994 and once again the PRD candidate, was out of the question. For years, Balaguer had warned that Peña would hand over the country to the Haitians. And he had a score to settle with Peña's running mate, Fernando Alvarez, who repeatedly challenged him for the Presidential nomination of the Reformista Party, then in 1994 defected to the white banner of Peña's PRD. Peña as President would not need the Reformista votes Balaguer controlled in Congress. Balaguer had a wrong to avenge, influence to preserve, and an image to protect. Peña would not help with any of these goals. Even though he had been weakened by his battle with cancer, diagnosed weeks after Balaguer's 1994 inauguration, Peña Gómez was still the biggest threat to Balaguer's control. The best way to keep him down was to rely on the old strategy: to call him Haitian, to suggest that as a black man he was emotionally unstable, to claim he was prepared to give the country away to foreigners who looked like him.

Leonel Fernández, the forty-two-year-old candidate of the Dominican Liberation Party (PLD), had followed Balaguer's old rival, Juan Bosch, faithfully. Campaigning under his first name to reflect his youth, Leonel convinced Dominicans that he was part of a new generation. He had boundless energy, a new face, and, more important, was not competing with the grand old statesmen of the past. Leonel had demonstrated that he understood loyalty and the importance of waiting his turn. There was another reason for Balaguer to support him. Leonel's party held only 2 seats of 31 in the Senate and 13 of 120 in the lower house of Congress. A President Fernández would need Balaguer's support.

Under the old code of brotherhood, there was a question of honor for Balaguer: he had a debt to repay Juan Bosch. A victory for Bosch's party now would give the country's other grand old leader a hand in the Presidency that Balaguer had wrested from him in 1990, and it would repay the United States for sending in the Marines in 1965. Though it had been politically expedient for Balaguer to have Bosch expelled and prevented from returning to power, this did not diminish his distaste for the great neighbor to the north.

A month before the election, Leonel's party alleged that massive numbers of Haitians, perhaps as many as a quarter of the Dominican Republic's 3.75 million voters, would try to vote using fake identification. Never mind that the number was absolutely implausible, given that the best guess was that there were only half a million Haitians in the country. Police swooped into the cane fields and into Haitian urban ghettos, demanding identity documents from anyone whose skin was dark. The police deported as many as three thousand illegal Haitian immigrants. Dominicans interpreted the move as an attempt to intimidate dark-skinned voters who might have wanted to vote for Peña.

Shadows of the 1937 massacre remained. Dominicans joked darkly that police came up to a group of people in the street and instead of asking them to pronounce *perejil*, as Trujillo's soldiers had asked Haitians, they asked them to say *otolaringólogo*, ear-nose-and-throat doctor. One man in the group threw up his hands and told the police, "Okay, okay, take me away. I'm Dominican, but I don't even dare to try to pronounce that."

Ominous ads appeared on television, with a forceful voice speaking in Haitian Kreyol over the picture of a Dominican flag and Spanish subtitles: "Haitians do not have the right to vote. Using falsified election documents is a crime. If you see anyone trying to vote with a forged voting card, report him to the authorities." Flyers went out to the communities where Haitians lived, warning them that they would be watched during the election.

The halls and rooms emptied quickly at the ghetto hotels behind the Modelo market, where Haitian merchants hawked their wares. "Everybody has left," said José Adame, a Dominican of Haitian descent who lived there. "After the elections they will all come back." In rapid-fire Haitian Kreyol, switching intermittently to Spanish, he told how police loaded illegal Haitian immigrants into a van to deport them. Because he is black and speaks Kreyol, they questioned him but let him go when they saw his Dominican *cédula*, or identity card.

As José continued, his tone took on a tenor amazingly similar to that of a Chicano in Los Angeles talking about new Mexican illegal immigrants. "I don't have a passport. I have a *cédula* because I was born here and my father is Dominican," said José. "But people who don't have their papers, the Dominicans have every right to deport them. They are illegal." He prompted a chorus of agreement from the other Haitians and Dominico-Haitians taking a lunch break and admiring the rooster one of them was preparing for that afternoon's fights.

For its part, the Haitian government downplayed the deportations. Just a few months earlier, hopes had been high for a lasting rapprochement between the two countries. In February, Aristide had turned over the Haitian Presidency to his elected successor, René Préval. That removed the personal enmity between Balaguer and Aristide as a major obstacle to Dominican-Haitian relations and led to an invitation to the new Haitian President to visit the Dominican Republic. In March, Balaguer himself had gone to the Santo Domingo airport to meet Préval and later conferred on him the Order of Juan Pablo Duarte, the nation's highest decoration. The leaders spoke about free trade across the island and about cooperating on environmental and other projects. After Balaguer's having opposed closer ties with Haiti for so long, this was an amazing development.

But in May, Balaguer's support of the PLD accusations flew in the face of the progress that had been made just weeks earlier. Some Dominicans even wondered if there was a connection between Préval's visit and his government's virtual silence regarding the deportations. Privately, Haitian officials clarified their motives: they feared that, against the backdrop of acute political tension surrounding the elections, vehement protests would only make things worse for Haitians in the Dominican Republic. They did not want inadvertently to intensify the persecution that was bad enough already.

At PLD rallies, fans waved giant stuffed lions in purple robes, representing Leonel the lion dressed in the party color. They had also gone out to get black monkey dolls, which they held in the mouths of the lions. They told racist jokes: A waiter asks President Balaguer what he would like to drink. "Well, since I'm President, bring me a Presidente beer," Balaguer says. Juan Bosch tells the waiter, "Since my name is Juan Bosch, bring me a J&B scotch." The waiter then turns to Peña and scoffs, "Well, I don't know what you can drink, because the bar's all out of *anis de mono* and Malta India." Monkey anise and dark Indian malt.

Peña's supporters fought back as best they could. The candidate himself contracted the historian Julio Genaro Campillo Pérez, head of the Dominican Genealogical Society, to research his family history. Published a week before the election, the book is filled with identity cards, baptism certificates, death certificates of Peña's parents. Father: Ogis Vincente, *Dominicano*, Agricultural Worker. Mother: Ana María Marcelino, *Dominicana*, Domestic Worker. Their faded photographs are identified by spidery handwriting on the side, confirmed by blotchy fingerprints, stamped in blurred ink with the official seals of the Dominican government. There are notarized consular letters, depositions from people who knew both Peña's birth family and his adoptive parents. Until the massacre of 1937, Peña's family had lived in Guayubín, not far from

Balaguer's hometown of Navarrete. But then, a few months after their second son was born, the parents fled to Haiti. A local farmer and his wife, the Peña Gómez family, took in the children and raised them.

Peña said the book "completely defeated" the issue of his nationality but not of his race. "To take away racism, they'd have to take the color out of my skin," he told a pair of foreign journalists.

As the election approached, Peña's party gathered for its last rally— a *mitin*, or "meeting," one of the words Dominicans adopted from occupying Marines. (Others were *zafacón* for trash can, from "safe can"; and *suape* for mop, from "swab.") Though Dominicans debate poll results for hours, the real measure of their election hopes is seen in the number of supporters they can attract to such rallies, which are held across the country. Giant speakers mounted on gaily painted cattle trucks blare music composed for the campaigns—merengues, *bachatas*, pop ballads, and even hip-hop and rap to please the youth from New York. Sometimes a live band plays from the truck. Other times, the vehicles are filled with party faithful dancing and waving.

Milagros Ortiz Bosch, the PRD senator from Santo Domingo, perched atop a white Jeep from which speakers blared Peña's soaring campaign ballad, *"Primero la gente,"* At last, at last, the people first! The Jeep started off from the tree-lined streets of Gazcue and headed up past Independence Park to Mexico Avenue, where the windows filled with cheering supporters. It bumped through the shantytowns in Villa Francisca between the Modelo market and the Ozama River. All the way, Dominicans ran alongside. They held their thumbs up, giving Peña's sign. Milagros—who, like the PLD's Leonel Fernández, went by her first name—threw them white baseball caps printed with Peña's name in blue. The Jeep then turned north and wound through the *barrio* known as Mejoramiento Social (Social Improvement), up to 24th of April *barrio* (named for the failed 1965 coup to restore Juan Bosch to power), and across the Ozama to the rally site in Los Mina. Now a Santo Domingo suburb, the community was founded in 1677 by runaway slaves brought here from Mina, in Angola.

A sea of PRD supporters, dressed in white and carrying white flags, filled the streets. The waves of white drove home the irony of the campaign against their candidate's blackness. Under their caps, the faces of the crowd displayed all the colors and features of the Dominican spectrum: brown, olive, red; African, European; kinky hair, wavy, straight; round noses, angular ones; fat and thin lips, all smiling and singing.

In the middle of the throng, an albino waved his arms high, shouting louder than anyone. "We're going to end misery and the racial discrimination they are using against Peña because of his color," said Adalberto Rodríguez Valdez. Rodríguez has Negroid features but white freckled skin and kinky blond hair. Still, he was not wearing a cap to protect him from the harsh sun. An electrical technician, he was born in Manzanillo almost forty years ago. "Peña is a Dominican! My grandmother is black, but that doesn't mean she's not Dominican!" he cried out, so passionately that his pale eyebrows furrowed over his blue eyes.

Later in the week, in his final rallying speech, Balaguer urged voters to vote for "authentic Dominicans." Yet after all, this is a country where nearly 80 percent of the population is mulatto. So he boomed out over the heads of throngs of party faithful dressed in red that Dominicans are not racist. "Dominicans are so proud of themselves and their color that they prefer black and mixed-race women to white women. Without a doubt, it's because the mixed-race children remember better than white children when the sky is most beautiful, that hour in the tropics when the sky becomes tinted with the deepening of the late afternoon."

Adding military to literary bombast two days before the election, Balaguer replaced the police chief with General Enrique Pérez y Pérez, a hard-liner from his first twelve years in office, those days of terror in *los doce años*. Doors slammed shut, and taxi drivers parked their cars at home. The streets emptied, and Dominicans sat quietly during the last twenty-four hours before voting began.

At 4 a.m. election day, the lines were already long at the polling stations. Under the new system designed to prevent people from voting twice, women went to the ballot boxes in the morning, men in the afternoon. The sun was high by the time women's names were checked against rolls and voting was allowed to begin.

Dressed in royal blue, Virtudes Reyes Meza held her voter identification card in front of her and clamored, "I voted in the last elections.

Why am I having problems now?" She had appeared on the voter roll, the *padrón*, as ineligible to vote because her birth certificate was registered late before the last election.

Reyes had been caught in recent efforts to clean up the *padrón*. The Central Electoral Board had combed through voter lists and eliminated names of voters who were dead or duplicated. Many voters were declared ineligible. At a number of polling stations, Dominicans protested loudly when officials told them they were listed as dead.

"Just because she registered late doesn't mean she doesn't have the right to vote," said a visibly upset Maribel Gassó, the Reformistas' Vice Presidential candidate. Reyes had worked for Gassó's family, and she had traveled from La Romana, more than two hours to the east, to vote.

In the afternoon the men were drunk, even though bars were closed and stores prohibited by law from selling alcohol from the day before elections until after voting was completed. Waiting to vote at Mano-guayabo, a scruffy western working-class *barrio*, the men stood around ribbing one another about politics.

"He's Haitian!" said a man in a striped shirt, teasing the dark-skinned man in front of him. "He's going to vote for Peña!"

The others standing around laughed as the man tried to defend himself but was drowned out. "Oh, come on," the victim said. "My skin is dark, but I'm Dominican. My parents are Dominican."

A third man interjected, "So what? Even if his parents were Haitian, he'd be Dominican. If you're born here, you're Dominican. If you go somewhere else, what nationality are you? Your parents are Dominican, but you're born somewhere else. The ones who are born in the United States are Americans."

The crowd did not want to hear his reasonable words.

"You can tell who they are," Striped Shirt continued, "even if they're born here. It's easy to see who's Haitian. When you want to know, all you have to do is get him to pronounce *perejil*. The Haitians can't say it."

The line moved on.

Back in Santo Domingo, the media staked out Balaguer's house to see what he would do. Just before the polls closed, Balaguer's limousine drove to his voting station but carried him away again without his casting a vote. He had acknowledged the elections but was making it clear that he did not respect them. This was also a snub to his own party's candidate.

When the results came in, everything was as expected. For the first time ever, international observers declared the Dominican Republic's voting process clean and fair. Peña was shy of the 50 percent—plus one vote—that would have given him a first-round victory. Leonel, in second place, had catapulted himself into the leading spot for the second round. Peynado pulled in a humiliating 15 percent of the votes.

Political experts had seen through Balaguer's strategy months ahead. The old President knew better than to give Leonel an easy first-round victory; he wanted the new President to be indebted to him for votes he would deliver in the second round. Balaguer had split his support between the Reformistas and the PLD, giving Peynado just enough support to keep him from bolting the party and to prevent either Leonel or Peña from winning in the first round. Balaguer now had six more weeks before the country chose a new leader.

In those six weeks, Balaguer made one last move to control history. In a sweeping series of gestures that were no less dramatic for being anticipated, he approached his old rival Juan Bosch and worked to cement an alliance supporting Leonel. This silenced Balaguer's own party's disgraced candidate, Peynado, who had been threatening to join Peña in the second round. Then, in one triumphant rally, the two octogenarians Balaguer and Bosch joined hands with Leonel and raised their arms together, a trinity of power pledging that their new National Patriotic Front would keep the country safe from foreign incursions.

Less than a week before the second round, the mood is festive at the Manoguayabo cockfighting arena. Conversation is loose and jovial as the cockers slice the natural spurs from the roosters' legs and carefully replace them with artificial spurs wrapped around with clean white tape. The two cocks being prepared at the moment are white and red, the colors of Peña and Balaguer.

"Look," says one man between sips of Presidente, "the white is going to go against the red. Just like Tuesday!" He guffaws.

"No, no," says another. "White and purple. And the purple is going to win!"

"Red and purple are the same, don't you know?" says the first. "And white is clearly the better one."

"No way," says a third man. "The purple one has it."

By 11 p.m. on election night, June 30, the results were clear and held steady until the final count the next morning: Leonel Fernández 51.25 percent, José Francisco Peña Gómez 41.75 percent, a margin so wide that it was impossible to contest.

What happened the morning of July 1 had never occurred before in the Dominican Republic. Gone was the fear that used to hang over the mornings after elections. The streets around the bright purple-and-yellow PLD headquarters were jammed for blocks in all directions by cars and people celebrating. The ones who could not afford champagne shook up coconut soda and sprayed the sweet fizz over the dancing masses.

The tall white PRD headquarters were nearly deserted, the halls filled with defeat. But by the afternoon of July 1, Peña conceded graciously. Leonel, in his victory press conference, was conciliatory. Behind the moment of calm, however, the Great Man myth had not disappeared from Hispaniola. It was hard to forget that things had ended up as Balaguer intended. Balaguer's time was over, but he was not gone.

The winter after Leonel Fernández was inaugurated President, doctors told Peña that his pancreatic cancer, which had been in remission during the election campaign, had returned. He began a new round of treatments. But now that it was certain that he would never be President of his country, the longtime politician began giving up. Slowly, the cancer was winning. But the PRD was reluctant to admit that he would soon be gone. By the time midterm elections approached in May 1998, party members were fighting among themselves and could not even agree on a candidate for mayor of Santo Domingo. To save the party, Peña agreed to run, against the objections of his close friends, who said his health would not stand up to the rigors of the campaign. On the night of Sunday, May 10, 1998, Peña died. The day before, he had caught cold in a rainstorm while campaigning for mayor of Santo Domingo.

President Fernández declared three days of national mourning and ordered that José Francisco Peña Gómez be buried with honors normally accorded only to heads of state. But when the President attended Peña's wake, PRD supporters threw garbage at him, so he stayed away from the funeral.

Quietly, some intellectuals spoke of a curse that destroyed anyone who opposed Balaguer. They remembered Narcisazo; Orlando Martínez; Antonio Guzmán, who won the election in 1978, forcing Balaguer to step down, but committed suicide weeks before his term ended; and now Peña.

Months after he conceded power to his handpicked successor, Balaguer holds court, though not in his walled, elegant powder-blue mansion overlooking Máximo Gómez Avenue. Geographically, he is still at the center of power: next to the papal nuncio, kitty-corner from the U.S. consulate, and across the street from the National Library and theater complex. But Balaguer's quarters are in the simple back wing of the house, above the garage. The apartment has always been a retreat, and it contributes to the image of a man who has sacrificed his life for the good of his country. Now Balaguer has withdrawn even further inside.

He has been in deep, deep silence for months, rarely appearing in public except when photographers are persistent enough to snap a picture of his daily walk in Mirador Park or his visits to the graves of his family. Balaguer's aides had planned a spectacular concert for his ninetieth birthday, a month after he gave up office. But he stayed home.

His only public overture came in December, when he gave away his collection of books about Columbus to the Pedro Henríquez Ureña National University. It was as if he were symbolically casting aside his power: "This rough magic I here abjure," Prospero pledges. "I'll break my staff, bury it certain fathoms in the earth, and deeper than did ever plummet sound I'll drown my book." But is Balaguer giving up? Not necessarily. Inside his walled retreat, he maintains a parallel court and the constant threat that he will unleash his words once again to determine the future of the young President he helped elect.

Outside his mansion, Dominicans wait in front of the gates in the hopes of conveying their personal requests to the President himself. In the old days many more hopeful gathered here. Now they are few. The visitors who come are the small group of people he has always taken care of and the once-powerful generals and kleptocrats who hope he will protect them by exercising the moral power he still holds. Newspapers are filled with opinions on whether Balaguer should be forced to reveal the fate of Orlando Martínez. Rumors are swirling that arrests will be made and that they will reach as high as General Pérez y Pérez, now retired again after a brief stint the previous spring as police chief. Inside Balaguer's property, these men, once so powerful, come to make sure they still enjoy his protection. They are still under his shadow. Every so often, President Leonel Fernández comes to ask the advice and blessing of the old man. Except for those of Balaguer's old-time intimates, his visits are virtually the only contact between this house and the real world outside.

A car drops off a woman not much more than three feet tall. Her kinky hair is brushed severely back from her dark face. Chin held high, in a bright-blue dress and tiny black patent-leather platform sandals, she waves the gate open imperiously and marches in. A few minutes later, another tiny woman appears outside the walls. Dressed in cutoffs and a loose shirt, she has unruly hair and a broad smile. "*Hola*, Severina!" the soldiers standing around welcome her. She greets them, then starts sweeping with a broom cut short. Every day as she has for years, Severina sweeps clean the house and sidewalk. Balaguerologists say the two dwarfs bring the former President luck, following Spanish royal tradition.

Occasionally, the soldiers stationed in front of the house admit a supplicant to Balaguer's front yard looking for the chance to ask favors of his intimates passing in and out each day past a row of chairs under the brilliant red-orange flowers of a flamboyant tree. His face shaded by a baseball cap, a long-retired soldier is one such supplicant, hoping for a letter to help him get a visa for family members to join him in Venezuela. After a stint in the Dominican army he had moved to Caracas, where he now sells watches and other sundries. He begins to tell his story: about how, when his first marriage fell apart, he could no longer stand his native country. "My first wife was a foreigner. Spanish. Her name was Sol María Bravo Carpintero." *Bravo* means "angry." Baseball Cap's face contorts as he recalls how aptly she was named. "She fought with me so much that we couldn't live together anymore."

Intimates of Balaguer begin arriving, and Baseball Cap stops the story. With the long, skinny-legged stride that many older Dominican men have, he approaches them to ask for help. A stocky mulatto in dark glasses and carrying a 9mm pistol strides in. He is Balaguer's son, Saturnino, the only one of his many children whom Balaguer has acknowledged as his. The stocky man holds his weapon out to the side, like a comic-book gangster, as he shakes Baseball Cap's hand. Saturnino gives Baseball Cap the name of the aide who can fill his request. Then he heads down the driveway to Balaguer's waiting room in the garage.

Generals and kleptocrats sit in white plastic patio chairs along the wall of the garage. It is as if Balaguer is mocking these wealthy men by keeping them waiting there. Pérez y Pérez is there, complaining about the secondhand smoke from the plump young man smoking a cigarette next to him. In another corner, several soldiers in fatigues are watching Westerns. A stick-thin woman, heavily made-up and wearing an expensive-looking white flowing pantsuit, breezes in and greets everyone, then disappears into the mansion.

Balaguer's black Lincoln pulls in. This means it is time for the old man to come out for his daily walk. An elevator lowers him gently from his quarters upstairs, down into a brown-and-green carpeted hall that is icily air-conditioned. The old man moves slowly down the hall with a side-to-side wobbling motion, like a windup doll, but purposefully. Balaguer stretches his hand out to greet a visitor. Neither firm nor weak, his grasp is a simple acknowledgment. His voice, in greeting, is a monotone. Under his trademark black fedora is baby-fine white hair, full on the sides, thinned on top but not bald. His skin is almost translucent, except for several sun or liver spots. His beautiful gray suit fits well over his hunched shoulders and sunken chest.

Joaquín Balaguer is the very picture, in the late twentieth century, of the Prospero whose words he read as a teenager, of the wise duke who harnesses the power of an enslaved spirit and deformed monster toward the achievement of his goals. Prospero's epilogue to *The Tempest* could be Balaguer's own. The aged duke and magician has commanded Ariel to whip up a tempest that will ground a ship carrying his traitorous brother and his brother's men. Through the resulting chaos, Prospero rights the wrongs done to him. With the storm calmed, Prospero reconciled with his brother who betrayed him, his mantle passed on, he reviews his life and asks his audience to judge whether the violent means to which he resorted justify the end:

Now my charms are all o'erthrown,
And what strength I have 's mine own;
Which is most faint: now, 'tis true,
I must be here confin'd by you,
Or sent to Naples. Let me not,
Since I have my dukedom got
And pardon'd the deceiver, dwell
In this bare island by your spell;
But release me from my bands
With the help of your good hands,
Gentle breath of yours my sails
Must fill, or else my project fails,
Which was to please. Now I want
Spirits to enforce, art to enchant;
And my ending is despair,
Unless I be reliev'd by prayer,
Which pierces so that it assaults
Mercy itself and frees all faults.
As you from crimes would pardon'd be,
Let your indulgence set me free.

As Prospero's words echo, Balaguer's cheeks soften. He is nodding slightly as he smiles broadly. His monotone has broken, an invitation to laugh. Then his levity is gone. He is brisk, not unpleasant but moving on, refusing to judge himself. He climbs into his black Lincoln, which will take him to the park for his walk at noon, the hottest time of day, to defy the sun.

Across the Water

¡Oh Nueva York mi dolor descamado!
¡Oh Nueva York Humanidad sub-yacente!
Por ti entendí que la primera
definición de la Patria es la nostalgia.

Oh, New York, scales ripped from my pain!
Oh, New York, underlying Humanity!
You taught me that the first
meaning of Fatherland is nostalgia.

—*Sherezada "Chiqui" Vicioso*
from "Nueva York 1987"

On a hot July day in 1992, beginning at the humble home near the Lion's Club where Kiko García played basketball as a boy, mourners pushed slowly through the streets of San Francisco de Macorís. Hundreds of Dominicans, even many who didn't know him, joined the procession as it jammed the roads on the way past the homes of childhood friends who remembered him from the years before he left for New York, past the church, and on to the crumbling old municipal cemetery. The graves were jammed so tightly around the narrow walkways connecting them that many mourners had to wait in the small park outside the arched gateway. There was room enough for just a few family members, cemetery employees, and journalists to pick their way through the labyrinth of vaults and over the piles of rubble to the place where Kiko García would be laid to rest. The grave was not yet marked with his name and the dates of his life and death: July 6, 1968–July 3, 1992—not quite twenty-four years.

Under more common circumstances, a young man brought back dead from New York to San Francisco would be a tragedy only for the victim's family and friends. It would not move the residents of the rest of the city beyond a passing nod and certainly would not bring them out into the streets in protest. In 1991, 160 former residents of San Francisco had died in the United States, many of them in drug-related incidents.

Though it is only the third-largest city in the Dominican Republic, San Francisco has sent more emigrants to New York than any other Dominican hometown. It is as synonymous with young drug dealers as San Pedro de Macorís is with major-league shortstops; La Romana, with polo, golf, and international luminaries at the luxury resort, Casa de Campo; Baní, with the sweetest mangoes; Samaná, with whales mating in the bay each January; Puerto Plata, with sun-baked Germans and Canadians on package tours.

Hispaniola's contours blur and disappear on the horizon, far below the wings of the airplanes taking off from Santo Domingo and Puerto Plata, rising above the Atlantic to New York and Miami, thirteen flights a day on American Airlines. Far below, too far to see, tiny boats called *yolas* set out each week to cross the shark-infested Mona Passage from the tiny Dominican seaside town of Miches to Puerto Rico. All those boats and planes carry Dominicans who, when they arrive and try to set up new lives in the United States, replicate the struggle back home. But slowly, and from afar, they have been changing the nature of that struggle.

Most of the time, the drug dealers and loan sharks brought back to San Francisco in caskets died at the hands of equally or even more disreputable characters. (Like the man called "Negro," who went to collect a debt from a drug dealer, who asked how he wanted it repaid, *"En plomo o plata?"* Lead or silver? Negro didn't have a chance to answer: he got the former.) "Good riddance," was the town's typical response to criminals buried there. But this time was different. Dominicans marching at Kiko García's funeral pressed themselves on foreign journalists to tell their story. "They have brought back a lot of young men who died because they were involved in drug trafficking, and the people didn't flood into the streets like this. We knew they were drug traffickers, so we didn't protest their deaths," said Joel Zayaz, a tall curly-haired youth who had played basketball with García when the two were younger.

Despite his friends' insistence to the contrary, Kiko García had indeed been arrested for selling drugs to an undercover police officer in 1989 and later pleaded guilty. But unlike many of the other men buried in the San Francisco cemetery, he did not die from the bullet of another small-time loser. Kiko was killed by a policeman in Washington Heights, a New York City neighborhood where cops and Dominicans don't get along.

On the night of July 3, 1993, New York police officer Michael O'Keefe was driving down St. Nicholas Avenue with two other cops in a car unmarked but well known for its LOCAL MOTION bumper sticker. A tall Dominican, lurking in front of a reputed drug building at the corner of 162nd Street and Amsterdam Avenue, caught O'Keefe's eye. When he saw a bulge that looked suspiciously like a gun in the young man's waistband, the officer got out of the car to investigate, while his partners drove around the block. O'Keefe later recounted in grand-jury testimony that he entered the lobby of the building and saw Kiko, who tried to flee and then turned around to fight back, a .357 Magnum in hand. The Dominican and the cop struggled for the weapon. As O'Keefe's radio transmitted his frantic calls for help, two shots rang out, two bullets ripped through Kiko García.

In the hazy hours after the killing, word and rumor spread. The uncertain facts faded next to the gravity of a simple event: a Dominican youth had died at the hands of an American policeman. Kiko's family and friends remained adamant that the young Dominican had done nothing wrong. Two women in the building where Kiko died said they had seen O'Keefe shoot him in the back, and the community erupted in outrage. Months later, a grand jury cleared the officer of this charge. (It noted, among other evidence, that the women could not possibly have seen the struggle because their landing did not afford a view of the lobby.) But the important thing was that, in the minds of the people who lived there, what the women said happened could have happened.

The George Washington Bridge, linking New Jersey and Manhattan, is the principal feature of Washington Heights. Over thirty years, this largely Jewish and Irish neighborhood has become inhabited by Dominicans, who have informally renamed it Quisqueya Heights, after the Indian name for the land they left behind. In Quisqueya Heights, where the taxi drivers, nurses, doctors, and most business owners are Dominican, it is easy to live for decades without having to learn English. There's a money-transfer store on every corner for sending money back home to families on the island. The 1990 census counted 332,713 Dominicans in New York, and most of them lived in Washington Heights. But just a few years later sociologists and demographers guessed that twice that number was a more accurate assessment. Not even half of those Dominican immigrants have completed high school (a 1990 study showed that more than 60 percent of Dominicans over the age of twenty-five did not have their diplomas, a statistic much worse than that for Haitians, of whom only 35 percent in New York had failed to complete secondary education; some of this disparity may be attributable to the fact that Kreyol-speaking Haitians did not find it as easy to get by without English as did the Spanish-speaking immigrants and so learned English more quickly and thus adapted better). Washington Heights is one of New York City's poorest neighborhoods, with more than a third of the Dominican households below the poverty line and with unemployment at more than twice the rate of the rest of New York.

An undercurrent of desperation has always run through Washington Heights, at least ever since Dominicans began moving there after the civil war in their own country in 1965. And there was no escape valve when Kiko García faced off against Michael O'Keefe and lost. Hard-working Dominicans still lived in fear of violence because, in this most crowded of Manhattan's police precincts, with twice as many people per cop as the city average, crime and drugs were rampant in the neighborhood. But many Dominicans burned with anger at what they believed was the department's readiness to write off all Dominicans as drug dealers.

The officer fired his gun at a particularly explosive time, just as hopes for change had begun to rise: nine months earlier, Washington Heights had elected Guillermo Linares, the first Dominican-American member of the City Council, in a special election held to fill the newly created District Ten seat, which had been drawn to represent the growing population there. It was hoped that with time the Dominicans' new political voice could have eased tension. But in July 1992 the sense of possibility made the situation at hand worse, not better; reality fell even further short of the Dominicans' hopeful dreams.

Dominicans have sent their young men north for a long time. The merengue star Juan Luis Guerra sings, in his hit "Visa para un Sueño" (Visa for a Dream), of lines of people waiting at five in the morning in front of the American consulate hoping for a visa that would allow them to go to New York and look for a new life. By 1992 nearly a million Dominicans, one in eight, lived in the United States, and the number was growing quickly. By 1994, two years after the riots, the U.S. Immigration and Naturalization Service would count 51,047 legal Dominican immigrants entering the United States in one year alone; though that represented a peak, the flow continued to be steady, at around 40,000 legally admitted during each of the next few years, with at least as many illegal immigrants making it north as well.

The more Dominicans went abroad, the louder the calls sounded from home for them to keep sending money. By 1996 they would be wiring a billion dollars back to their country each year. On their frequent trips back and forth, they carried televisions, VCRs, mountains of diapers, clothes, tennis shoes, cosmetics in piles of King Kong–sized suitcases—either bought in the little stores lining Manhattan's St. Nicholas Avenue or carried empty from the island and lugged back full. The wealthier Dominicans were in Miami, whose tropical heat and Latin culture reminded them of the best things at home. A large community mushroomed in Boston and the outlying areas of Lawrence and Lynn, and there were others in Rhode Island. But far and away the most emigrants settled in New York, particularly in Washington Heights and the South Bronx.

There was even a name for them. The phrase *Dominican Yorks* first described all Dominicans who lived abroad. But with the narcotics boom of the 1980s, when the number of young Dominican men dealing drugs in New York ballooned, *Dominican York* took on a selective, pejorative meaning: it alluded only to those young drug dealers with their neon license-plate trim and gold-plated hubcaps on their fancy new BMWs, their thick gold chains (*cadenuces*, laden with chains, was another name for them), and their gaudy houses built with fast-won new riches. The working-class Dominicans, who often held down two or three jobs to make ends meet, sent money home bit by bit, and, if they were lucky, made it home for the Christmas trip they saved for all year, were the *dominicanos ausentes*, the absent Dominicans, or *los que viven fuera*, those who live abroad. Though the hardworking absent Dominicans made up the majority of the community in New York, the Dominican Yorks were the ones who caught public attention.

In the middle of the long, hot summer, mourners headed out of Kiko's wake in Washington Heights chanting: "Who Killed Kiko García? Police, Assassins." Somebody threw a bottle, someone else followed suit; broken glass sprayed everywhere. Whiffs of tear gas grew into clouds that mixed with the sharp smell of burning tires. Riots erupted over seventy square blocks. Flames rose from more than two hundred fires: a police van, 120 cars, and 14 blazing buildings. Police arrested 139 people for disorderly conduct and assault. Officials counted 90 people injured, including 74 policemen. This storm of violence left behind a vacuum of stunned disbelief.

A week after the riots, in the quiet following Kiko García's funeral, his mother, Regina, sat in her living room in her hometown, San Francisco de Macorís. Her husband, Danilo, had died fifteen years earlier, before he could finish building their five-room house, which has never been painted. "If Kiko had been a drug trafficker, we wouldn't be living like this," Regina García sobbed. If he'd been a successful drug dealer, he would have built a confection of a house, one with boldly painted superfluous Deco detail and a satellite dish, like so many others around San Francisco de Macorís. If he'd been wealthy, he certainly wouldn't have had to work as a Manhattan grocery-store clerk.

Nor would Regina have had to go back to her cramped New York apartment and resume her job assembling car parts in a Hackensack, New Jersey, factory. Regina García raised her nine children alone, and in 1987 she moved to New York. A year later, Kiko joined her. "When Kiko came to New York, he said nothing bad would ever happen to him because he wasn't involved in any trouble," Regina said between the sobs shaking her whole body and leaving her gasping for breath. Kiko's sons —Henry, six years old, and Amilca, seven—buried their faces in her knees and wept.

In Santo Domingo the day after Kiko's funeral, another family mourned a son who died in New York. During the riots, Dagoberto Pichardo fell to his death from the seventh floor of a building as police pursued him because they believed he was throwing rocks from the roof. His dream, too, was over. The Pichardo family left their home in San

Francisco de Macorís to set up a shoe store in Santo Domingo twelve years earlier; Dagoberto married his high-school sweetheart, Christian Lantigua, in 1987, and the young couple decided it would be best for him to go to New York to earn enough money to send to his parents and for her to continue her architectural studies. Two days after their daughter, Laura, was born that same year, Dagoberto left for New York. A year later, his older brother, Luis Manuel, joined him. "I don't want anyone to confuse us with Dominican Yorks or anything like that," said Luis Manuel. Bit by bit, Christian bought the materials to build a house with the money Dagoberto sent home from his flower-shop job in New York. As she and their two children pressed handprints into the cement of his fresh grave on Friday, July 10, 1992, the house, five years after they began imagining it, was still nothing but a foundation and walls. Two hundred friends and family watched and sobbed.

The Spanish word *cementerio* reflects, better than does the English word for cemetery, the fact that the resting place for the dead is filled with cement. In San Francisco de Macorís, cement is poured at a dizzying speed to build mansions, some paid for with drug money. It is poured slowly to raise modest homes like Regina García's and Christian Lantigua's, paid for with factory and delivery wages painstakingly set aside. Cement quietly covers the graves of Kiko García, Dagoberto Pichardo, and the others who came back in coffins—sometimes a steady stream, one after the other, sometimes a handful each month. Unfinished houses, sealed graves.

President Balaguer told reporters that Dominican officials in the United States "have obtained the assurances of American authorities and the mayor of New York that they will carry out an exhaustive and impartial investigation and, if it uncovers anything, they will apply the appropriate punishment to those responsible. The facts are lamentable, but responsibility for them lies not with the entire Dominican colony but with a very small part of that group." Spaced between these official words was a silence, a failure to acknowledge the two dead young men, a distance deliberately maintained between the Dominican government on the island and the Dominicans in New York. Certainly, Balaguer must have considered the unpleasant facts of the situation a threat to his own image as well as to that of the Dominican Republic. But it is doubtful that he could have imagined the extent to which what happened in Washington

Heights accelerated a process cutting to the heart of the conditions that had fed conflict on Hispaniola.

For a long time, Dominicans had defined themselves in terms of other places: indebted to Spain for a cultural heritage, and definitely *not* Haitian. When Dominicans started arriving in the United States, however, they were forced to confront a different conception of themselves. Immigrants of mixed-race descent, who had been considered white or light-skinned back home, now discovered that in the United States they were "black" and that many of their new neighbors, whose eyes had not learned to distinguish shades of color, might easily mistake the darkest of them for Haitians. At the same time, they were lumped into a cultural mix of Hispanics, whatever that was: they certainly did not consider themselves to have much beyond language (and hardly even that, considering how different their rapid Caribbean Spanish was from other Latin American versions of the tongue) in common with the Mexican flower vendors or the Peruvian and Ecuadorian trinket vendors, and they had long resented the way Cubans and Puerto Ricans seemed to look down their noses at Hispaniola.

Their absence strengthened their longing for the place and people they had left behind and thus heightened their consciousness of what it meant to be Dominican, as a concept understood independently, not in relation to Spain or Haiti. They would not forget Mother's *sancocho*, prayers to the Virgencita, the red-orange flowers of the flamboyant tree, the season to pick *nísperos*, the gritty voices of the old men performing *perico ripiao* music, the taste of *habichuela con dulce* at Lent, the way to drink beer properly (a half degree below freezing and the bottle covered in gray "ash"), the color of the sunrise over the Caribbean, the *campesino* calling his goat: *Chivo! Chivo!* This awareness was germinating amid the pervasive cultural and commercial force that was the U.S.A., an influence so strong that it made holding on to true Dominican traits even more urgent, lest the homeland disappear from their collective memories.

In turn, the growing presence of Dominicans, especially their formation of a cultural island of their own within New York City, represented a change in the nature of immigration to the United States. They and other recent West Indian and Latin American immigrants were different from the Europeans who had crossed the ocean a century earlier: most of these newcomers were not white, and they came by airplane on flights that lasted just a few hours instead of by slow transatlantic sea voyages. Unlike the immigrants of the Industrial Revolution, who looked back as little as possible, these groups kept up with what was going on at home by phone and occasional trips back. And, most important of all, the Dominicans and their contemporaries were putting their energies not into blending into their new homeland but toward replicating what they had left behind.

This meant that at first they did little to improve their lot in the urban ghettos into which they had moved. They were too busy earning money to invest time in a place where they regarded themselves as temporary residents, just passing through until they had enough to go back home. Certainly, the small businesses the Dominicans started and even the meager wages they earned injected life into previously abandoned urban areas. (The journalist Joel Millman has described this process convincingly in *The Other Americans: How Immigrants Renew Our Country, Our Economy, and Our Values*.) But these immigrants were more concerned with life elsewhere and felt they could do little as their neighborhoods grew more crowded and crime—much of it related to drug turf wars—grew worse: in 1992 forty-seven New York owners and employees of corner stores, *bodegas*, were killed by robbers.

Besides, what could they have done? Many of them did not speak English, much less hold citizenship: it took time before recourse to the American civic structure became a realistic option; the creation of District Ten in 1991 had been an important victory, as had efforts in the 1980s to get the school district to respond to the needs of the new immigrants, but there was still a long, long way to go. What is more, participating in American politics required mastering a new set of rules, for the Great Man model of leadership was of little use in the United States. The place was too big for any one leader, especially when becoming successful meant taking on a new language and culture. Those were the reasons the Dominicans at first failed to confront some of the conditions that led to Kiko Garcia's death and its violent aftermath. But what happened made it impossible for them to be silent any longer. It took a social explosion, but after so many years of being drowned out by the Great

Man myth, the Dominicans who left, the absent ones, would slowly find a voice.

In a photo Jacob Riis took in 1888, men stand along a back alley known as the most violent of Manhattan's immigrant slums: "Bandits' Roost," a name not inappropriately evoking the territory of a fierce old cock. One tough, leaning against a post that makes him appear as if he is holding a shotgun, peers out suspiciously from below the brim of his hat. The other residents line the street defiantly, glaring from their windows at the photographer, planted firmly atop a porch railing, feet firm atop a staircase. This is *our* street, they seem to say. In the aged photo, rows of laundry, a vain effort to preserve cleanliness in the soot-filled tenement alleys, flutter above their heads.

In Riis's *How the Other Half Lives*, the turn-of-the-century work of photos and text documenting New York tenement life, the immigrant community of lower Manhattan resembled in many ways that of the Dominican world that now exists at the other end of the island in Washington Heights: it was one of hard, hard work against a background of poverty and neglect. The major difference was that, unlike the way the Dominicans have gathered in one place, the immigrants of a century ago were thrown together. In one of the ghettos Riis studied, where the population was roughly half Irish, half Italian, windows were barred in iron and policemen patrolled the streets warily. The Irish blamed the police presence on two troublemaking German families, while the Chinese blamed the Irish: "A Chinaman whom I questioned as he hurried past the iron gate of the alley, put the matter in a different light. 'Lem Ilish velly bad,' he said," Riis wrote. Others, no doubt, blamed the Italians, in an old but ongoing story: the next-least-fortunate always find a group worse off than themselves, the Irish against the Germans against the Italians against the Chinese during the Industrial Revolution; the Dominicans against the Haitians on Hispaniola; the Germans against the Turks in Europe; the Serbs and Croats hating each other in Bosnia.

But differences can dissipate, and did so in the United States as the twentieth century progressed and the new citizens born there focused on pursuing the American Dream. The (by and large white) European immigrants who had arrived during the Industrial Revolution learned English. Their descendants intermarried, creating new generations of

Americans freed from—and largely indifferent to—the struggles of their parents' homelands. Culture became a pastime taught in schools or preserved in restaurant decor. The past receded.

Assimilation in the middle part of the twentieth century was made easier, of course, by laws that limited the arrival of new immigrants, particularly those from Southern Europe. In 1924 the National Origins Act established quotas on new arrivals in such a way as sharply to limit growth in the population of Slavs, Jews, and Italians, while giving more flexible treatment to Northern and Western European immigrants. The result of the law was to cut down dramatically on immigration for the next four decades, through the rest of the booming 1920s into the Great Depression, past the establishment in 1935 of Social Security and the subsequent widening of the United States' safety net of government-provided social services. As World War II approached, it was this national origins–based, closed-door policy toward immigrants that tied President Roosevelt's hands as he tried to seek ways to help Jews escape Europe.

Things did not change substantially until the civil rights movement began to put pressure on domestic attitudes about discrimination. American policy toward immigrants finally loosened in 1965, with the passage of the Hart-Celler Immigration Reform Act and its resulting loosening of rules in order to promote family unification. Though the supporters of the law had conceived it with Eastern European refugees and their families in mind, the immigrants who began arriving in the late 1960s thanks to Hart-Celler, and kept coming over the next three decades, were something else altogether. There were fewer of them relative to the rest of the population than during previous waves—foreign-born residents made up around 9 percent of the population by the mid-1990s compared to more than 13 percent from 1860 to 1930—but these new immigrants were more visible: they looked and acted different. They were far more likely to have dark skin and less likely to pick up English and assimilate quickly than their predecessors of a century before. Nor was assimilating a clear priority: instead of Americanizing as fast as they could, the new groups, including Dominicans, created their own small islands within the United States; while this strategy provided a strong support network for new arrivals and kept the old country alive, it also kept them apart from the residents of their new home and thus made it harder for them to push for what they wanted. They remained as alienated from mainstream America as the old tenement groups had been in Jacob Riis's time. Still, they were divided over how long they wanted to remain that way.

To dream a new life in a strange cold land requires a certain innocence. For most Dominicans, that innocence soon disappears in a place like Washington Heights or the South Bronx. Another funeral, four months after the Washington Heights riot, took place on a gray night in late November as the first hard cold of 1992 was gripping New York. A photographer had been murdered in a robbery gone bad, his life and death yet another snapshot of the frustrations of the city's hardworking Dominicans.

José Cuevas grew up in a poor *barrio* of Santo Domingo, where he, his five brothers, two sisters, mother, and father all lived on his father's scant policeman's salary. "At dinner time he would take his plate outside and give his food to poor people," recalled Freddy Graciano, a childhood friend who, like Cuevas, moved to Washington Heights. Cuevas didn't lose his spirit. He left Santo Domingo in 1973 and took a string of jobs in New York. Hoping to open his own business one day, he saved his money over the years, earned from jobs in factories, at the Dominican consulate, in a laundry, and shooting photos for the Dominican newspaper *Listín USA*. Each week, he documented Dominican athletes on community baseball teams. He was all over not just Washington Heights but Manhattan, on assignment to City Hall, the United Nations. (He chuckled over the photograph he took of Cuba's Ambassador Ricardo Alarcón puffing on a cigar in a United Nations lounge.)

The afternoon he died, Cuevas left his newspaper job early to sign the lease on a small laundry he planned to open with his partner. As the two men returned to Cuevas's apartment building at 172nd Street near Broadway, his partner walked ahead up the lobby stairs and turned around when he noticed Cuevas had fallen behind. Cuevas was talking to two men who, before his companion could react, shot Cuevas in the chest, took twenty dollars from the dying man's pocket, and fled.

On the night of the funeral, a wreath of yellow and white flowers lay in the lobby where Cuevas died. Six candles burned in honor of St. Anthony, restorer of things lost and patron of the poor and needy. How much had changed since Kiko García died! This time, the Dominican community pulled together instead of tearing itself apart with rage, as it had done in the summer. So many people crowded into McGonnell Funeral Home that the staff had to close the doors three times to let the mourners move through in shifts.

Guillermo Linares, the mild-mannered Dominican educator working on his Ph.D. at City University who is also the community's representative on the City Council, came to McGonnell's. The Thirty-fourth Precinct commander, Nicholas Estavillo, came to the funeral, too; he had won city support for splitting his precinct in two to take some of the strain off the overcrowded police facilities. Even Mayor David Dinkins appeared, looking properly somber as Miguelina Cuevas cried out: "I want justice for my husband!" Politicians, police, and activists pledged their support for solving the crime.

Almost a year later, Linares ran for reelection for a full term (he had first won in a special election), and Mayor Dinkins was facing a bruising race against Rudolph Giuliani, the former prosecutor who took a strong "tough on crime" stance. And right in the middle of the campaign, a second Dominican firestorm exploded when police tightened their enforcement of parking rules in a long-controversial city ticketing program and towed double-parked cars blocking a fire lane in Washington Heights. A hundred people gathered on Friday night, October 8, along 175th Street, to protest. During a long and angry evening, police arrested five people for obstruction and assault. As the crowd was breaking up, Pedro José Gil, a twenty-two-year-old Dominican immigrant, looked down from the roof of his six-story tenement building over the police cars about to leave. Angrily, he heaved a thirty-pound bucket of spackling compound over the lip of the roof; the bucket struck Officer John Williamson, twenty-five years old, in the head, and he died instantly.

Williamson left behind a grieving fiancée and many outraged colleagues. Gil fled to Santo Domingo, where relatives persuaded him to return to New York, and he was arrested on charges of second-degree murder.

By itself, towing cars from a fire zone hardly justifies an outpouring of indignation, much less one that leads to a death. But in a community where life is defined in terms of Us versus Them, it doesn't take much for a minor disagreement with the police to escalate. And for the rest of the city, too, the towing issue was blown far out of proportion. Dominican Yorks in Manhattan and Haitian thugs in Port-au-Prince were side by side on the top of the front page of the October 12, 1993, *New York Times*: "Haitians Block Landing of U.S. Forces: Envoys Flee Port as Their Cars Are Struck." "SUSPECT ARRESTED IN BUCKET SLAYING OF POLICE OFFICER—POLITICAL STORM PERSISTS—DINKINS ADMINISTRATION SAYS ITS TOWING POLICY WILL CONTINUE—GIULIANI STILL CRITICAL."

The mayoral candidates, of course, took sides: the incumbent Dinkins, the conciliator, versus the challenger Giuliani, the enforcer. Since neighbors had tipped off the police to Gil's identity, Mayor Dinkins thanked the Dominican community for their "hard work, their caring and their compassion." But Giuliani nonetheless hammered him, using the Dominicans as an example of how Dinkins had let "drug dealers" and "urban terrorists" take over upper Manhattan. ("Dominican" was unsaid but understood.) Dominicans, just like Haitians working in Dominican cane fields, measured up as less than human.

Washington Heights might as well have been another country trying to invade Manhattan. In reality, it is another country. The exodus from Santo Domingo to New York, from one island to another, was no escape. It merely moved the ring in which Dominicans lived. And because many of the Dominicans who lived in Washington Heights were reluctant (or unable) to conceive of themselves as part of the bigger city instead of as tied to a land far away, they could do little to combat the false image of themselves as a group dominated by drug dealers and hooligans: an easy target for scapegoat-hungry politicians.

On November 4, Giuliani won the race for mayor.

Quietly, Linares was reelected.

The walls of the New York City councilman's office are covered with photos of him with Bill Clinton, Mario Cuomo, and other Democratic Party heavyweights. There is also a certificate signed by President Joaquín Balaguer declaring Guillermo Linares a *caballero*, a gentleman of the highest order. The question of how to blend in, and with whom, is documented there behind picture frames.

From the time of Linares's first City Council campaign in 1991, he had maintained a strong focus back home: his campaign materials included a letter from his mother on the island, in the little town of Cabrera. And he made frequent trips back to the island for fund-raising and rallies (just as politicians from Santo Domingo soon found that such trips to New York for elections back home were a political necessity). But he was firmly rooted in the United States nonetheless. A nonprofit community-development group he helped found in New York City celebrated Dominican history and culture, but Linares made clear that looking back should not prevent Dominican-Americans from recognizing that they had a new home: "It was all in helping create pride in our heritage, in our own origin, but it was always in the spirit of elevating and preparing us for the struggle here."

Guillermo Linares's parents had fled to New York in 1965 amid the turmoil that followed the end of Trujillo's dictatorship, painfully recognizing that the income from their small farm in the north coast town of Cabrera could not provide for the education of their seven children. When they brought their oldest son, Guillermo, to New York, they expected that the fifteen-year-old boy would stay only for a while.

"I never thought of going back until I was in my college years," Linares said. "Up until that point, I was struggling to learn English, I was struggling to cope in school, and I was working always to help the family. The day after I arrived here, I had a job in a grocery store." (After a few years at the job, robbers held up the grocery and pointed a shotgun at his head; he escaped being shot but quit the job to work in a supermarket.) Through his high school years, the shy student felt disconnected from his childhood on the family's Dominican farm. "The environment that received me here did not have ways of acknowledging those experiences," Linares said. "My name was no longer Guillermo. It was Willy."

In college he studied Latin American history and learned about the connections between his adopted country and the Dominican Republic. "I began to realize that my years growing up on a farm were very relevant to me, to a large part of my life here, that my family and their struggle were all very relevant. It took me five years to rescue my name." Newly armed with a past as well as a present, he had to decide who he wanted to be. Two years into college, he followed his parents' urging to become an American citizen. With the money he earned driving a taxi for five years, he put himself through the rest of college and became a teacher. "I realized that I was in the United States not by accident, that there was a context that connected the United States and the Dominican Republic and there was an economic context of interest in both places. It is here we need to organize, here we need to participate, here that our children are growing up: *here*. Here that we need to fight for their education, the access, and the respect, because we do make a contribution."

As a teacher, Linares became an activist pushing for the needs of Dominican students, who were neglected even though they had rapidly become the largest ethnic group in the Washington Heights schools. From the start, getting people to focus on life in the United States had been the biggest obstacle to his efforts; the fact that few were citizens meant American politicians had no reason to listen to them. The way Linares and other Dominican community leaders had finally pulled their community together was through the school district, where parents could vote for school board members even though they did not have the right to vote in regular elections. Through the 1980s, Dominican activists convinced the Washington Heights school district to offer bilingual education and other services to help immigrants, to build new schools and add teachers to meet the rapidly growing student population. Dominicans got themselves elected to the school board in growing numbers and pushed for the inclusion of Dominican cultural icons in education: one school was named after Salomé Ureña, the grande dame of Dominican poetry. Linares eventually became school board president and used that post to leap to citywide politics.

Meanwhile, the schools in Washington Heights were filling with Dominican role models. In 1994, Euclid Mejía (whose Dominican father had named him for the mathematician in hopes that the name would be an omen for his intellectual growth) became the first Dominican principal of a New York high school, at one of the city's largest and most troubled institutions, George Washington High School, where three-quarters of the students were Dominican.

Linares's connections back home had given him political weight as the Dominican community joined together to elect one of its own, marking a major milestone. But that kind of rallying behind the flag of the old country had a dark side to it as well: the same dark side Balaguer and Trujillo before him had exploited in their nationalist rhetoric. And it would come back to haunt Linares in the wake of a battle over who has the right to do business in Washington Heights and neighboring Harlem.

The issue was a proposal by the New Jersey corporation Pathmark to build a giant supermarket on a vacant lot in East Harlem, just east of Washington Heights. Dominican owners of small supermarkets and corner *bodegas* all lined up against the project. To be sure, Pathmark was an economic threat: fifty-three thousand square feet of supermarket competing with two hundred small merchants (and the huge distributors who supplied them but who went unmentioned because it contradicted the argument that the little guys would be hurt). The giant corporation also stood to receive $7 million worth of tax credits, subsidies, and interest abatements; the *bodegueros* argued that they had paid high interest rates for loans to set up their tiny stores in a crime-ridden neighborhood where they received no special help from the city.

But killing the proposal would deny the community jobs and lower prices. It would also send a signal to other investors that they would have trouble bringing their business to the neighborhood. The majority of people in East Harlem and Washington Heights stood to benefit. To soften the impact of the Pathmark project on the Dominican and Puerto Rican supermarket owners in the neighborhood, Linares pushed a program creating a fund to provide loans and help refinance local merchants and to develop an eight-thousand-square-foot shopping center for local store owners. But that did not appease the Dominican store owners.

When Linares voted to approve Pathmark, they plastered storefronts and light posts in Washington Heights with flyers reading: *"Linares TRAIDOR!"* Linares, Traitor. In pressing their point, the *bodega* owners—and the politicians who courted them—relied on the old tactic that Balaguer, and Trujillo before him, had used successfully for so many decades. They portrayed the Pathmark debate not as being over what was best for the community or the Dominicans who lived in it but on cultural and nationalistic terms as an issue of who was a true Dominican (absurd considering Linares's background). The same people who had rallied behind him in 1991 were now attacking Linares for "not being Dominican enough." No matter that he defeated another Dominican in his first primary race. Never mind that his experience and dilemma were quintessentially Dominican. The charge "not Dominican enough" had nothing to do with that.

The insults stung. "My loyalty is to this country, but that is not to be interpreted as a denial of my country of origin," Linares said two years after the battle, choosing his words carefully but letting his pain show through. "This is the country of my children, and this is the country that opened its arms to me and gave me the opportunity to get to where I have come."

Things were very different in New York after the crisis in 1965, when U.S. immigration laws changed and it became easier for Dominicans to emigrate to the States. (Even before the Hart-Celler Act and the Dominican civil war, U.S. officials in Santo Domingo had already begun making it easier for Dominicans to get visas, under the logic that migration would serve as a political safety valve during a particularly turbulent period; from 1961 to 1963 the number of visas granted to Dominicans quintupled, from under two thousand to nearly ten thousand.) One Dominican who came in shortly after the civil war, José Fernández, became an important player in the Dominican political scene in New York City as well as in Santo Domingo. Unlike Guillermo Linares, who had focused his efforts in the New York political arena, Fernández remained active primarily in the Dominican political system. His political niche was extremely unusual but appropriate to the strange status of the Dominicans who lived permanently between two worlds: Fernández won office and a mandate to represent Santiago Province—even though he made his home in New York—and the absent Dominicans in the Dominican Congress.

More than three decades after he had come to Manhattan, José Fernández reminisced as he sat at a broad table in the Dominican Liberation Party (PLD) office, at 158th Street and Amsterdam, three flights up a staircase smelling of a mix of ammonia and fried chicken so persistent that the odors seemed to have embedded themselves in the paint. It was easy to tell which floor the PLD was on because the door had been painted the party color, purple. Inside, the television constantly played videos from Santo Domingo of giant rallies with swaths of people clad in purple, speeches by the candidate, ads urging people to vote. The walls were covered with news clippings and giant portraits of Leonel Fernández and Juan Bosch.

José Fernández (who is not related to Leonel) had always been a supporter of Juan Bosch, and at the time he left Santo Domingo he was active in the Dominican Revolutionary Party (PRD), which at the time was Bosch's brainchild; he left the PRD when Bosch did in 1973 to create the new Dominican Liberation Party. When José Fernández arrived in New York, he remained an active ally of Juan Bosch, though it was hard to give as much time to politics as he would have liked. He found a job stitching leather coats and worked his way up to foreman at the coat factory. He went back to school, taking courses at Lehman College and a semester of English at Columbia University, but his English never quite got to where he wanted it. He gave most of his attention, in any case, to his home country, where his parents still lived. His father died in 1987, and his mother stayed in Santiago and refused to come to the United States to visit. Only one of his three brothers came to the States, and then only for surgery that he did not survive.

Going back and forth between New York and Santo Domingo for twenty-one years, politicking all the time, never quite saving enough money to go home for good, Fernández finally found an answer to his political yearnings. In 1993, as the Dominican Republic geared up for the 1994 election, the PLD decided that the best way to convince Dominicans abroad of its attentiveness to their concerns was to elect one of them to the Dominican legislature. So the leaders of the more than seven hundred PLD members in the United States and Canada (from the five boroughs of New York City, New Jersey, Providence, the Boston area, Philadelphia, Montreal) met to choose one absent Dominican to run for office representing them in Santo Domingo. Fernández won this spot, but he had to win a second nomination from Santiago: he took a leave of absence from his job so he could campaign back home. His political work was a success, and he won the seat.

The victory was bittersweet, however. Fernández had to commit to spending half the year away from his wife and children—Vladimir in high school, José in junior high, and Maciel in fourth grade—in New York. "Many times, in the airplane, I realize that I am part of two societies, that both have things that pain me and that I love. The saddest moment is when I have to leave the States, get on a plane, leave behind my wife and three children, and go where duty calls, because I was elected to a function, a responsibility I care for a lot," he said. "But my heart stays here in New York. When I am there, by phone I always have to call at three or three-thirty in the afternoon to see how the day was at school, if my children are doing their homework."

In Santo Domingo, José Fernández struggled against the suspicion and resentment that came from the same mentality that had greeted news of the Washington Heights riots in 1992. Dominicans regarded the emigrants, even the ones who sent back money, with deep skepticism. "When I speak of the Dominicans abroad, it's as if I am speaking of foreigners," Fernández said. "My fellow citizens in the Dominican Republic don't realize I'm speaking about people who are just as Dominican as they. The Dominicans back in the country think I am referring to another society." Before long, he will be. "Our children, born here, are Americans; their culture and mannerisms are North American."

Like José Fernández, many other absent Dominicans were realizing that their own children would never share their feelings about their homeland. This was made even more painful by the fact that they knew they were watching the land of their childhood slip away from them: they faced the same resentment and envy that color their homeland's attitudes to its diaspora. But that did not prevent them from trying to hold on.

"Even though we live here, we invest back there," said Froilán Barinas, a dentist in Washington Heights and a member of a small group of professionals who belong to the PLD in New York and helped raise $250,000 for the 1996 Presidential campaign. "We have many people who work hard and contribute back home." But they all knew that back in Santo Domingo, lawyers tried to charge them five times as much as they charged those who had never left; doctors charged double. Dr. Barinas felt cold stares of distrust from Dominicans at home when they learned where he lived, so he did his best not to reveal it. "When I go back, I try not to stand out as a Dominican living in New York. I take off my ring and wristwatch."

Héctor Cabrera, another PLD man in New York, studied diligently for his master's in marketing, became a middle manager at Coca-Cola in New York, and after six years in the United States achieved financial success—but it was modest compared to that of the drug dealers with their fancy new cars. "I'm not the model. I'm only an example of failure," he remarked incredulously.

If the experiences of the PLD faithful were sad, then those of the devotees of the Dominican Revolutionary Party (PRD) were even more so, for they threw their lives into trying to elect a candidate who could never be allowed to win back home. In March 1996, as the last snowfall of the winter began, hundreds of Dominicans crammed into the Washington Heights headquarters of the PRD to see José Francisco Peña Gómez. New York and Miami are regular stops on any Dominican politician's campaign trail, to raise money and to convince Dominicans to call their families back home to make voting recommendations. Rafael "Fiquito" Vásquez, who was running the PRD in New York, watched hundreds of taxi drivers, schoolteachers, social workers, supermarket owners, and small businessmen line up to wait for the candidate. "Peña himself has estimated that half his campaign money came from New York," he said.

The main meeting room filled quickly, and organizers finally opened the reserved seats to the crowd. When it seemed no one else could fit in, they darkened the room and played a video of a rally two days earlier in Santo Domingo. The Caribbean sun threw the images into sharp relief, and the waiting crowd cheered and chanted as the speakers blasted Joaquín Balaguer for forcing them to flee to New York in order to make enough money just to get by. By the time Peña arrived, the audience was no longer inside a run-down building under a soggy snowstorm at 176th Street and Wadsworth Avenue but 1,543 miles away, amid a crowd of sun-drunk spectators on the streets of Santo Domingo.

New York turned into a crucial campaign ground for the election in Santo Domingo. Ubiquitous bumper stickers (the two parties estimated that they printed fifty thousand between them) decorated gypsy cabs in Washington Heights and the South Bronx—white with blue letters for Peña, purple and yellow for Leonel. Purple-robed stuffed lions were displayed in car seats and windows, and the PLD even rented a giant balloon one weekend.

Between the May 16 first round and the June 30 final round, the rallies in the United States took on added urgency. Peña and Leonel arranged final hurried visits north to raise money. In mid-June, Peña supporters again jammed into the Wadsworth headquarters to see their candidate. One, Dinorah Hilario, sat in the outer office helping to co-ordinate the throngs of volunteers. Though her college degree was in accounting, she was working as a home-care nurse in Queens, where she has mostly lived for the seven years since she left the Dominican Re-public. In two weeks she was due to take her U.S. citizenship exam, and the next day she would return to Santo Domingo to help monitor voting for the PRD.

She hadn't yet had time to get a new voting card in her hometown, Nagua, so she couldn't vote herself; but as soon as she had citizenship papers, she would register as a Democratic voter. Thanks to a change Peña had forced through in the 1994 revision of the Dominican consti-tution, Dominicans like her, naturalized in the United States, didn't lose their right to vote in the Dominican Republic. "We have to take part in politics here in New York," she explained. "If we don't take care of ourselves, we'll fail because of the same problems that sent us here in the first place." Dominicans in New York spoke often of those problems, and the reference had become a catchall phrase for poverty, reliance on a paternalistic government rather than on political institutions that gave everyone a voice, failure to provide education and health services; the list went on and on as a blueprint of the developing world.

Nearby, Rosa Pérez was another PRD volunteer helping with ar-rangements for the arrival of the candidate. Vice president of the Bronx Dominican Social Democratic Women's Federation, she also worked with the Association of Dominicans Helping Their Provinces, sending wheelchairs, food, medical supplies, whatever they could, back home. "One grain of sand at a time, we send things home to help our country," said Rosa Pérez. "Far and away most of us think: Tomorrow I'm going home. But then ten years go by, and we're still here." She herself spoke no English, though she had lived in New York for a decade, ever since she left San Cristóbal, the town where Trujillo was born. But she didn't need English for her hair salon and clothes businesses in Washington Heights, where everyone was in the same situation.

At the last minute, word came that Peña would not appear. Tri-umphantly, the party hacks whispered that he was meeting with Jacinto Peynado, the defeated and disgruntled candidate of Balaguer's Reformista Party, and that his plan was to cement a last-minute alliance against

Leonel. (The meeting happened, but the alliance never came to pass.) The party faithful in New York were hoping that their envelopes of money would salvage Peña's campaign, and they cheered when his wife, Peggy Cabral, materialized in his stead.

Dressed elegantly, her hair held up with a gold pin, Doña Peggy swept into the room, her reserved dignity contrasting with the enthusiasm of the crowd. At a long bank of tables in the large back room, she patiently and politely sat with New York PRD leaders to receive a long line of taxi drivers, supermarket owners, and local party operatives all dressed in their best clothes. Over the previous months they had sent not only money but equipment to Peña in Santo Domingo: fax machines, trucks, flags, hats, T-shirts, buses. Now they were being asked to search their pockets one more time. Each person came up to the table, congratulated Doña Peggy, and handed over an envelope. For nearly four hours the envelopes kept coming; the take was at least $150,000.

Peña's supporters in New York lost the election, but they were still ahead of where they had been before it took place, for the candidate who won, Leonel Fernández, was the most convincing evidence that, however slowly, the absent Dominicans were changing what their compatriots at home said about them. Leonel knew what Peña's supporters in Washington Heights wanted, because, even though he represented another party and defeated their candidate, he was still one of them: he had grown up in New York City.

"We lived alone, my mother and brother and me, in a small apartment. Two Hundred West Ninety-fifth Street, Apartment One. I still remember that," Leonel said softly when I interviewed him in his small law office in the fashionable Naco district of Santo Domingo a week after his election.

Leonel, struggling with English, had to repeat second grade at Public School 75. But soon he mastered the language and began to read voraciously at the neighborhood branch of the public library. He laughed about his choices: "I didn't have anyone to show me which books. I read just to read, anything: biographies of Lou Gehrig and Babe Ruth, a book about little animals, *The Last of the Mohicans.*" His mother, Yolanda Reyna, worked as a night nurse, then slept until noon, and worked again in a factory in the afternoon. When he was old enough, Leonel got a delivery-boy job with a forty-dollar weekly salary; his tips more than doubled the take-home pay. His older brother, Dalcio, worked at a dry cleaner. As the boys grew, their mother was able to leave her factory job and instead do sewing work on the weekends.

To make sure her sons remained as Dominican as they were now American, she brought home Dominican newspapers every day to keep up with what was going on in the Dominican Republic. Nearly every corner *bodega* sold *Listín Diario, El Siglo,* and *El Nacional.* (There had been no Dominican newspapers when José Fernández arrived.) The food on the table and the banter around it were Dominican. Yet Yolanda Reyna worried that the four months Leonel spent in Santo Domingo during vacations from school weren't enough to keep him from losing touch with the country he had left when he was seven, the country to which she longed to return. Worse, she feared the temptations of the city would be too much for a teenager already "wasting" his afternoons playing basketball with his friends at Brandeis High School. A teenage boy loose in New York could get into a lot of trouble. She thought Leonel's friends and his job were taking too much time away from his studies.

When he finished high school at seventeen years old, in 1968, Leonel returned to the Santo Domingo *barrio* of Villa Juana. There, his new companions turned him on to a whole new world: Mao Tse-tung, Albert Camus, Jean-Paul Sartre, Ernest Hemingway, Régis Debray. "When I came to Santo Domingo, I was extraordinarily amazed that living in a lower-middle-class neighborhood the only concerns of all the young people were intellectual," Leonel recalled.

Despite occasional lapses into the byzantine rhetoric he learned under Juan Bosch, Leonel has the earnest optimism of someone who spent his teenage years in the United States. He openly said he had modeled himself on President Bill Clinton, who is only a few years older than he, and words he used—"globalization," "civil society," "creating institutions"—evoked Clinton. "They even call me and my Vice President, Jaime David, 'Clinton and Gore with mustaches,' " Leonel chuckled. The night before, the Dominican President-elect had spent three hours on the Internet perusing CNN Online.

Books from a mid-Manhattan public library were piled at the end of the long conference table in Leonel's office. Several books more were stacked on a shelf: *Reinventing Government, Changing America, In Pursuit of Excellence.* The President-elect had sent an urgent E-mail request to a New York friend, who brought the books down. The books were stamped with a due date of July 18, two weeks hence; the friend would take them back to New York and return them.

Like Clinton, Leonel portrayed himself as a man of the people, someone who could listen to what citizens needed and turn their requests into reality. "I want to hold a town meeting with the absent Dominicans and tell them, 'Explain your problems to me. I want to hear what you have to say,'" he said. And sure enough, a few weeks later, hundreds of Dominicans lined up outside Salomé Ureña High School in Washington Heights to attend his first town meeting.

"One of the things I see as the biggest worry of Dominicans living in the United States is that the new generation of Dominican children born in the United States are losing their roots," Leonel said. "The problem is one of jobs and economic security that they don't find in the Dominican Republic. That's what motivates them to leave. They must have access to health care, education, social security. They don't have that here, and that's why they emigrate. I want to change that image. I think it is important to incorporate the Dominican community in New York into the decisions we make here. I want them to know there is a Dominican President who will be thinking about the problems of Dominicans living in New York."

Instead of being less Dominican for having grown up away from the country where he was born, Leonel appeared to be a typical Dominican person living between two cultures. "I eat at my mother's home every day. We eat *la bandera Dominicana*"—the Dominican national dish of rice and beans and a little chicken or beef. "I don't know how to eat properly. My grandmother spoiled me. If I don't eat that meal, I feel as if I haven't eaten."

His double loyalty was made all the more poignant by the astounding and paradoxical recommendation he made to the absent Dominicans shortly after he took office: the best way for them to help their country was to become U.S. citizens. Leonel himself had kept his green card as a permanent resident of the United States. His message was that Dominicans could embrace life in the United States but still remain loyal to their motherland. It was stunning to hear from the President of a country whose leaders for years had wrapped themselves with the national flag and denounced outside interference as threats to Dominican sovereignty.

The President embodied the experiences of Guillermo Linares, José Fernández, and the million-plus Dominicans in the United States. But his plea to his compatriots abroad to seek U.S. citizenship had a particularly urgent ring in light of a dramatic change in U.S. laws, which represented a shift away from the relatively permissive environment that had ushered in Caribbean immigrants since 1965. In August 1996, the month Fernández took office in Santo Domingo, the United States enacted the Personal Responsibility and Work Opportunity Reconciliation Act, a piece of legislation that was Orwellian in name and directed in no small part toward immigrants, who, its proponents argued, were costing taxpayers too much. The Congressional Budget Office estimated that the law would save the federal government $25 billion by the year 2002, and nearly half of that savings would come from excluding legal immigrants from the Social Security, Medicaid, and food-stamp rolls. In September, President Clinton signed into law the Illegal Immigration Reform and Immigrant Responsibility Act, which strengthened U.S. efforts to fight illegal immigration.

The laws responded to a clamor against immigrants that had been growing louder since the beginning of the decade, when the country was mired in deep recession. The anti-immigrant argument had begun with a series of English-only movements, then gathered momentum to include California's Proposition 187, an initiative to deny social benefits to immigrants, on the 1994 ballot. When the Republicans won a congressional majority in landslide midterm elections that year, it was after a campaign full of rancorous rhetoric in favor of cutting welfare benefits across the board and limiting immigration. Ostensibly, the issue was welfare benefits, as opponents of immigration claimed that newcomers were using expensive public services, many of which had been created during the mid-century immigration lull. Politicians argued that taxpayers could not afford to give welfare and education to masses of new immigrants: the waves of Europeans who came with the Industrial Revolution didn't get Social Security, so why should their descendants pay for the upkeep of the newcomers who were taking away American jobs?

The debate in the United States had acquired a tone jarringly similar to the Haitian bashing that continued on Hispaniola. In America as in the Dominican Republic, the argument that immigrants take jobs was disingenuous because few citizens would accept the poor working conditions and pay that immigrants would. In the United States, however, those who opposed immigration had to be more careful to couch their argument in economic terms and treat the cultural and racial aspects of the issue delicately. (In the Dominican Republic, of course, there is no social safety net for Dominicans, much less for the Haitian immigrants there; Dominicans themselves must emigrate to make up for what their government fails to provide.)

Part of the reason the debate resonates so strongly is that the immigrant is so like the rest of us: our ancestors went through the same struggle; and like so many Americans, immigrants are simply seeking jobs at livable wages. Because of this similarity, it is easier to blame outsiders when an American worker loses a job than it is to fault an abstraction like injustice or economics or a large entity like a corporation or a government. At the same time, the only way morally to justify attacks on the weak is to deny that they are like us. In politics the victims of collective rage are faceless, sterilized, stripped of human qualities so that in blaming them we can feel safe.

Ironically, the efforts to cut down on immigration were what finally encouraged the Dominicans in New York to establish deeper roots in their new home. In 1990 only 18 percent of Dominican immigrants in the United States had become naturalized citizens, compared to 50 percent or more for many Asian immigrants. But that began to change quickly, even before the welfare-reform law passed in 1996, for two reasons. One was that the 1994 constitutional change in Santo Domingo, allowing double citizenship, reassured Dominicans that they would not lose their citizenship back home if they were naturalized as Americans. The other was that Dominican community leaders could already see what was happening and thus had anticipated that they needed to convince people to become citizens.

By forcing states to take on greater financial responsibility if they wanted to keep extending benefits to legal immigrants, the new laws prompted an even more startling shift in New York City. Mayor Giuliani, whose anti-Dominican rhetoric had weighed heavily in his first election, changed his tune dramatically and began to take the immigrants' side in the welfare debate; he became a national spokesman in favor of preserving benefits. There was a financial logic to his position, of course, in that welfare cutbacks would hurt the city, which had long paid more than it received back in federal and state funds. But Giuliani's public stance also confirmed that the mayor of the nation's biggest city recognized the importance of immigrants as a vital part of the urban economy.

The changes put in motion by the immigrant welfare debate had another positive effect for the Dominicans, too: the greater visibility of the immigrants, and their growing tendency to apply for citizenship and register to vote, caught the attention of politicians citywide, who began to court the Dominican vote. Slowly the Dominicans were beginning the integration process that generations of European immigrants had done before them. But the Dominicans were doing it their own way.

Close to ten o'clock the night of the 1996 U.S. elections, Bill Clinton was far ahead. Buying a drink at a corner store near the 168th Street subway stop in Washington Heights, a young Dominican danced out into the street, waving his arms in victory and shouting, *"Bi' Cli'to' ganoooo!"* Clinton won! The Dominicans hoped that with Clinton's reelection, pressure to limit immigrant benefits would stop. (In fact, they would be able to take some comfort in 1997 from a new law that restored Social Security and Medicaid benefits to elderly and disabled immigrants who had been receiving them before the 1996 laws tightened the purse strings. But that was not enough to undo the changes that had already gone into effect.)

At the Audubon Bar & Grill at 166th Street and Broadway, a crowd of Dominicans was gathering to celebrate Clinton's win and, more important, the election of the first Dominican to the New York State Assembly. Adriano Espaillat, a community activist, had just defeated the incumbent, John Bryan Murtaugh. The band was playing *bachata*, the music of the Dominican countryside. Almost no one was speaking English. Around the edges of the room, however, some people were tarring the festive mood with their whispers: "Next we're going to elect a *real* Dominican to the City Council." Espaillat, unlike Guillermo Linares, had allied himself with the supermarket owners and Harlem politicians who opposed the Pathmark project.

Long after vote counts ended, the new assemblyman came in, his black hair shining under the TV cameras. Standing beside him were his beaming grandparents, in their nineties with thick glasses and white hair, who had lived half a century in the United States without learning English. His parents were there, too, as were his wife and children. Espaillat was glowing. The Dominicans had made it.

But each step forward was accompanied by one step back. Three months later, at Espaillat's inauguration at the jam-packed auditorium of Salomé Ureña High School, two Dominican priests and a rabbi blessed the ceremony. Then Espaillat received the political benediction of an array of Latino and Harlem politicians repaying him for having opposed the Pathmark project. (Noticeably absent was Guillermo Linares.) The largely Dominican-American audience belted out the Dominican national anthem with Adriano's brother leading them. When he switched to "The Star-Spangled Banner," however, they stumbled, awkwardly mumbling, just moving their lips or humming along with the music: they were still caught between two worlds, not living completely in either one. And the same was true back home.

Not so many coffins come back to San Francisco de Macorís since they brought Kiko García home in 1992. The old municipal cemetery used to get thirty bodies a month before the riots after his death, but the number has fallen to three or four a month, and weeks go by without a new coffin arriving. In New York, police have cracked down on drug dealing.

Enough money has come in now from the absent Dominicans that there's not such a sense of urgency to leave. The town itself feels as if it has been someplace else and come back. Across the street from the industrial park, on the highway into (or out from, depending how you look at it) San Francisco de Macorís, road signs in front of Club Julius announce in a mix of badly mangled Spanish and English: JULIUS NIGTH CLUB: PARA VOTAR EL STREE, a promise that the Julius will take your stress away. Spotted with satellite dishes, this whole town, like the club, exudes a sense not just of transience but of wanting to be someplace else. The Las Vegas–meets–Miami Beach architecture of the Julius, the statues of men in togas out front, the promise of sex and decadence: all this caters to the new money and sense of success that has come into San Francisco de Macorís from New York. Referring to the questionable taste of the emigrants who made their money from drugs, *The Washington Post* dubbed the architectural excess of the nightclub and the sprouting homes in the suburbs nearby "narco-deco."

Afternoon sun peeks through the arched windows of Club Julius and glints off the mirrors in the otherwise dark expanse of the striptease club, a spacious arena of tables spaced wide enough apart to make it easy for the dancers and waitresses to make their way across the floor. The walls are painted black, complementing the black-and-red exterior. There's a piano bar in the back, but there's no piano, and the chairs are piled up in a corner. It has been closed for a year now, and Club Julius is for sale.

It's three in the afternoon and Carolina is keeping shop, empty shop, until two American visitors walk into the Club Julius. A young male friend lolls at the bar counter while Carolina serves the visitors a Presidente beer, not so cold that it freezes when poured, but close, just right. As she pours, her forefingers are conspicuously clean. It is two days after the 1996 Presidential election, and those who voted still sport fuchsia fingers dyed in indelible ink to prevent their voting twice.

"I haven't applied for my *cédula* yet, so I can't vote," she explains, blushing. That is why she is here alone this Tuesday afternoon. Later, Carolina confesses that she's only seventeen, not old enough for a voting card. The other women who work here, the dancers who follow their shows with *negocios*, business, as she politely puts it, are still back in their hometowns, to which they traveled to vote. Most of them are from Santo Domingo, the capital, where they grew up with more knowledge of *negocios* than you might find in once-sleepy San Francisco.

When they finish dancing, they lead their aroused customers back to one of the rows of stifling tiny rooms behind the Julius. In the heavy afternoon, the air in the halls to the rooms is still and damp, laden with mold spores. Even in full daylight, no light reaches into the rooms; they are darker by day than at night, when they are dimly lit.

Though it's quiet this afternoon, Carolina insists that business is good at the Julius. Customers come from all over the Cibao valley, and even from as far as Santo Domingo, two hours away. When Dominicans come back from New York, this is the place to go.

Carolina is on break from high school. Summers, she takes a small room here and works every day. In the fall, when school starts again, she goes back to her hometown of La Vega, less than an hour away by car, and only works at the Julius on weekends, waitressing and dancing. When she talks about dancing, her eyes light up.

"I don't do *negocios* as the other women do," Carolina says matter-of-factly, without defiance. "I just dance. And I don't dance nude either. I keep on my top and panties." But she has higher ambitions, aspirations that have only come about because the country has changed enough that she can dream of these things. She studied dance in La Vega and wants to study more, not just dance, maybe go to New York like her cousins, like the many young men from the Cibao who have gone north. "I want to study engineering," she says. "I'm good at math." She's seen the buildings go up all around town, financed with money from up north, and knows that engineers can make a good living even here.

Where will she be five, ten years from now? A college-educated engineer? Still at the Julius? Gone to New York? She tells the story of her dreams with wide-eyed conviction that they will come true. Even though the odds are against that happening, she wants so badly for it to be that it would be cruel not to want to believe too.

The Other Side

Rele O,
Lamize pa dous O, Rele O
Amwe O,
Lamize pa dous O,
Rele O.
M pral cheche
Lavi'm lot Kote O.

Sing out Oh,
Misery isn't sweet, Sing Oh
Help me Oh,
Poverty isn't sweet Oh,
Sing out Oh.
I'm going to look for life
On the Other side oh.

—*Traditional* rara *lyrics performed by Rara La Fleur Ginen*
Bel Air, Port-au-Prince, Haiti

Carnival celebrants parade down Santo Domingo's Malecón. Elaborately masked *diablos cojuelos*, La Vega devils, with sequins and beads dripping from their bright silver satin robes, twirl and feint. They run from one side of the road to the other, slashing at the edges of the crowd with whips tipped with cloth balloons meant to stun their victims. *Lechones*, with horned masks notable for their long, duck-like curved lips, dance in large groups. These come from the town of Santiago.

Just ahead, a dozen skimpily clad transvestites-for-the-day prance along, jeering at one another and flirting with the men looking on. Other men dressed up as ugly, large-breasted women tiptoe while others taunt them with shouts of *"Roba la gallina!"* Steal the hen! Cracking whips at one another and at the crowd, *toros*, bulls, surrounded by their entourage stride confidently down the Malecón.

A group of half-naked men run down the seaside boulevard; some are streaked in paint applied in stripes and patterns meant to look as if they are from traditional African tribes. A pair of teenage boys are covered entirely in red paint and nothing else as they parade, holler, and rush up to spectators, whom they threaten to embrace. Rustling and shaking, other paraders dance along, too, covered from head to toe in thick clumps of grass or palm fronds.

A tiny man, his young blue eyes twinkling in a wrinkled face that appears prematurely aged, is dressed in a baggy suit, thick glasses, and a black fedora: he is a Balaguer in the midst of his people, with two young mulatto men following him dressed in gangster suits and waving guns, pretending to be bodyguards. Farther down the route, a group of teenagers in homeboy pants, New York–style, blast the crowd with hip-hop music from the boom boxes they brandish.

At the end of Santo Domingo's Carnival parade route, the paraders and crowd swarm around *el obelisco macho*, one of the many monuments Trujillo had built in his honor (though one of the few that remain). This phallic obelisk has been repainted with the images of the Mirabal sisters, the three butterflies whose deaths mobilized their country against the dictator more than three decades ago. As evening falls, the parade spills down past the obelisk and into the Colonial Zone. Wizened old ladies peer out of their windows as the African revelers, the European devils, the mischief makers, the criminals, and the misfits pass by. The women rest their wrinkled cheeks on the wrought-iron bars as they watch the tired paraders head home.

Pigeons roost for the night in the ruins of the hospital of San Nicolás de Bari, where time has stood still since Sir Francis Drake destroyed the structure in the sixteenth century. Along the Ozama River, the coral walls of Columbus's old home, the Alcázar de Colón, glow orange against the night sky. Across the river, the Columbus Lighthouse is covered with dark streaks left by polluted rain, thickened by smoke from Santo Domingo's army of diesel generators. As the night darkens, the lighthouse's giant beam turns on and traces a ghostly crucifix in the sky as a reminder of a history that refuses to remain in the past.

These old and new structures are physical testimony to what has happened over the course of five hundred years in Santo Domingo, but the pageant surrounding the annual Carnival and Independence Day celebrations contains the real history of Hispaniola. The participants have broken their island's story down to represent the groups that have played out events the way they are remembered now: the indigenous Taino that Columbus met on Hispaniola in 1492, the slaves brought from Africa to harvest cane in the New World, the spirits and devils of local legend, the youth of New York. At Carnival, the loudest voices come from those who are usually silent: the strongman President is transformed into a smiling, wizened old man who provokes only laughter, while those who represent the Taino, the slaves, and the misfits are the most powerful and admired paraders. For a short time the masses are more powerful than the Great Man. And men, who the rest of the year pride themselves on their *machismo*, can show off as women at Carnival. Briefly, traditional roles are reversed.

While Carnival symbolically breaks society's rules, it also subtly reinforces them. Behind the whole spectacle is an undercurrent of sexual tension, role reversal, and the harmless release of violent urges. In theory it is all in fun, but the underlying message is that the voiceless are allowed this luxury only once a year. The performance takes place against a backdrop of the constant threat of real violence, whether as the result of political repression, drug wars on the streets of New York, or the increased likelihood of day-to-day conflict brought on by the pressures of poverty and frustration. (In Haiti, the connection between Carnival and politics was explicit: while President Aristide was in exile, musicians were harassed for performing Carnival songs that openly opposed the violence perpetrated by the military regime.)

Santo Domingo's national celebration ends several weeks of Carnival gatherings that have taken place across Hispaniola, different in each city and town according to the local customs and culminating on February 27, Dominican Independence Day, which sometimes coincides (but more often does not) with the traditional Shrove Tuesday celebration in Europe and elsewhere in Latin America. Santo Domingo's version of Carnival is a local adaptation of a universal cultural trope: the celebration of differences and the glorification of aggression.

This annual ritual resembles others that also are constructed to isolate instances of conflict and project them against a backdrop that is sterilized of real consequences, so as to transform struggles into experiences that unite groups around them: for instance, a football game, a Greek tragedy, a horror movie, a boxing match. Many of these phenomena are culturally acceptable (though subject to varying degrees of debate), but others—like the cockfight—remain, for many people, repulsive.

Yet the sometimes horrifying nature of the fight is what makes it so compelling, for it is rooted in the same impulses that cause humans to create rituals out of violence: attention to the fight is, in effect, an examination of something that is an unavoidable part of life. Witnessing a barnyard cockfight in the fourth century A.D., St. Augustine concluded that it was only natural that such a combat would take place in a barnyard, so observing it was merely to study things as they were. Still, he could not help but lament the abject deformity of the vanquished rooster. "And yet, by that very deformity was the more perfect beauty of the contest in evidence," he mused. The ugliness of the defeat was part of the order of things, for without such hideous phenomena, beauty would be less evident; he extended this logic to behavior that at first glance appeared cruel or distasteful but was still, by his thinking, a necessary part of the way society worked.

The battle fascinates the human observer because it is natural; the fans of the cockfight are simply glorifying base aspects of human nature that can also be seen in the animal world. But if that is the case, then why is it that aggression and violence are part of the order of things? Why do the cocks fight? They fight for territory and power, "for the sake of the supremacy of the hens subject to them," as St. Augustine surmised.

If human experience mirrors that combat, we could say that the space we contest is more complex: it can be physical, economic, emotional, or cultural. On Hispaniola, the struggle is for all of those, magnified by the island's enclosed and subdivided geography. Its history has been particularly turbulent. But every country holds the potential for violence, and it does not always erupt. When we watch a cockfight (metaphorically or, as on Hispaniola, in reality), are we letting the animals go to battle for us?

Noel Modesto "Nabú" Henriques doesn't go to the cockfights anymore. Tropical vines snake around the yard and walls of his crumbling house in Santo Domingo's beautiful but run-down Gazcue district, not far from the Colonial Zone. Training and fighting gamecocks require a not inconsiderable investment of time and money. Nabú's time is past. He is over sixty years old now. But the sport is still in his blood.

Nabú's uncles, Juan Tomás and Modesto Díaz, were two of the country's most renowned *galleros* in the 1950s, before they helped to plot the assassination of Trujillo and were murdered in retaliation. Dominicans still remember Modesto's famous cock El Lecherito with reverence. Nabú learned the sport from his uncles.

"Did you know roosters don't sweat?" Nabú asks. He is giving instructions in the fine points of the sport and the expertise needed to train the best cocks. "If you put a group of young cocks together in a pen, they will fight. If you place a mature rooster, even a turkey, for that matter, in the pen with them, they will be afraid of him and not fight." But that is true only for part of the year. Beginning in June, the birds' plumage changes, and until October's Festival of San Andrés, it is down season for cockfights. Thundershowers drench the country nearly every afternoon, and the roosters' dynamic changes completely during the transition leading to the fall hurricanes. Nabú warns: "In the rainy season, they will no longer recognize each other and will then fight each other to the death."

The conviction that a strong fighter is needed to keep order below created the type of leaders on Hispaniola who have used their own unsavory methods to prevent their people from acting on urges to rebel and write a different history. Under this model, violence on Hispaniola has taken place in cycles. The sequence begins like this: one leader prevents people from expressing frustration and from making initiatives on their own to change. He discredits even the possibility of forming democratic institutions that could channel anger into constructive ends; instead, he stays in power by nurturing his own cult of personality and by diverting citizens' attention toward a nationalistic and racist political agenda so that instead of recognizing his failure to improve their lot they blame their neighbors across the island. But a man has only a lifetime in which to rule and not even that, since the minute his power begins to ebb, the next aspiring personalistic leader is waiting to dethrone the old President. So his reign ends in chaos and fighting as those below establish the next father figure, who again rules by cult of personality combined with a culture of fear.

That is what happened when Trujillo died, and, no doubt, it was the biggest fear of many Dominicans as Balaguer prepared to leave office in 1996. But in putting their faith in the myth of a father-leader to keep order and protect them, the people of Hispaniola showed little confidence in their own abilities to defuse tension. They either stayed in their places, buying into the myth, or left the island to seek new lives in the United States. But those do not have to be the only choices, for the people on the island have shown they have a tremendous capacity to transcend the pressures that feed aggression.

At the station close to the Modelo market, the bus fills with *madansara*, the Haitian women who carry wares back and forth from Santo Domingo to Port-au-Prince. Between the women merchants, seats fill with other travelers returning home or visiting relatives in the Haitian capital. Buses make the five-hour trip from Santo Domingo to the Dominican border town of Jimaní for fifty pesos.

When each bus stops in Jimaní, money changers swarm around it, exchanging gourdes for pesos. Motorcycles and small pickup trucks take the travelers down the road to the border at Malpasse, the Bad Pass. After passing migration, they can walk through huge iron gates to Haiti. Just out of the Dominican gate, as they enter the no-man's-land between the two countries, a score of motorcycles block the way. The motorcycle drivers are jockeying for passengers to carry to the Haitian side.

Dalbert carries no visa or even, for that matter, passport. So he bribes the soldiers to let him through the gate. His reasons are simple: renewing his passport costs money, and the visa on top of that. But with no passport, he pays ten pesos to the Dominican guard, a few U.S. dollars to the Haitian guards, and he is back in Haiti, ready to take another truck for the last twenty-three miles to the capital.

Inside the tap-tap waiting to leave from the border at Malpasse to Port-au-Prince, a woman is angry. She has brought huge bags full of goods onto the bus and wants to travel with the bags on the seat next to her and at her feet. The people sitting next to her argue. "Why don't you put it on the top of the truck? That's where all those things should go." She yells back at them that they are hers, that she will keep them with her. She makes such a fuss that the others leave her alone and continue waiting for the tap-tap to fill so it can begin the last leg of the trip to Port-au-Prince: just twenty-three miles, but traveled so slowly they will take an hour and a half to cover.

Another wave of travelers crosses the border from the Dominican Republic, moves through migration, and walks to the bus. The woman still doesn't want to move her things. The driver rushes up and argues with her. Onto the top of the truck go her bags, big white sacks with the faded red picture of Dominican President Balaguer emblazoned on the sides. All the passengers grumble as the driver guides more and more people into the tap-tap, past the point where it is full. The heat is unbearable. Through the painted slats on the sides of the truck, he pokes people in the ribs until they move over. Finally, he slams the back door shut. The truck waits again, until he gets a sugary fruit drink and is ready to go.

As soon as the tap-tap starts moving, the women pull out scarves and plastic bags to cover their heads. They do it mechanically, as if they have made this trip so many times that their hands have memorized the motion. Their wraps are meant to protect them from the dust but seem symbolically to shut out the heat, the noise, the pushing inside the tap-tap. The gears grind. As the truck picks up speed, dust rises inside, covering everything with a fine film. Voices rise as the angry woman picks a fight with the woman sitting three seats over. The whole truck is arguing now, with no one in particular or with everyone, declaiming in voices loud enough to drown out the engine. A woman yells at her little boy to sit down. There is no space for the boy, who looks about seven years old but is probably at least ten or eleven. He is trying desperately not to sit on his infant brother's head. Disgusted, the woman with the baby turns away and takes up the fight with the angry woman, who hasn't shut her mouth since the tap-tap left the border. Insults fly, curses hurled in Spanish. Everyone has forgotten the point. It is the spirit of arguing that is important.

"What are you screaming in Spanish for?" another woman yells. "This is Haiti!"

The woman with the child in her arms turns around and concentrates her fury on this new object. Her entire body strains as she leans toward the aggressor.

A Dominican man next to her grabs her shoulders. "Calm down!" he orders her in Spanish. "How can you act like this with that baby? If anything happens to that baby, it will be your fault."

The other passengers join in to stifle the argument. They calm down for the rest of the tortuous trip to the capital. The fight has distracted them from the heat, the dust, their cramped legs, and the bone-cracking discomfort of the hard wooden benches on which they sit as the tap-tap lurches and bumps down the rough road. Under the seats, chickens— tied three together—peck at the shoes of the travelers.

"Merci, monsieur!" comes the cry, signaling a wish to stop, from the back of the tap-tap. Someone reaches up to the canopy to touch two wires together. The wires light a red bulb in the cab. The truck stops to let off the angry woman with the bags. As her sacks are hauled down from the top of the tap-tap, a soldier along the side of the road surveys its occupants. He walks close along the edge of the truck and uses the butt of his gun to jab the passengers in the ribs. The dust settles and the heat rises, no breeze inside. Finally, the tap-tap moves again, on toward the outskirts of Port-au-Prince, another trip completed.

"The average normal civilized human being witnesses aggression only when two of his fellow citizens or two of his domestic animals fight, and therefore sees only its evil effects," the sociobiologist Konrad Lorenz has written in *On Aggression*, his study of animal behavior and how it can help us to understand human aggression. But this impulse is not good for nothing, Lorenz argues: it unites a species against attackers; it results in the stronger members of a group protecting the weaker members; and it diminishes tension within the group once a pecking order has been established. In his view, aggression is a needed life-preserving instinct; what is more, it often leads to and accompanies the formation of bonds of community.

If aggression is necessary, then the problem becomes what to make of the continuum of increasingly aggressive actions: "from cocks fighting in the barnyard to dogs biting each other, boys thrashing each other, young men throwing beer mugs at each other's heads, and so on, to bar-room brawls about politics, and finally to wars and atom bombs." Lorenz questions the causes of the lowly cockfight and applies his findings to the most destructive types of human behavior: What feeds conflict? Why does a fight escalate? When can it be defused? How is its disturbing element transformed from a destructive force into a unifying one?

The cornered rat, the cock in a ring, the boisterous young man: all of them fight to defend territory. When a creature is attacked, its options are to fight back or flee. If a losing fighter cannot escape, his struggle becomes even more desperate. Fights intensify when there are no options. So the answer becomes finding a proper escape route, which can be through physical separation, by seeking safety in groups, or by another route that involves creation rather than destruction.

The most interesting means of escape is symbolic. Aggression can be directed away from its true object and guided into harmless (or even productive) channels, often in the form of habit and ritual. Animals develop their own rituals for courtship and to establish order; humans do the same, developing elaborate cultural rites. Here we have another reason for the human fascination with ritual violence, with the cockfight being one of its more dramatic forms: not only does the animals' battle represent an aspect of human conduct (as St. Augustine saw it), but when surrounded by rituals of community, it dissipates aggressive urges. The counterpart to the blood spilled at the center of the event is the bond that forms around it, made even stronger by the fact that blood is a metaphor for family ties.

On Hispaniola, geographic, economic, and political pressures have intensified urges to aggression and elaborate mechanisms for escape. One of these escape mechanisms has been geographic and can be seen in the form of the million Dominicans and million Haitians who have taken up residence in the United States (and in the form of the cane cutters, merchants, and construction workers who left Haiti for the Dominican Republic). Another has been the seeding of rich myths and rituals, like the cockfight, the parallel religious spirit world of Vodou, even the development of prowess in storytelling and dramatic presentation that can transform the tiniest interaction into an act of assertion.

Especially during times of conflict, Dominicans and Haitians have drawn lines clearly establishing divisions between groups, delineated by race, culture, language, and nationality (Dominicans or Haitians, the people who stayed or those who left, the privileged or the impoverished, educated or illiterate, black or mulatto or white, Spanish or Kreyol or French or English). These divisions have been played out in the form of the island's tragic history and have been fortified by cultural myths and competing versions of history. Like the dual nature of aggression itself, these stories have the power to sustain or destroy; often they do both simultaneously.

In seven years the fish in Viriato Sención's ten-gallon aquarium has grown so big it can hardly turn around. El Pinto stares menacingly out; through the glass, you can see the indentations where it has bashed its head repeatedly against the walls of the aquarium. "One time, it tried to commit suicide by leaping out. It broke the aquarium and landed on the floor," says Viriato. "We had to fill the sink with water and keep him there until we could get a new aquarium."

Viriato spends the days writing his way out of his small overheated apartment in the South Bronx. Half of him is solidly placed in New York, half back on Hispaniola; he is trapped between the two places in a deep personal exile. Viriato was one of the original members of Juan Bosch's Dominican Revolutionary Party (PRD) fighting against the Trujillos. After the 1965 civil war ended and Balaguer was elected in 1966, Viriato left Santo Domingo to live in exile in Puerto Rico. When he returned to Santo Domingo four years later, he met Balaguer's sister, Emma. With her, he founded a charity, the Cruzada del Amor, the Crusade of Love. When Balaguer lost the 1978 election to Antonio Guzmán of the PRD, Sención left behind the Presidential palace of Joaquín Balaguer, the President's sister, Emma, and the world of cronies looking to pull out a few bucks for themselves.

In 1979, Viriato picked up, with hardly a penny to his name, and moved to New York to work operating a printing machine at a Queens factory. When he returned to Santo Domingo seven years later, Balaguer had been reelected. Viriato went to see Emma, who asked him to come back to stay. But one look at the world he had left convinced him he would never return. "I said I would never again set foot in that house of intrigue," he said. The first day back in New York, he began writing a novel that re-created the world he knew in Santo Domingo. He purged that life by writing of the torture chambers of the Trujillo and Balaguer regimes, of the deceit in the Presidential palace and at the highest levels of the Church. The resulting novel, *They Forged the Signature of God*, was a best-seller in Santo Domingo. But it did not win him back his country.

He tells the story of a friend from Santiago who spent nearly a dozen years building a large house that remains empty. Renting it out would be a tacit admission that she has given up on her dream of going back for good. But everyone knows she never will. After so many years in New York, her life is in Manhattan, not in Santiago. "She's invested all her money in a house she'll never live in," Viriato says, shaking his head. The woman's story is even sadder because it is like his own; he, too, can never go back. But he will never be able fully to embrace New York, either. His wife, Milagros, became a U.S. citizen a few years ago, but Viriato resists. "If I stay Dominican, I can write with as much force as I want. I can criticize what I want and have moral weight behind my words that I wouldn't if I were an American citizen," he says.

But his words sound like an excuse, masking a reality he can't articulate: Viriato cannot bring himself to sign a piece of paper rejecting the place where he lives in his mind. He is in permanent exile from two countries at once, two homes battling inside his head. His physical departure from Hispaniola was only a partial reprieve.

The counterpart to the Dominicans exiled outside their country is a community of people exiled within Hispaniola; like Viriato, they are caught between competing worlds. In a *batey* outside Santo Domingo, Ramoncito Cariño pulls a chair onto the packed dirt in front of the cane barracks where he grew up. Nearby, his sister Elma is sitting with her friends. A little girl, bright-eyed and barefoot, lolls on his knee and looks adoringly up at her daddy.

Ramoncito can't vote because he never exchanged his old identity documents for the new magnetized voting cards issued before the 1994 elections to make it harder for the government to falsify votes. When it was time to sign up for the fancy new cards with fingerprints, a signature, photograph, and metallic image all encased in hard plastic, there was a rumor going around that anyone who seemed Haitian would not be given one. Ramoncito decided to avoid trouble.

He pulls out a birth certificate, issued when he was a teenager because his parents hadn't registered him when he was born, as happens with many children of Haitian cane cutters. The name written on the stamped and signed paper is Raymond Cheli. It means Raymond Dear, written the way the Dominicans heard his parents say the *r* in the French word *cheri*. He's translated the name into Spanish as Ramón Cariño. His friends call him Ramoncito, Little Ramón, Raymond Dear.

"I've lived all my life here," Ramoncito says in Spanish, as he fingers the paper of his birth certificate, soft and creased from so many foldings. He folds it once more, slowly, and returns it to his worn wallet. "Most people call me by my name in Spanish. I speak Spanish better than Kreyol. I've never been to Haiti. So I'm almost Dominican."

Ramoncito hovers between not just the racial and linguistic divisions of the island but also the class barriers. He sings *bachata*, the music of Dominican brothels and cafeterias, the ballads of the lower class and the desperate. It is the music of choice on the *bateyes*, in the slums across the Ozama River from Santo Domingo's Colonial Zone newly remodeled for tourists, and in the countryside of the Cibao. Only recently, it has begun to attract the middle class too.

Sitting outside a Santo Domingo café one evening, waiting to perform, Ramoncito finds himself at a table with some upper-class Dominican kids. Trying to impress an American woman sitting with them, one youth, who looks about nineteen years old, starts rattling on and on about the Internet, the 1990s rich-kid toy that has replaced stereos and cars as the ultimate status symbol. "Shareware . . . Download . . . HTML, URL, World Wide Web . . . I have *two* servers, Codetel *and* TriCom," he rambles in English, ignoring the quiet *bachatero* and the fact that nobody seems particularly impressed by or is even listening to his cyber-babble. Ramoncito sits quietly, thinking about the words he will sing in the popular songs "¿Quién Te Engañó, Mujer?" (Who tricked you, woman?) and "Sal D'e'ta Casa" (Get out of this house), thinking about the ever-so-slight rasp he hopes will disappear from his throat. The nights have been chilly recently. He's afraid he is coming down with a cold.

Once it comes time to perform, the middle- and upper-class crowd, many of them kids who study in the States, applaud wildly in approval and sing with him the closing bars of "Sal D'e'ta Casa." Ramoncito has a sense of balance projected unself-consciously.

The real show follows later, after the café crowds are left behind.

Stopping afterward for fried chicken and boiled yucca with red onion and vinegar, Ramoncito and his guitar players break out into a spontaneous performance as they sit in plastic chairs at an all-night open-air restaurant off the highway on the way back to the *batey*. He throws his head back and thrusts the lyrics, sweet and smooth, out of his throat. Though much *bachata* is sung in a nasal old-man's whine, Ramoncito's voice floats, bell-clear, angelic, controlled. He looks around at his audience, directing phrases at them with focused glances out of his sharp eyes and long eyelashes. His songs elevate suffering and release it.

All around the *bachata* trio, working-class men, still grimy with the day's dirt, lay back in their chairs and tip their ash-cold bottles of Presidente beer in approval at the impromptu performance. They join in, shouting requests. Ramoncito is belting out for them all the pain of living. They have no idea he is only almost Dominican.

For each other, Dominicans and Haitians fit exactly the social construct known as the Other, which the French-Bulgarian critic Tzvetan Todorov has explained in this way: "beings whom everything links to me on the cultural, moral, historical plane; or else the other are unknown quantities, outsiders whose language and customs I do not understand, so foreign that in extreme instances I am reluctant to admit they belong to the same species as my own." The Other can be an abstract idea, another individual, a group to which one does not belong. Identifying the Other and asserting one's position relative to it involve three processes: a value judgment, an assessment of distance, and, ultimately, identification or rejection. We ask first if this Other is good or bad, better or worse, loved or hated, above or below. Then we can place ourselves on a spectrum of distance or nearness to the characteristics we have assigned the Other. With that information we can decide whether to identify with or reject the Other. Affirmation depends on denial, making each decision an implicit rejection; without exhaling, it is impossible to inhale. In this process, everyone becomes an echo chamber or a hall of mirrors (to use Todorov's images). We are defined not only by what is within us but by reflections off those around; they become what is within. For this reason, the Other that is rejected most violently is often the one that most resembles us, an interior Other: the one we need most.

In his book *The Conquest of America*, Todorov uses this concept to explain the process of redefinition that the Spanish conquistadores underwent when they arrived in the New World. That meeting between Europe and America was the ultimate encounter between Self and Other, not just a geographical event but a psychological one that affected Europe as much as it did the Americas.

Hispaniola, as the place where that shift in consciousness began, is still undergoing a negotiation between Europe, Africa, and America: all these Others exist at once at the heart of the ongoing struggle on the island. And Todorov's conception of Self and Other can explain why Dominican and Haitian leaders, in their very similarity, have chosen to emphasize the differences between their two countries. The things they have in common are the most painful elements of their tragic history: brutal leaders, poverty, rejection by the outside world, and long episodes of violence (directed most often at those who have the least power to defend themselves). "Each time the ideologues look in the mirror, they find there that the Dominican is almost, I would venture to say, the double of the Haitian," the Haitian sociologist Franz Voltaire remarked at a Dominican conference about the two countries. "Evidently, every time he looks in the mirror, he finds the Haitian there, and tries to break the mirror, in the sense of saying: this does not exist."

But it does. *Bachata* blares from three open-air bars clustered at the mouth of the Nigua River, an hour or so by road west of the Columbus Lighthouse. In October 1796 it was here that slaves in Spanish Santo Domingo first rebelled against their colonial masters. Two hundred slaves, aware of France's promise to end slavery in the west of the island, burned down the cane in the surrounding fields and slaughtered cattle. Two hundred years later, Nigua remains an African community, in both religion and skin color, linked to Haiti's history and a reminder of all the Dominican Republic's past that is shared with its neighbor. The inhabitants of Nigua are darker than the Dominicans of the Cibao or the mulattoes of the capital. In Nigua, the African spirits do not hide so much behind the masks of Roman Catholic saints as they do in the rest of the country. Windows and doors are decorated with the magical rhomboid shape to protect residents. Just back from the main road, in the *hounforts* in the style of Haitian Vodou temples, Dominicans invoke Papa

Legba and the pantheon of saints whose names are the same as those in Haiti. But they also honor their own, peculiarly Dominican spirits.

Houses are painted in red and green for Belié Belcán, the most powerful Dominican Vodou spirit. He brandishes a machete and knife, like the sword of his Catholic counterpart, St. Michael the archangel. Belié Belcán is skilled in negotiation and diplomacy, enforced by brute strength and steel if need be: he intervenes, as all the *lwa* do, to resolve human conflicts. He is a powerful, solitary male figure, a statesman and strongman, an African-influenced version of Hispaniola's Great Man myth. He has not been co-opted or distorted by governments for their own good. Belié Belcán is all the more powerful for having been relegated to anonymity.

In the realm of myth this powerful male archetype, who is superhuman, exists in opposition to another character, the one who is less than human but just as necessary. This role is filled by the immigrants of Hispaniola. Haitians cut the cane Dominicans will not touch; in New York, the newest Dominican immigrants work in factories, Laundromats, and hospitals or become nannies and maids, performing low-wage services that Americans will not do.

The immigrant is Hispaniola's Caliban. Prospero loathes his half-human slave but depends on him to find food and do work that he cannot do. "We cannot miss him: he does make our fire, fetch our wood, and serves in offices that profit us," he says of the gruesome figure. When his service to Prospero is finished and the duke leaves the island, Caliban is left alone, reviled but necessary as a counterpart to the happy court returning to Milan: he is the Other within, the one they most want to expel.

Shakespeare's storms happen in a set time, a controlled environment, both on stage and within *The Tempest* itself. Conflicts between the actors are confined to the space of a ship tossed on the waves, with the guarantee from the beginning of the play that "no, not so much perdition as an hair" will fall on any of the ship's occupants: the struggle is taking place in safety. In an abstract setting, the dividing lines of society are recast into harmless seams rather than deep faults; they can be bridged, and people can cross from one side to the other. Control defeats chaos, love erases hate, humanity triumphs over monstrosity, civilization over barbarism, all within an imaginary arena, controlled by a master who does not allow base impulses to escape his control and who believes that without him all will return to chaos.

On Hispaniola, the ongoing interplay of the Prospero and Caliban archetypes has not been confined to a safe, imaginary realm. Ordinary men have co-opted the image of the magician-teacher, assumed that role in a real world, and projected the subhuman qualities of Caliban onto those who serve them. This tendency to mythologize has sustained Hispaniola's people by casting a light of wonder and destiny onto their stories when gray reality is unattractive; but in producing Trujillos and Duvaliers in all their incarnations, and by reducing its struggling immigrants to less than human, the story of Hispaniola has retold itself only in the form of tragedy. The new struggle for Dominicans and Haitians is to replace destructive myths with sustaining ones, in a slow and painful process.

In spring 1997 there was an air of change in Santo Domingo. Bright white and yellow lane markers had been painted on the city's many newly repaved streets in an effort to bring a feel of progress. Brand-new Burger Kings and Taco Bells filled Winston Churchill Avenue. Even McDonald's, which for years had decided Moscow and Beijing had more investment-friendly climates than Santo Domingo, had set up a Dominican franchise. (Down Winston Churchill Avenue, McDowell's restaurant flaunted its golden arches in proud defiance of the Americans' inability to enforce trademarks in this little country in its shadow.)

The grounds of the National Palace were being remodeled (though some Dominicans grumbled about the dubious wisdom of bringing geese in to wander the grounds). In the outer office of President Leonel Fernández, a security detail gathered around a computer terminal to check Toyota prices on the Internet. A new economic plan was partly in place, after he had introduced it much as a professor would, via three lectures on national television in which he used a pointer and diagrams to explain what he wanted to do. The President had proposed modernizing the state, integrating the economy with the world, selling shares in the bankrupt state businesses to private investors, even fixing the ever-decrepit state electricity company. His intentions were good: instead of ruling by decree and arbitrarily imposing his own policies as Balaguer had done,

Leonel said he intended to allow legislators to discuss his proposals and come to a consensus.

But the limited progress that Leonel had achieved had not done much to conceal the suffering of the many people in Santo Domingo who barely made a living. As he spoke of democracy and consensus, taxi drivers were striking over rising fuel prices. Teachers were threatening to stop work, too. Congress was refusing to approve the President's economic proposals. The blackouts for the moment were less frequent, but only because the government had found temporary funds to pay for supplies to the state electricity company; its money would soon run out, and blackouts would become worse than ever. And the old Haitian scapegoating, never buried far beneath the Dominican political landscape, came back as strong as ever.

Boys still crowded almost every intersection on Winston Churchill to sell newspapers, peeled oranges, loofahs, mandarin oranges, and *nisperos*, brown fruit with a deep-orange, rich molasses-tasting center (avocados and mangoes would not be in season until summer). The fruit was delicious, but it hardly counted as a decent living. One afternoon, a small dark boy, maybe ten years old, lifted the afternoon copies of *Ultima Hora* and *El Nacional* up to the window of a passing car. He did not answer the driver's friendly greeting. When the man pressed him, the boy made a *hmmmmmm* sound and motioned as if to signal that he could not speak. *"W pale Ayisyen?"* the driver asked. Do you speak Haitian Kreyol? The boy's face lit up. He understood the words, but it would take more prodding before he would answer. He had been pretending to be deaf so the Dominicans would not know he was Haitian.

His fear was not unfounded, because the Dominicans had expelled twenty thousand Haitians in the previous weeks. The State Sugar Council, still broke in December as the harvest was supposed to be beginning, had been forced to ask the government for money so it could cut the sugarcane, again using Haitian workers to do the job because it could not afford Dominicans. The sugar company recruited sixteen thousand Haitians just before the President announced his economic austerity plan and proposals to sell off the old state companies that had always been sources of corrupt income for political cronies.

An unpopular President, prodded by hard-liners within his party (and within that of Balaguer, who was already wavering in his support of his young successor), allowed the Interior Ministry to resort to the easiest, most cynical trick of Dominican politics: diverting attention (and, by implication, blame for economic problems) to the Haitians.

Police patrolled the streets looking for Haitians, especially in Santiago (ostensibly to dismantle a Haitian beggar network). The Dominican agricultural authorities even announced that they would keep out Haitian pigs, which the officials said carried hog cholera.

Leonel tried to put the best light on the situation by pointing out that at least these deportations had been done with the cooperation of the Haitian authorities and that efforts were made to deport the Haitians as humanely as possible. "Nobody can deny the Dominican government's right to return undocumented workers to their country. Every day Dominicans come back, expelled from Puerto Rico, and we don't say anything. Every day, when the U.S. repatriates Mexicans from the border, nobody protests, because they know the U.S. has the right," Leonel said. But despite his protests, the deportations merely showed that despite the intentions to change things for the better, it would be a long time before any Dominican government gave up its favorite tool for distracting the citizenry.

As political struggles continued in the world of men, the champion fighting rooster Bacundú was resting peacefully in José Then's retirement home. José Then had a new winner, even more impressive than Bacundú. His new champion was all black, had killed nine opponents in sixteen minutes, and bore the terrifying name Chupacabras, the Goat Sucker, after the spectral monster that terrorized Mexico, Central America, and Puerto Rico when it roamed the countryside draining the blood from farm animals around the time Fernández had been elected the year before.

It had been nearly a year since Quique Antún's candidate, Jacinto Peynado, lost the elections to Leonel Fernández. In the newspapers, rivals in Balaguer's party were giving interviews criticizing Antún, trying to force him out of his post as secretary-general. But at the cockfights on a Saturday afternoon, he was buoyant. His bird was a winner, the first time in a long time. He had just made 100,000 pesos, around $7,500, on one bet alone. Dr. Angel Contreras clapped Quique Antún on the back. Contreras's own rooster lost today, but he was celebrating with Antún. Through his colleague's victory, he won, too.

For here is the flip side of the culture of the cockfight and its central paradox: in celebrating violence, rituals like this one reveal the possibilities for reconciliation. Myth can sustain just as it has the power to destroy.

At dusk the mist rises from the cane fields at Palave, just outside Santo Domingo. As the deep gold of the sunset hits, the mist ignites against the remaining dark clouds of a late-afternoon rain shower hovering like smoke over the horizon. When the French- and Kreyol-speaking Haitians occupied Santo Domingo in the nineteenth century, these fields were called Palais Bel, beautiful palace, after the coral mansion that graced a small hill above the cane. Like the once-steady walls of the palace itself, now in ruins, the words "Palais Bel" have since disintegrated into Spanish sounds, Pa-la-vé. Flocks of small white Dominican herons, *garzas*, billow over the remaining stumps of the old palace walls and into the trees nearby the way they always do as the sun sets.

As dark settles, preparations begin for Carnival. Sugarcane is being harvested in the fields all around. For weeks before and after Mardi Gras, residents of the nearby towns and cane barracks dance and sing in the streets the whole night long. They celebrate aggression and sexual exuberance, music and dance, breaking all the limits set during the rest of the year.

Similar celebrations in Haiti, called *rara*, take place between Ash Wednesday and Easter, peaking in Holy Week, when the rest of the country shuts down and the yearly calendar of Vodou ceremonies is quiet. When Haitian migrant cane cutters transplanted the *rara* to the Dominican Republic, the Spanish attempt to pronounce the French *r* turned the word into *gagá*, an unintentional but appropriate play on the word's other meaning, "crazy."

There are various theories about where the name *rara* came from. In colonial days the 1685 Code Noir guaranteed the slaves of Saint-Domingue vacation time on Saturday nights and during Holy Week. *"Lalwadi,"* the slaves might have cried, creolizing the French *la loi dit*, the law says so! affirming the few days that were theirs and defying the plantation owners who might have said otherwise.

Anthropologist Harold Courlander suggests the word *rara* may come from a Yoruba adverb that means "loudly." During Carnival season there are often so many *raras* out on the roads that they inevitably meet at a crossroads and face off to determine which will turn aside to let the other pass. They dance faster, play louder. As the groups battle musically to establish right-of-way, members at the edges sometimes resort to physical struggles.

The procession begins at a cemetery, the domain of the spirits of the dead, of crossroads and highways. In Vodou cosmology a crossroads marks the path between the human and divine worlds, divided by a cosmic mirror. Maya Deren, a filmmaker and anthropologist who fell in love with Haiti in the 1940s, describes the crossroads as a metaphor for the depth of the mirror reflecting from one world into another. "It is, above all, a figure for the intersection of the horizontal plane, which is this mortal world, by the vertical plane, the metaphysical axis, which plunges into the mirror," she wrote in *Divine Horsemen*, her study of Haitian Vodou.

The crossroads and mirror express the unconscious, the world of the divine, departed ancestors, and the spirits. But they also have a political content. After the overthrow of Jean-Bertrand Aristide, Haitian Grammy-nominated roots-pop band Boukman Eksperyans warned the military in the hit song "Kalfou Danjere" (Dangerous crossroads) that the soldiers, too, would have to pass through the crossroads. The military banned the group from the 1992 Carnival celebrations. In the journey from this life to the next, the band warned, everyone must pass through the crossroads. The military murderers, the song implies, are turning away from the crossroads, where the Vodou deities judge their actions on earth.

Running through a mirror that reflects two linked but separate facets of the same world, the center post of Vodou cosmology is also a metaphor for the Dominican and Haitian border: reflecting worlds kept separate despite their similarities. The cross and the mirror, choice and reflection, divide and link Us with the Other: the hunter and the prey, the Dominican and Haitian, those to be glorified and those to be forgotten, the living and the dead. The line that divides myth from reality, east from west, north from south, self from Other, is, like the Dominican-Haitian border, not impenetrable.

Before setting out from Palave, the *gagá* salutes the Vodou deities who will safeguard their journey and bless the encounters that will take place on the way. It then moves out into the streets slowly, growing louder as the night deepens. By midnight the *gagá* has taken over the roads crisscrossing the cane fields of Palave.

Against a backdrop of laughter, singing, and shouts, the steady beat of drums and the insistent single-note calls of the *vaksin* trumpets swell up over the sharp points of cane. Above a rise in the road, the *gagá* appears, a mass of bodies filling the space between the cane stalks, tall as men, on either side of the road. At the head of a group, leaders crack whips, sharp, insistent. Behind them, players with drums and *vaksin* follow, playing amelodic but not unpleasant music. The *gagá* surrounds any passing car, demanding a toll before continuing slowly, still singing, down the road into the darkness.

During the rest of the year the swishing of the cane is the only sound here at this hour. Behind the *gagá* at Palave, a car full of Dominicans follows, blaring merengue so loud that even the insistent hoot of the *vaksin* in the *gagá* fades behind it. The two musics compete for control of the night air.

Suddenly the procession ahead stops. Shouts arise. Elma, a young woman from a nearby *batey*, has been dancing with a large, muscular young man not from the immediate area. She is tall and slim, with Yoruba cheekbones and fine long eyelashes. Her hair is cropped close. Even in a T-shirt and hand-me-down pants, she is elegant, sophisticated. If it were not for the haphazard scars on her face, childhood scrapes left untreated, she could hold her own on a runway with the elite models of Paris and New York. But tonight she is not moving with the controlled tension of a fashion model. Like the other young women in the *gagá*, she has been dancing with abandon, thrusting her breasts in the air and swiveling her hips.

The young man she has been dancing with has taken her suggestive movements as an invitation. Roughly, he tries to kiss her. She shoves him away violently. Furious, he sees a metal rod lying nearby and grabs it. Brandishing his new weapon soothes his hurt pride. Almost before he has fully raised the rod, Elma's friends and relatives, the young men of her *batey*, come to her defense. They pull the offender away from the group and beat him bloody.

To an outsider, the abandon of the dance looks like chaos and debauchery. It is not. The unabashedness of the *rara/gagá* can only take place within shared limits. A common code allows everyone space to perform without fear. The undulating hips, strutting chests and breasts, dancing buttocks, bare skin, and bawdy lyrics are not open provocations but a show, reenacting and releasing normally restrained drives.

As the *gagá* waits for the fight to finish, the Dominican car following the procession stops. Two young couples tumble out the doors. One of the young men zips around to the trunk and opens it, revealing giant speakers. His friend slips back into the front seat, ejects the merengue tape, and pops in a cassette of meren-hip-hop, a fusion of tropical brass riffs and hip-hop brought back from New York, urban music melding with countryside rhythms. The young Dominicans, taking advantage of the pause in the procession, begin dancing on the open road next to their car. One of the young men shows off, break dancing, his legs flying into the air as he bounces from one formation to another.

For the Dominican middle and upper classes, these fields represent the unwashed masses, the hordes of poor immigrants taking over their country. The forces of history, economics, law, police, governments, and leaders have all aligned against the Haitian cane cutters. They are scapegoats for the fact that one in eight Dominicans has been forced to seek work and a better life elsewhere. Officially, Haitians and Dominicans can never mix.

During Carnival, the festival that flaunts limits and rules, real conflicts briefly disappear as Dominicans and Haitians celebrate their differences and their common roots. Soon the cane cutters will go back to work; the politicians will attack one another again; the *yolas* filled with starving emigrants will keep leaving the island; the blackouts will continue.

But tonight at Palave, Haitian meets Dominican and blends in with New York. Haiti is no longer on the other side of the border, New York no longer across the water. They are here in the cane fields that have long represented the center of conflict between the Dominican Republic and Haiti. The three worlds have fused into one.

Glossary

A

an ba fil: under the wire or illegally, in Kreyol; refers to Haitian cane cutters who came to the Dominican cane fields without legal papers.

apagón: blackout, caused by chronic lack of maintenance and shortage of funds at the Dominican state electricity company; a blackout is often noted by the exclamation *¡Se fue la luz!* The lights went!

asson: a sacred gourd used to summon the spirits in Haitian Vodou.

B

bachata: Dominican country music, once seen as something liked only by the lower class but popularized in the early 1990s, especially after Juan Luis Guerra and his group 4:40 released their recording *Bachata rosa*, a highly produced commercial interpretation of the musical style.

bajo mundo: the lower- and middle-class cockfighting arenas of the Dominican Republic.

baka: the Dominican werewolf, cousin to Haiti's *loup-garou.*

barrio: neighborhood, often but not always bearing a connotation of being lower-class or crowded.

batey: barracks in the Dominican cane fields where cane cutters are housed; these structures are named after the central market areas during early colonial times. El Batey is the name of a community in Sosúa established by Jewish refugees in the aftermath of Trujillo's massacre of Haitians on the border.

bien-bien: a Dominican naked mountain tree spirit who robs gardens at night and, if discovered by humans, wails so plaintively that anyone who hears it will be overcome with sadness forever.

blan: in Haiti, a foreigner; though this word is from the French *blanc*, meaning white, a *blan* can have very dark skin: Haitian Americans and African Americans are called *blan.*

blancos de la tierra: literally, whites of the earth; colonial-era Dominicans used this term to refer to their darker skin color, which resulted from intermarriage.

bodega: a small grocery store; the dream business of Dominicans who emigrate and want to return one day to their country with enough money to start a modest enterprise; grocery stores that proliferate in New York's Washington Heights also take this name.

bolo: a rooster bred to have no tail feathers; two turn-of-the-century Dominican political groups called themselves *bolos pata prieta* (black-legged *bolos*) and *bolos pata blanca* (white-legged *bolos*).

botánica: a store that sells religious articles like chromolithographs of the saints, candles, small statues, and ritual waters and oils; common in Santo Domingo's Little Haiti and in New York's Washington Heights.

botpippel: Kreyol for boat people, the refugees who fled first the Duvalier regime, then later the repression by those who led a coup to expel Aristide.

boujwazi: in Haiti, the high bourgeoisie, the elite class that opposed Aristide's Presidency.

bracero: cane cutter; derived from the Spanish *brazo*, for arm.

C

caballero: a gentleman.

cacique: an Indian chief, the indigenous counterpart of the Spanish colonial *caudillo*.

cadenú: "chain wearer," a derogatory term for certain Dominican emigrants, taken from the gaudy gold chains worn by many drug dealers; plural is *cadenuces*.

campo: the Dominican countryside, which has achieved an almost mythical status as *campesinos* have left for the cities and for New York.

cañaveral: cane field.

caudillo: the strongman on a horse, a type of leader common throughout Latin America.

cédula: Dominican identity card also used for voting; redesigned after the 1990 election to deter voting fraud; an earlier version of the *cédula* contained a space where the bearer's race was listed but with the word *indio* often used instead of *negro* or *mulato*.

cibaeño: a native of the Cibao, the Dominican Republic's fertile central valley; cibaeños are often the butt of redneck jokes by other Dominicans.

ciguapa: a female mountain spirit whose feet are backward so that she can never be traced when she lures a handsome young man back to her lair; the Dominican poet Josefina Báez has used the image of the *ciguapa*, always seeming to go backward, to describe the plight of Dominican women living in New York but caught between two countries, always thinking of the place they left behind.

cimarron: a slave escaped to the mountains during Spanish colonial times (see *marronnage* below).

cocolo: a bald-headed rooster; also, a cane cutter from the English-speaking Caribbean, especially the island of Tortola, brought to the Dominican Republic during the sugar boom in the early twentieth century.

colmado: a Dominican corner kiosk that is not just a convenience store but also an important Dominican gathering place, where people stand around and drink ice-cold beer (ideally, a half degree above freezing, which can only be achieved if there is enough electricity to keep the freezers going) or sit and play dominoes or tell stories and show off.

colono: a private Dominican sugar producer; *colonos* sell to the Consejo Estatal del Azúcar (CEA, the State Sugar Council), which then exports the sugar, usually at preferential prices to the U.S. market.

coludo: a breed of rooster with tail feathers.

criador: in the Dominican Republic, a man who breeds and raises fighting cocks.

criollo: Dominican creoles, the descendants of Spanish explorers.

cubrirse: to bet against yourself in a cockfight as a hedging strategy to keep from losing money when your rooster is losing.

D

diablo cojuelo: a costumed Carnival character from the town of La Vega.

Dominican York: a derogatory term for Dominican emigrants living in New York.

dominicanos ausentes: the "absent Dominicans," an affectionate, nostalgic term for the country's emigrants.

Doña: a term of respect for an older Dominican woman; sometimes used as a noun for an older woman.

E

escabeche: a vinegar sauce used in traditional Dominican cooking and part of José Then's favorite recipe for cooking a fighting cock that has died in a fight. (p24)

F

flamboyant tree (franboyán): the royal poinciana, a tree with feathery leaves and flaming red flowers that is a Dominican national symbol.

fritay: plantains, bits of meat, pork fat, and other food deep fried in oil over open fires on street corners by Haitian women.

fucú: jinx or curse, especially when referring to *el fucú de Colón*, the curse associated with Christopher Columbus's name; the word is thought to come from words for magical spells used in languages spoken in Togo, Nigeria, and Sierra Leone.

G

gagá: the Dominican version of rara, the Lenten Vodou processions in Haiti.

gagaire: a Haitian cockfighting arena; *gagè* in Kreyol.

gallera: a Dominican cockfighting arena; the central social activity of many small towns.

gallero: a Dominican cockfighter.

gallo: rooster.

golpe de sangre: a mortal blow in the Dominican cockfight.

gourde: the Haitian national currency; one "Haitian dollar" is still five gourdes, according to the fixed exchange rate to the U.S. dollar set in 1927 during the U.S. occupation of Haiti; the gourde was allowed to devalue after the 1986 fall of Baby Doc Duvalier and in the late 1990s was trading at more than twenty to the U.S. dollar.

guayabera: a formal linen shirt worn by men; also called *chacabana* in the Dominican Republic.

H

hounfort: a Vodou temple.

houngan: a Vodou priest.

I

indio: a description of a range of skin colors of mixed-race Dominicans, used to imply a color that results from Indian heritage without making mention of African ancestry.

ingenio: a sugar mill.

J

juez de valla: the referee at a Dominican cockfight.

K

kòk kalite: a champion Haitian fighting rooster; the nickname for Jean-Bertrand Aristide when he began campaigning for President under the sign of the rooster.

kongo: a derogatory term for a recently arrived Haitian cane cutter in the Dominican Republic; the word alludes to slaves recently off the boat from Africa.

konpa-direk: a five-beat Haitian music style similar to the Dominican merengue.

Kreyol: Haiti's language; the word displays its origin as one of the family of languages called Creoles to reflect that they are a mix, most often of African and European languages.

L

Lavalas: Aristide's political movement when he ran for election in 1990, named for a cleansing torrential flood.

lechón: a Carnival character, with horns and a flat hog's snout, from the city of Santiago.

los doce años: Balaguer's first twelve years as President, 1966–1978, a period of repression and intimidation by his thugs, called *la banda colorá*.

lòt bò: the other side, in Haitian Kreyol; used to refer to Haitians living in the United States or the Dominican Republic.

lwa: spirit, in Haitian and Dominican Vodou (often spelled *lua* by Dominicans).

M

machismo: the hyper-male set of mannerisms adopted by Caribbean and Latin American men.

macuteo: the common practice by police in the Dominican Republic of asking for bribes; the word is taken from the Haitian *tontons macoutes* (see below).

madansara: a Haitian merchant woman, named after the tiny black finch whose calls are shrill and persistent; the female bird often works herself to death carrying food to her young.

mambo: a Vodou priestess.

marronnage: flight to the mountains by slaves in Saint-Domingue.

merengue: the Dominican national dance, similar in rhythm to Haiti's *konpa-direk*.

met tet: the master of the head, from the French *maître tête*; in Haitian Vodou, the spirit *(lwa)* that gives direction to a devotee.

mítin: Dominican political rally, taken from "meeting."

mona: a rooster used not to fight but to provoke the two birds that are about to begin a cockfight.

morena/moreno: an often affectionate Dominican term for a dark-skinned woman or man.

morir soñando: "to die dreaming," the name of a favorite Dominican drink made from orange juice mixed with milk.

mulato/mulata: mixed-race, of African and European descent.

N

nèg: man (regardless of skin color) in Haitian Kreyol; adapted from the French *nègre*, for Negro.

ñame: a Dominican yam.

P

padrón: Dominican voter roll.

palabra de gallero: the cockfighter's word of honor.

pelo bueno/pelo malo: good hair (straight and shiny)/bad hair (kinky); expressions Dominicans use to refer to race.

perejil: parsley; the word used by Dominican soldiers during the 1937 massacre to identify Haitians, who could not pronounce the *r* and the *l* properly.

perico ripiao: a peasant style of music; literally, "ripped parrot."

pesador: a cane weigher who measures the *braceros'* cane so that the workers can be paid for what they have cut.

peso: the Dominican currency, around fourteen to the dollar during the mid-1990s.

poto mitan: the center post of a Vodou temple; the *lwa* descend through this supporting pole.

Q

quinceañera: a girl's fifteenth birthday party, a special occasion for the whole family.

quiquí: a rooster bred only to grow spurs, which are then cut out of its legs and used to arm other roosters.

R

rara: Haiti's Lenten processions, accompanied by rowdy music and loosely associated with Vodou, especially its crossroads deities, who protect the roads where the *rara* bands march.

S

sancocho: a Dominican stew made with root vegetables, meat, and a saffron or achiote base.

suape: mop in the Dominican Republic, from the U.S. Marine term "swab."

T

tabla: in cockfighting, a drawn match; also called *empate*.

tambora: a small Dominican double-headed drum made of hollowed-out logs; a national symbol associated with the merengue and *perico ripiao* styles of music.

tap-tap: a brightly painted Haitian truck or bus.

ti comersant: a little merchant, part of the informal economy, especially a trader who goes back and forth between the Dominican Republic and Haiti.

tiguere: a young Dominican tough who hangs out in the streets and makes mischief.

tontons macoutes: the paramilitary force established by François Duvalier and named after a Haitian folk character, Tonton Macoute, the Uncle Strawsack who kidnapped children in a straw satchel.

traba: a farm where roosters are bred, raised, and trained.

trapiche: one of the first sugar mills, powered by animal labor.

V

vagabundo: a good-for-nothing; a vagabond.

vaksin: bamboo trumpets used in *rara* and *gagá* celebrations.

viejo: a Haitian cane cutter who has lived for many years in the Dominican Republic and has been given authority over other cane cutters.

Vodou: Haiti's folk religion, a mixture of African and Roman Catholic elements.

Y

yola: a rickety boat used to carry Dominicans to Puerto Rico in hopes of living in the United States; from a Taino word for boat.

yuca: the root of the yucca, or cassava, plant, a staple of the Latin American diet; poison made from the same plant was what Taino Indians used to kill themselves to escape slavery at the hands of the Spanish colonists.

Z

"Zafa!": the exclamation used to undo a jinx, especially the Columbus jinx.

zafacón: garbage can, an expression Dominicans adapted from the U.S. Marines' use of the word "safe can"; this word is also sometimes used to pun the piquant slang expressions "Zafa! Coño!"

Bibliography

Much of this book is based on the author's reporting for publications, including *Newsday*, *Newsweek*, *The Christian Science Monitor*, *The Boston Globe*, *Listín USA*, *NACLA Report on the Americas*, *In These Times*, *The Nando Times*, *Chicago Tribune*, *The Montreal Gazette*, *St. Petersburg Times*, *San Francisco Chronicle*, *Business Latin America*, *Dow Jones Emerging Markets Report*, *IFR-LatAm*, and *AméricaEconomía*. In particular, the article "Democracy Comes to Hispaniola," which appeared in the Fall 1996 *World Policy Journal*, summarizes many of the issues in the book.

The reporting involved hundreds of interviews in the Dominican Republic, Haiti, and New York City from 1988 through 1997. Other sources included the many Dominican daily newspapers, particularly *Listín Diario*, *El Siglo*, and *Hoy*, and the weekly magazine *Rumbo*; and the Haitian newspapers *Haiti Observateur*, *Haiti Progrès*, and *Haiti en Marche*. Background also includes reports in the U.S. press, particularly *The New York Times*, *The Washington Post*, and *The Miami Herald*. Another reference is the City University of New York's Dominican Studies Institute publication *Punto 7 Review: A Journal of Marginal Discourse*, which includes essays, fiction, and poetry dealing with Dominican immigration and identity issues.

GENERAL HISPANIOLA REFERENCE

Alvarez-Lopez, Luis. "A Selected Bibliography." In Luis Alvarez-Lopez, Sherrie Baver, Jean Weisman, Ramona Hernández, and Nancy López. *Dominican Studies: Resources and Research Questions*. New York: CUNY Dominican Studies Institute, 1997.

Dold, Gaylord. *Dominican Republic Handbook*. Chico, Calif.: Moon, 1997.

Moya Pons, Frank. *The Dominican Republic: A National History*. New York: Hispaniola Books, 1995. Moya's bibliography on Dominican-Haitian relations is published in Wilfredo Lozano, ed. *La cuestión haitiana en Santo Domingo*. Miami and Santo Domingo: North-South Center/FLASCO, 1992.

ROOSTERS AND COCKFIGHTS

Césaire, Aimé. *La Tragédie du roi Christophe*. Paris: Présence Africaine, 1963. This play about Haiti's last emperor begins with a Haitian cockfight in which the battling roosters are named for the rival rulers of the north and south.

Dundes, Alan. *The Cockfight: A Casebook*. Madison: University of Wisconsin Press, 1994.

Geertz, Clifford. "Deep Play: Notes on the Balinese Cockfight." *Daedalus* 101, no. 1 (1972): 1–37. The classic anthropological essay on the cockfight. Reprinted in Dundes, *The Cockfight*.

Girouard, Tina. *Sequin Artists of Haiti*. New Orleans: Contemporary Arts Center, 1994. Discusses the use of the rooster as a political symbol in Vodou flags after the coup against Aristide.

Gold, Herbert. *Best Nightmare on Earth*. New York: Touchstone, 1991. A contemporary travelogue with a chapter on *le combat de coqs*.

Niles, Blair. *Black Haiti*. New York: Grosset & Dunlap, 1925. Contains a chapter titled "The Black One Is Your Cock."

Pichardo, José M. *Gallos y galleros*. Santo Domingo: Sociedad Dominicana de Bibliofilos, 1985. Pichardo's book is illustrated by Dominican artist Guillo Pérez, who has done a series of cockfighting paintings, many of which are included in Adriano Rodriguez's extensive personal collection of rooster art.

Rodriguez, Adriano. *El gallo de pelea*. Santo Domingo: Editora Corripio, 1983.

Seabrook, W. B. *The Magic Island*. New York: Literary Guild, 1929. A travelogue written during the 1915–34 U.S. occupation of Haiti, this book recounts a tale of trickery and pride in a chapter about a cockfight, "Polynice and His White."

THE 1937 MASSACRE

Castor, Suzy. *Migraciones y relaciones internacionales: El caso haitiano-dominicano*. Santo Domingo: Editora Universitaria UASD, 1987. A

Haitian historian, Castor drew on documents from the Mexican national archives.

Cuello, José Israel. *Documentos del conflicto dominico-haitiano.* Santo Domingo: Taller, 1985. A Dominican publisher, Cuello has compiled the files of the Dominican Foreign Ministry into a comprehensive and sobering book.

Vega, Bernardo. *Trujillo y Haiti.* Vol. 1, *1930–1937.* Santo Domingo: Fundación Cultural Dominicana, 1988. Also, his *Trujillo y Haiti.* Vol. 2, *1937–38.* Santo Domingo: Fundación Cultural Dominicana, 1995. Vega, a Dominican economist and historian who became ambassador to the United States after Leonel Fernández's election, has worked in the U.S. and Dominican national archives extensively and compiled his research, reproducing many key documents.

GENERAL DOMINICAN-HAITIAN RELATIONS

Balaguer, Joaquín. *La isla al revés.* Santo Domingo: Fundación José Antonio Caro, 1983. This racist book, by the seven-term Dominican President, is a clear example of "official" discourse on Dominican-Haitian relations and the roots of intergovernmental conflict and migration policy.

Corten, André. *L'État faible: Haiti et République Dominicaine.* Montreal: Editions de CIDIHCA, 1989. A Belgian sociologist examines the role of the two countries' weak, kleptocratic states in ongoing tension.

Moya Pons, Frank. *La dominación haitiana, 1822–1844.* Santo Domingo: UCMM, 1978. A history of the Haitian occupation of Santo Domingo.

Muñoz, María Elena. *Las relaciones dominico-haitianas: Geopolítica y migración.* Santo Domingo: Editora Alfa y Omega, 1995. An outline of historical and economic roots of Haitian migration to the Dominican Republic and conditions leading to the massacre.

Peña Batlle, Manuel. *Historia de la cuestión fronteriza dominico-haitiana.* Ciudad Trujillo: Editora Sánchez Andujar, 1946. A virulently anti-Haitian book by a Trujillo apologist.

Price-Mars, Jean. *La République d'Haiti y la République Dominicaine.* 3 vols. Port-au-Prince, 1953. A broader historical perspective on Dominican-Haitian relations, by the eminent Haitian scholar.

TRUJILLO

Crassweller, Robert. *Trujillo.* New York: Macmillan, 1966. An authoritative account of the dictator's rule.

Diederich, Bernard. *Trujillo: The Death of the Goat.* New York: Little, Brown, 1978. The gripping story, told by a journalist, of the plot to assassinate Trujillo, including the initial involvement of the United States and its eventual betrayal of the conspirators, most of whom died in the tragic aftermath.

RACE IN THE DOMINICAN REPUBLIC AND HAITI

Franco, Franklin J. *Los negros, los mulatos y la Nacion Dominicana.* Santo Domingo: Editora Nacional, 1969.

Guzmán, Daysi Josefina. "Raza y lenguaje en el Cibao." *Eme Eme, Estudios Dominicanos* 2, no. 11 (March–April 1974): 3–45. A scholarly essay detailing the way Dominicans refer to racial types.

Labelle, Micheline. *Idéologie de couleur et classes sociales en Haïti.* Montreal: University of Montreal Press, 1978. A sociologist treats historical and recent variations on the theme of race and class in Haiti.

COLUMBUS

Cassá, Roberto. *Historia social y economica de la República Dominicana.* Santo Domingo: Editora Buho, 1987. Another solid Dominican history.

Klein, Herbert S. *African Slavery in Latin America and the Caribbean.* New York: Oxford, 1986.

Las Casas, Bartolomé de. *Historia de las Indias.* Mexico: Fondo de Cultura Economica, 1951. No one describes better the horrors of the Spanish colonial rule.

Moya Pons, Frank. *Manual de historia dominicana.* Santiago: Universidad Católica Madre y Maestra, 1977. Adapted into English as *The Dominican Republic: A National History.* New York: Hispaniola Books, 1995. The most comprehensive Dominican history, from Columbus's arrival to the present. A revised version of this book in 1992 provoked government attempts to have it banned because of its account of election fraud in 1990. Moya Pons also critiques the quincentennial celebration of Columbus's arrival in the New World in an impassioned and concise booklet, *El choque del descubrimiento*. Santo Domingo: Taller, 1992.

Reid, Alastair. "Waiting for Columbus." *The New Yorker*, February 24, 1992. A wry account of the history and hoopla surrounding Columbus.

Williams, Eric. *From Columbus to Castro*. London: Andre Deutsch, 1970; New York: Harper & Row, 1971. Colonization and slavery portrayed from a Caribbean-wide perspective.

THE HAITIAN REVOLUTION AND HAITIAN HISTORY

Bellegarde-Smith, Patrick. *Haiti: The Breached Citadel*. New York: St. Martin's Press, 1990.

James, C.L.R. *The Black Jacobins*. New York: Random House, 1963. The classic work on the Haitian Revolution.

Ros, Martin. *Night of Fire: The Black Napoleon and the Battle for Haiti*. New York: Sarpedon, 1994. Originally published as *Vuurnacht: Toussaint Louverture en de slavenopstand op Haïti*. Amsterdam: Uitgeverij de Arbeiderspers, 1991.

Trouillot, Michel-Rolph. *Haiti: State Against Nation/Origins and Legacy of Duvalierism*. New York: Monthly Review Press, 1990. Extensively treats the 1806 division of Haiti into north and south, the conflicts between Henri Christophe and Pétion, and the long-term implications of the economic and political mechanisms built during those early years of independence. Trouillot's *Silencing the Past: Power and the Production of History*, Boston: Beacon, 1995, analyzes the historical narrative surrounding the Haitian Revolution, Columbus, and the Holocaust.

SUGARCANE CUTTERS

Báez Evertsz, Frank. *Braceros haitianos*. Santo Domingo: Taller, 1986.

Corten, André. *Port au Sucre: Prolétariat et prolétarisations: Haiti et République Dominicaine*. Montreal: Editions de CIDIHCA, 1986. A Belgian sociologist examines the role of the sugar industry in the ongoing tension.

Corten, André, Carlos Manuel Vilas, Mercedes Acosta, and Isis Duarte are compiled in *Azúcar y política en la Republica Dominicana.* Santo Domingo: Editora Taller, 1976.

International Labor Organization. "Report of the Commission of Enquiry appointed under Article 26 of the Constitution of the International Labor Organization to examine the Observance of certain International Labor Conventions by the Dominican Republic and Haiti with respect to the Employment of Haitian Workers on the Sugar Plantations of the Dominican Republic." November 1983.

Latin American Faculty for Social Sciences (FLACSO). *La cuestión haitiana en Santo Domingo: Migración internacional, desarrollo y relaciones inter-estatales entre Haití y República Dominicana.* Santo Domingo: FLACSO/North-South Center, 1992. A multidisciplinary overview of the situation on the *bateyes,* via a compilation of papers from a conference held December 2–4, 1991, published the following year by FLACSO and the University of Miami's North-South Center. The book looks at legal, labor-market, geographical, and economic issues behind the controversial cane-worker system.

Lawyers Committee for Human Rights. *A Childhood Abducted: Children Cutting Sugar Cane in the Dominican Republic.* New York: Lawyers Committee, 1991. Documentation of human-rights abuses in the cane fields. Supplemented by frequent interim reports, press releases, and testimony to the U.S. Congress, UN Economic and Social Council, and the Inter-American Commission on Human Rights, especially in the period 1990–92. Other reports published in conjunction with Americas Watch and the National Coalition for Human Rights.

Lemoine, Maurice. *Bitter Sugar: Slaves Today in the Caribbean.* Chicago: Banner Press, 1985. Originally published as *Sucre amer: Esclaves aujourd'hui dans les Caraïbes.* Paris: Nouvelle Societé des Éditions Encre, 1981.

Marrero Aristy, Ramón. *Over.* Santo Domingo: Taller, 1940. A Dominican novelist writes on the cane fields in a book also notable for its presentation of Dominican peasant dialect.

Moya Pons, Frank. *El batey.* Santo Domingo: Fonda para el Avance de las Ciencias Sociales, 1986. A study of Dominican cane fields originally intended to serve as the basis for policy recommendations to the PRD government. The 1986 elections, however, brought Balaguer back to power and the recommendations were never implemented.

———, ed. *Forum: Posibilidades de dominicanización de la zafra azucarera.* Santo Domingo: Editora Amigo del Hogar, 1988. Number 27 of an occasional series. A transcription of a debate between sociologists on whether it is feasible to increase Dominican participation in cane cutting.

National Coalition for Haitian Rights. *Beyond the Bateyes: Haitian Immigrants in the Dominican Republic.* This report was published in May 1996 as part of the group's Caribbean migration initiative.

Plant, Roger. *Sugar and Modern Slavery: A Tale of Two Countries.* Atlantic Highlands, N.J.: Zed, 1987.

U.S. Department of State. *Country Reports on Human Rights Practices for 1990.* Report Submitted to the Senate Committee on Foreign Relations and the House Committee on Foreign Affairs, 102d Congress, 1st Sess. S. Prt. 1022-5, at 588-98. Also see GSP Subcommittee of the Trade Policy Staff Committee, 1990 GSP Annual Reviews, Worker Rights Review Summary, Case 18-CP-90, April 1991.

HAITI, FROM THE DUVALIERS FORWARD

Abbott, Elizabeth. *Haiti: An Insider's History of the Rise and Fall of the Duvaliers.* New York: Touchstone, 1988; updated 1991. A vivid description of the Pope's visit, which is widely recognized as a turning point for the Baby Doc regime.

Aristide, Jean-Bertrand. *In the Parish of the Poor: Writings from Haiti.* Translated and edited by Amy Wilentz. Maryknoll, N.Y.: Orbis, 1990.

Aristide, Jean-Bertrand, with Christophe Wargny. *Jean-Bertrand Aristide: An Autobiography.* Maryknoll: Orbis, 1993.

Diederich, Bernard, and Al Burt. *Papa Doc: Haiti and Its Dictator.* New York: Penguin, 1969.

Prince, Rod, with Jean-Jacques Honorat. *Haiti: Family Business.* London: Latin America Bureau, 1985.

Wilentz, Amy. *The Rainy Season.* New York: Simon & Schuster, 1988. The book follows Aristide through the early days of his political career.

THE UNITED STATES AND HISPANIOLA

Black, Jan Knippers. *The Dominican Republic: Politics and Policy in an Unsovereign State.* Boston: Allen & Unwin, 1986. A political scientist examines the two decades after the intervention.

Bosch, Juan. *The Unfinished Experiment: Democracy in the Dominican Republic.* New York: Praeger, 1965.

Gleijeses, Piero. *Dominican Crisis: The 1965 Constitutionalist Revolt and the American Intervention.* Baltimore: Johns Hopkins University Press, 1978.

Kryzanek, Michael J., and Howard Wiarda. *The Politics of External Influence in the Dominican Republic.* New York: Praeger, 1988.

Logan, Rayford. *Haiti and the Dominican Republic.* New York: Oxford University Press, 1968.

Lowenthal, Abraham. *The Dominican Intervention.* Baltimore: Johns Hopkins University Press, 1972.

Martin, John Bartlow. *Overtaken by Events: The Dominican Crisis from the Fall of Trujillo to the Civil War.* New York: Doubleday, 1966. This includes a detailed account of the conflicts between Bosch and Duvalier.

Schmidt, Hans. *The United States Occupation of Haiti, 1915–1934.* New Brunswick, N.J.: Rutgers University Press, 1995.

Szulc, Tad. *Dominican Diary.* New York: Delacorte, 1965. A blow-by-blow journalist's account.

Welles, Sumner. *Naboth's Vineyard: The Dominican Republic, 1844–1924.* 2 vols. New York: Payson & Clarke, 1928. A history of U.S. involvement in Santo Domingo, including efforts to annex the Samaná Peninsula, in the period following the Haitian occupation, by the self-described "sometime chief of the Latin America division of the Department of State of the United States and American Commissioner to the Dominican Republic from 1922 to 1925."

Wiarda, Howard J. *Dictatorship, Development and Disintegration.* Vol. 1. Ann Arbor, Mich.: Xerox University Microfilms, 1975.

Wilson, Larman. "La política exterior de la Republica Dominicana y Haiti." *Eme Eme, Estudios Dominicanos* 1, no. 6 (May–June 1973): 19–37.

JOAQUÍN BALAGUER

Balaguer, Joaquín. *Memorias de un cortesano de la "era de Trujillo."* Santo
Domingo, 1988. Strangely dry and impersonal, very little of the book
is a memoir in the sense of revealing anything about the author's
personal life. Instead, it includes correspondence with other Presidents
of the hemisphere and addresses Balaguer's relationship with the dictator who was his mentor. The one moment with any feeling is when
Balaguer tells the story of the boyhood episode in which he gave mangoes to invading U.S. soldiers. The book remains controversial for the
page Balaguer left blank with the promise that after his death it would
be filled in with the details of the death of activist Orlando Martínez
under the repressive *doce años* regime.

Díaz Grullón, Virgilio. *Antinostalgia de una era.* Santo Domingo: Fundación Cultural Dominicana, 1989. A memoir of the Trujillo regime.

Lorenzo Perelló, Ramón, ed. *Perfiles de Balaguer.* Santo Domingo: Fundación Pro-Cultura Dominicana, 1993. Edited by a Balaguer aide, this
is the official collection of essays by Dominican intellectuals about
Balaguer.

Rodríguez de León, Francisco. *Balaguer y Trujillo: Entre la espada y la
palabra.* Santo Domingo: Artes y Ediciones Caribe, 1996.

Victoria, Roberto. *Los 10 mandamientos de Balaguer.* Santo Domingo:
Offset, 1995. Written by a disgruntled former aide who was later
reinstated and became head of the Dominican mission to the United
Nations.

DOMINICAN IMMIGRATION

Duany, Jorge. *Quisqueya on the Hudson: The Transnational Identity of
Dominicans in Washington Heights.* New York: CUNY, 1994. Part of
a series of occasional monographs on immigration from the City University of New York's Dominican Studies Institute.

Fischkin, Barbara. *Muddy Cup.* New York: Scribner's, 1997.

Forum 27: La migración dominicana a Estados Unidos. Santo Domingo:
Editora Amigo del Hogar, 1988. A panel of social scientists debates
migration issues.

Grasmuck, Sherri, and Patricia R. Pessar. *Between Two Islands: Dominican International Migration.* Berkeley: University of California Press,

1991. The cover illustration is a family photo sent from the Cibao, where children pose in front of a Brooklyn Bridge backdrop, to the father working in New York.

Hernández, Ramona, and Francisco Rivera-Batiz. *Dominican New Yorkers: A Socioeconomic Profile, 1997.* New York: CUNY, 1997.

Hernández, Ramona, Francisco Rivera-Batiz, and Roberto Agodini. *Dominican New Yorkers: A Socioeconomic Profile.* New York: CUNY, 1990.

Kasinitz, Philip. *Caribbean New York: Black Immigrants and the Politics of Race.* Ithaca, N.Y.: Cornell University Press, 1992. Though only a small portion of this book directly treats Dominicans, its analysis of racial politics in New York is valuable.

Klein, Alan. *Sugarball.* New Haven, Conn.: Yale University Press, 1991. The economics and social effects of U.S. recruiting of Dominican baseball players.

Millman, Joel. *The Other Americans: How Immigrants Renew Our Country, Our Economy and Our Values.* New York: Viking, 1996.

Pessar, Patricia. *A Visa for a Dream: Dominicans in the United States.* New York: Allyn & Bacon, 1995.

Portes, Alejandro, and Luis E. Guarnizo. *Capitalistas del tropico: La inmigración en los Estados Unidos y el desarrollo de la pequeña empresa en la Republica Dominicana.* Santo Domingo: FLACSO, 1991. An analysis of migrant micro-enterprise in the United States and the Dominican Republic.

Ruck, Rob. *The Tropic of Baseball: Baseball in the Dominican Republic.* Westport, Conn.: Meckler, 1991.

Torres-Saillant, Silvio, and Ramona Hernández. *The Dominican-Americans.* Westport, Conn.: Greenwood, 1998. Two scholars, well known in the Dominican community for their research on Dominicans as an ethnic minority, discuss education, health issues, drugs and violence, arts, faith, food, gender, and race.

FICTION

Alexis, Jacques Stephen. *Compère Général Soleil.* Paris: Gallimard, 1955. English translation forthcoming: *General Sun, My Brother.* Translation and introduction by Carrol F. Coates. Charlottesville: Caraf Books/ University of Virginia Press, 1999. A novel about the massacre written by a Haitian who was later stoned to death by Duvalier for his political organizing against the dictator in Haiti.

Alvarez, Julia. *In the Time of the Butterflies.* Chapel Hill, N.C.: Algonquin Press, 1995. *How the García Girls Lost Their Accents.* Chapel Hill, N.C.: Algonquin Press, 1991. *¡Yo!* Chapel Hill, N.C.: Algonquin Press, 1997. Novels about Dominican history and the immigrant experience by a writer who came to the United States as a girl when her parents fled the Trujillo regime.

Bell, Madison Smartt. *All Souls' Rising.* New York: Pantheon, 1995. A historical treatment of the Haitian slave revolts.

Benedict, Helen. *Bad Angel.* New York: Dutton, 1996. A novel by an American journalist about a teenage Dominican mother in Washington Heights.

Carpentier, Alejo. *The Kingdom of This World.* New York: Knopf, 1957. Originally published in Spanish as *El reino de este mundo.* Mexico: EDIAPSA, 1949. The story of Boukman, the Jamaican slave and *houngan* who was instrumental to the start of the Haitian Revolution.

Danticat, Edwidge. *The Farming of Bones.* New York: Soho Press, 1998. A novel written by a Haitian-American woman about the 1937 massacre.

Desquiron, Lilas. *Reflections of Loko Miwa.* Translated by Robin Orr Bodkin. Charlottesville: Caraf Books/University of Virginia Press, 1998. A novel about class prejudice and religion in Haiti.

Díaz, Junot. *Drown.* New York: Riverhead, 1996. A collection of short stories by a Dominican-American writer painting a brutally honest portrait of the growing pains of young people caught between the Dominican and U.S. urban Latino cultures.

Galván, Manuel de Jesús. *Enriquillo: Leyenda histórica dominicana.* Santo Domingo: Taller, 1975. Originally published in 1882, this novel romanticizes the myth of Dominican Indian heritage.

Prestol Castillo, Freddy. *El Masacre se pasa a pie.* Santo Domingo: Taller, 1973. A Dominican novel about the 1937 massacre.

Sención, Viriato. *They Forged the Signature of God.* Willimantic, Conn.: Curbstone, 1995. Originally published in Spanish as *Los que falsificaron la firma de dios.* Santo Domingo: Taller, 1992. A surreal rooster's head stares out from the cover of the English version of this Dominican novelist's best-selling roman à clef about the Trujillo and Balaguer regimes. In one of the novel's most gripping passages, Sención describes a cockfight in which a rooster becomes possessed by its owner's rivalry with the town bully, kills the bully's cock, then leaps out of the ring and kills the bully. The novel fictionalizes Balaguer as the enigmatic and evil Dr. Mario Ramos. When it was published in Santo Domingo, the novel provoked an uproar for its depiction of recognizable characters in recent history. The book won the nation's highest literary prize, but Balaguer would not allow it to be conferred. Several short stories in Sención's *La enana Celania y otros cuentos* (The midget Celania and other stories) (Santo Domingo: Taller, 1994) also fictionally treat the Balaguer household.

MUSIC AND CULTURE

Austerlitz, Paul. *Merengue!* Philadelphia: Temple University Press, 1997.

Averill, Gage. *A Day for the Hunter, Day for the Prey: A Social History of Haitian Popular Music.* Chicago: University of Chicago Press, 1997.

Courlander, Harold. *Haiti Singing.* 1939. Reprint, New York: Cooper Square, 1972. Includes an interpretation of the origins of *rara*.

McAlister, Elizabeth. "Men Moun Yo (Here Are the People): Rara Festivals and Transnational Popular Culture in Haiti and New York City." Ph.D. diss., Yale University, 1995.

Pacini-Hernández, Deborah. *Bachata: A Social History of a Dominican Popular Music.* Philadelphia: Temple University Press, 1995. A sociologist discusses the class and race implications of Dominican music.

RECORDINGS

Boukman Eksperyans. *Kalfou Danjere.* Mango Records, 1992.

Caribbean Revels. Smithsonian Folkways CD SF 40402, 1991. Recordings of *rara* and *gagá* celebrations with comments by Verna Gillis and Gage Averill.

Juan Luis Guerra y 4:40. *Ojala que llueva café.* Karen Records K-126, 1988. *Bachata rosa.* Karen Records CDK-136, 1990. *Areíto.* Karen Records CDK-146, 1992. *Fogaraté.* Karen Records CDK-165, 1994.

Rhythms of Rapture: Sacred Music of Vodou. Smithsonian Folkways CD 40464, 1995. In conjunction with the UCLA/Fowler Museum's Sacred Arts of Haitian Vodou art exhibit.

VODOU

Brown, Karen McCarthy. *Mama Lola: A Vodou Priestess in Brooklyn.* Berkeley: University of California Press, 1991. This book includes an account of a Haitian woman's time in Santo Domingo as a *madansara*.

Courlander, Harold. *The Drum and the Hoe: Life and Lore of the Haitian People.* Berkeley: University of California Press, 1985. This classic work, originally published in 1960, is still in print in paperback.

Deive, Carlos Esteban. *Vodu y Magia en Santo Domingo.* Santo Domingo: Taller, 1992. Though often sketchy and not always accurate, this remains the most extensive source on Dominican Vodou.

Deren, Maya. *Divine Horsemen: The Living Gods of Haiti.* 1953. Reprint, New York: Macpherson Documentext. The book accompanies a video documentary of the same name. New York: Mystic Fire Video, 1985.

Hurbon, Laënnec. *Les Mystères du Vaudou.* Paris: Gallimard, 1993.

THE TEMPEST

Césaire, Aimé. *Une Tempête: D'après "La Tempête" de Shakespeare. Adaptation pour un théatre nègre.* Paris: Seuil, 1969. A Caribbean-influenced adaptation of Shakespeare's play.

Fernández Retamar, Roberto. *Caliban and Other Essays.* Translated by Edward Baker. Minneapolis: University of Minnesota Press, 1989. Essays on Caliban and Latin American identity.

Henríquez Ureña, Pedro. "Ariel." In *Obras Completas.* Santo Domingo, 1976. The essay, written in 1904, commenting on Rodó's influential essay.

Ponce, Aníbal. *Humanismo burgués y humanismo proletario.* Havana, 1962.

Rodó, José Enrique. *Ariel.* Cambridge: Cambridge University Press, 1967. When published in 1901, this elitist book-length essay influenced scholars across the Americas.

Shakespeare, William. *The Tempest.* Edited by Frank Kermode. New York: Routledge, 1994. This edition contains extensive notes and criticism of the play.

Wood, Nigel, ed. *The Tempest.* Bristol, Penn., and Buckingham: Open University Press, 1995. See especially Howard Felperin's "Political

Criticism at the Crossroads: The Utopian Historicism of *The Tempest*."

OTHER READING

Alland, Alexander Sr. *Jacob A. Riis: Photographer and Citizen.* New York: Aperture, 1973.

Lévi-Strauss, Claude. *The Savage Mind.* Chicago: University of Chicago Press, 1966. Reflects on myth, language, truth, and perceptions of other cultures.

Lorenz, Konrad. *On Aggression.* New York: Harcourt Brace, 1966. Questions about the nature of aggression and its role in animal and human societies.

Riis, Jacob. *How the Other Half Lives: Studies Among the Tenements of New York.* 1901. Reprint, New York: Dover Publications, 1971.

Todorov, Tzvetan. *The Conquest of America.* New York: HarperPerennial, 1992. Originally published as *La Conquête de l'Amerique.* Paris: Seuil, 1982. A literary criticism of the Spanish discovery of the Other through the colonization of the Americas.

Index